AUTONOMY, CARE AND FAMILY LAW

There is a tension at the heart of family law and policy between the increasing influence of individual autonomy and the demands of caring for children. Individual autonomy envisages decisions made in one's own best interests, whereas decisions around care are often made for the good of the family, and may conflict with the caregiver's individual interests. Whereas individual autonomy valorises economic self-sufficiency, caregiving responsibilities constrain choice and conflict with paid work. This book explores this tension to consider how, given changing social trends, family law and policy should take account of caregiving responsibilities on parental separation. Crucially, it suggests that we need to rethink family law by placing care at its centre.

This book draws on original empirical data to explore the experiences of parents in England and Wales, where the division of paid work and care is considered a choice, and Sweden, where parents are encouraged to work full-time, supported by wellfunded state childcare. This comparative perspective sheds light on whether the clash between the ideas of autonomy and care could be reconciled in a more gender equal society.

The book argues that caregiving is hidden from, and undervalued by, law and policy in both jurisdictions, underscoring the need for the proposed new approach. The law needs to think more deeply about what it means to care, and how the care provided by parents differs. Anna Heenan outlines how family law might look different if the proposed framework, based on placing care at the heart of family law, is adopted.

Autonomy, Care and Family Law

Anna Heenan

•HART•

OXFORD • LONDON • NEW YORK • NEW DELHI • SYDNEY

HART PUBLISHING

Bloomsbury Publishing Plc

Kemp House, Chawley Park, Cumnor Hill, Oxford, OX2 9PH, UK

1385 Broadway, New York, NY 10018, USA

29 Earlsfort Terrace, Dublin 2, Ireland

First published in Great Britain 2024

A catalogue record for this book is available from the British Library.

A catalogue record for this book is available from the Library of Congress.

Library of Congress Control Number: 2023943024

ISBN: HB: 978-1-50995-933-4
ePDF: 978-1-50995-935-8
ePub: 978-1-50995-934-1

Typeset by Compuscript Ltd, Shannon

For my family.

ACKNOWLEDGEMENTS

First and foremost, I would like to thank the participants to this research who were willing to share their stories and experiences with me. I am also grateful to the ESRC for the funding which made this research possible.

Enormous thanks are due to my PhD supervisor, Professor Anne Barlow, for her knowledge, support, and generosity. Likewise, Professors Anna Singer and Margareta Brattström hosted my visit to the University of Uppsala, and were generous with their time and insights into the Swedish system. Any errors in the understanding of the Swedish system are, of course, my own.

Particular thanks go to Professor Ambreena Manji, Dr Jess Mant, Dr Sharon Thompson and the anonymous reviewers for their comments on drafts of material for this book. I am also grateful to the former colleagues at Cardiff University (and, in particular, my Coffee, Research and Pastries Group) who discussed ideas with me. Once again, all errors are my own.

Finally, an enormous thank you to Andrew, not only for listening to me talk at you about this book and for your willingness to read drafts, but for your endless patience and support along the way.

CONTENTS

PART IV
PLACING CARE AT THE HEART OF FAMILY LAW

TABLE OF CASES

TABLE OF STATUTORY MATERIALS

PART I

Introduction

1

Autonomy, Care and Family Law

There is a tension at the heart of family law between the increasing influence of neoliberal ideas of autonomy and the need to respond to the practical demands of, and social expectations around, caring for children. This book explores that tension and suggests that the time has come for a new approach that places care at the centre of family law.

The concept of neoliberalism will be explored more fully later in this book, but in short neoliberalism is understood here as a system in which market values are used to inform responses to economic, political and social matters. Neoliberal-influenced ideas of autonomy valorise economic self-sufficiency and ideas of freedom of choice. These ideas appear to be premised upon the assumption that we live in a gender equal society; if everyone is to attain these ideals then there must be an assumption that everyone is (equally) capable of doing so. The view of a gender equal society seems to be accepted by the public to at least some degree, although attitudinal data suggests a complex picture. For example, a 2021 YouGov survey looking into global attitudes to gender equality found that 69 per cent of respondents in the UK (76 per cent of men and 62 per cent of women) believed that men and women were equal.[1] Further, 86 per cent disagreed with the statement that a women's place was in the home, and 92 per cent agreed that it was good for women to make a career of their own.[2] Additionally, 92 per cent (89 per cent of men and 94 per cent of women) agreed that 'women and men should generally get equal pay'.[3] Likewise, the 35th British Social Attitudes Report, published in 2018, found that 72 per cent of respondents disagreed with the view that a man's job is to earn money and a woman's job is to look after the home and the family.[4] The same percentage agreed that both men and

[1] M Smith, Global Report: Attitudes to Gender 2021' (YouGov, 8 March 2021) https://docs.cdn.yougov.com/cmzkyf80zr/YouGov%20-%20Global%20Gender%20Equality%202021.pdf accessed 28 April 2023 and You Gov, 'Global Gender Equality 2021' https://yougov.co.uk/topics/international/articles-reports/2021/03/08/global-report-attitudes-gender-2021 accessed 28 April 2023. This marks a slight decrease from the 2015 survey, in which 72% agreed with this statement: YouGov, 'Global Report: Attitudes to Gender' (2015) https://d25d2506sfb94s.cloudfront.net/cumulus_uploads/document/43qhq95qwn/YouGov_Gender_Results_Share_Website2.pdf accessed 28 April 2023.

[2] YouGov (2021) (n 1).

[3] Smith (n 1) and YouGov (2021) (n 1).

[4] E Attar Taylor and J Scott 'Gender' in D Phillips et al (eds), *British Social Attitudes: The 35th Report* (The National Centre for Social Research, 2018) http://www.bsa.natcen.ac.uk/latest-report/british-social-attitudes-35/gender.aspx accessed 28 April 2023.

women should contribute to the household income.[5] However, a 2019 survey by Ipsos MORI, in collaboration with the Global Institute for Women's Leadership and International Women's Day suggests that 49 per cent of respondents in the UK believed that there was more advantage in being a man (compared to 11 per cent who believed there was more advantage in being a woman).[6] Further, in the 2021 YouGov survey, there were differences between men and women's attitudes on key issues that would serve to advance equality between men and women. For example, 71 per cent of men, compared with 82 per cent of women, agreed that men should spend more time doing housework.[7]

The problem with neoliberal-influenced understandings of autonomy is that they fail to account for the demands of caring responsibilities and the ways in which such responsibilities are divided in society. As regards the former, caring has financial consequences for the carer; for example, it often entails some degree of career sacrifice. As regards the latter, despite perceptions of gender equality, the division of caring responsibilities in society remains gendered. In intact families with young children, fathers typically work full-time and mothers typically work part-time and perform a greater share of childcare.[8] As will be discussed, this reflects both structural constraints, such as the cost and availability of childcare, and cultural norms about what is expected of mothers and fathers in society.

This disconnect between prevailing neoliberal-influenced norms of autonomy and the demands of caring responsibilities is particularly problematic where parents separate. Informed by neoliberal-influenced norms of autonomy, increasingly the law expects both parents to become financially independent following separation.[9] However, whereas the breadwinner may be able to support him- or herself financially, part-time work has long-term financial consequences,[10] which can interfere with the ability of someone working part-time to be economically self-sufficient. Given the gendered division of caring in society, it is, therefore, unsurprising that women fare worse than men financially on separation.[11]

[5] ibid.

[6] IPSOS Mori, The Global Institute for Women's Leadership and Kings College London, 'International Women's Day 2019: Global Attitudes towards Gender Equality' (February 2019) https://www.kcl.ac.uk/giwl/assets/iwd-giwl-main.pdf accessed 28 April 2023.

[7] Smith (n 1) and YouGov (2021) (n 1). Note that while the summary of the report suggests that the question was about men doing equal housework, the wording of the report seems to be 'more housework' against the backdrop of research showing that men do less housework than women.

[8] See further Chapter 2.

[9] E Hitchings and J Miles, 'Financial remedies on divorce: the need for evidence-based reform' (2018) www.nuffieldfoundation.org/sites/default/files/files/briefing%20paper%20Jun%202018%20FINAL.pdf accessed 28 April 2023.

[10] M Costa Dias et al, 'The Gender Pay Gap in the UK: Children and Experience in Work' (IFS, February 2018) https://ifs.org.uk/publications/gender-pay-gap-uk-children-and-experience-work accessed 28 April 2023, 22–23.

[11] M Brewer and A Nandi, 'Partnership Dissolution: How Does it Affect Income, Employment and Well-being?' (Institute for Social & Economic Research, September 2014) www.econstor.eu/bitstream/10419/126462/1/79669074X.pdf accessed 22 June 2023, H Fisher and H Low, 'Recovery from Divorce: Comparing High and Low Income Couples' (2016) 30 *International Journal of Law, Policy and the*

While these financial consequences are significant, they are not the only effect of the incompatibility between neoliberal-influenced ideas of autonomy and caring responsibilities. As will be discussed, the importance placed upon paid work in England and Wales results in a situation where care is rendered invisible in society and its value is disguised. Yet care is central to what families do, and good care has a value. Care 'is a good part of life' which 'should be treasured and valued'.[12] It can also provide 'a source of meaning and value to life; a source of joy'.[13] Thus, not being able to care may also have costs. It is, therefore, problematic if care, which is so central to family life, is ignored by the family law framework. This book aims both to highlight care's current invisibility in family law and to suggest a new way forward in which care is placed at the centre of family law.

I. The Focus of this Book

This book and the research which underpins it focuses on the tension between neoliberal-influenced ideas of autonomy and childcare responsibilities and the problems this tension poses for the law on parental separation. Family law is, of course, broader than the law that applies on parental separation. However, separation raises intersecting legal issues, including the question of the arrangements that should be made for children and in respect of financial matters. It, therefore, provides a useful lens for exploring these issues more broadly.

Whereas at the level of the intact family it may be possible to reconcile the clash between neoliberal-influenced ideas of autonomy and the demands of caring, for example by one parent working and the other caring, this creates problems on separation where there is an increasing push towards both parties becoming financially independent. This book will focus on four key aspects of the law on separation: the financial consequences of cohabitation, financial provision on divorce, financial claims for children, and child arrangements on separation. It will evaluate the law's current approach to these issues and suggest how things could be done differently. While the focus of this book is, therefore, on specific aspects of family law, it is important to understand that these aspects of family law do not exist in isolation. The decisions people make around childcare are also shaped by the policy landscape. For example, childcare availability shapes the possibilities for reconciling care and paid work. For this reason, this book also explores the influence of family policy. As part of this exercise, it looks to Sweden, widely considered a leader in this arena, to offer a different perspective on how the clash between ideas of autonomy and childcare responsibilities

Family 338; H Fisher and H Low, 'Who Wins, Who Loses and Who Recovers from Divorce?' in J Miles and R Probert (eds), *Sharing Lives, Dividing Assets* (Hart Publishing, 2009).

[12] J Herring, 'Making Family Law More Careful' in J Wallbank and J Herring (eds), *Vulnerability, Care and Family Law* (Routledge, 2013) 46.

[13] J Herring, *Caring and the Law* (Hart Publishing, 2013) 11.

might be reconciled and whether this might help to improve the visibility and value of care in society and the law.

This chapter begins by outlining the legal framework in England and Wales in each of the four areas of family law outlined above. The law will be analysed in greater detail in Chapter 3, but this section is intended to provide a summary which can be used as a reference point for later discussion. The chapter goes on to explain the methods used in the research project upon which this book is based, before reflecting on the impact of the Covid-19 pandemic which occurred after this research was carried out. Finally, chapter outlines are provided for the rest of the book.

II. The Legal Framework in Outline

A. The Financial Consequences of Cohabitation

In England and Wales, cohabiting couples do not have any relationship-based financial claims against one another when they separate. This means that if, during their relationship, one partner was the breadwinner and the other took care of their children it is not possible for the carer to make financial claims for their own maintenance.[14] As the next section will explore, such claims are available to married couples.

Where one or both partners own property, it is possible to bring proceedings in property law; these claims are open to all co-owners of land and are not unique to romantic partners. What is different where a cohabitant brings a claim to establish an interest in property owned by their partner is that the Supreme Court has suggested that the relevant law is that of constructive, rather than resulting, trusts.[15] The key distinction is that while the law of resulting trusts focuses on the financial contributions made by each party, the law of constructive trusts focuses on their intentions. In theory, therefore, if the partners intended to share the property equally then it does not matter if one has contributed less. Nevertheless, in the absence of a clear intention to share property ownership, caring responsibilities do not carry the same weight as financial contributions in establishing an interest in property.

B. Financial Provision on Divorce or Dissolution

In England and Wales, couples have a choice of two formal mechanisms for relationship recognition: marriage and civil partnership. The latter was introduced

[14] It is possible to make claims for a carer's allowance as part of a financial claim for children. This is discussed in the section on financial claims for children below.

[15] *Stack v Dowden* [2007] UKHL 17.

at a time when marriage was only open to opposite-sex couples and was intended to give same-sex couples access to the legal rights offered by marriage. Since 2014, marriage has been open to same-sex couples,[16] and civil partnerships were extended to opposite-sex couples in 2019.[17] Given that numbers of new civil partnership formations are very low,[18] and the legal consequences of both relationships are the same,[19] this book refers to marriage throughout.

Marriage does not, of itself, affect property ownership. However, financial claims are available when a marriage ends by death or divorce. On divorce, there is a discretionary system which allows the court to make a combination of financial orders depending upon the circumstances of the case. These include orders for periodical payments,[20] lump sums,[21] orders dealing with property[22] and orders dealing with pensions.[23] Income, capital and pensions are dealt with together as a single issue, and these different aspects may be offset against each other. For example, a spouse might receive a greater share of property in return for not receiving any spousal maintenance, or for not receiving a share of the other spouse's pension.

In deciding what combination of orders to make the court is directed to consider a list of statutory factors in section 25 of the Matrimonial Causes Act 1973. Case law makes clear that the overall objective in considering these factors is to reach a fair result,[24] and that fairness has three strands: needs, compensation and sharing.[25] In most cases, the court is only concerned with needs because the assets are not sufficient to do more than meet those needs. Need is 'a very broad concept with no single definition in family law'[26] and needs are interpreted in light of the parties' standard of living throughout their marriage. In most cases, the key needs are for housing and income.[27] However, in bigger money cases needs have included, for example, provision to keep horses.[28] Caring responsibilities are relevant to the determination of needs: if one partner has a lower earning capacity because of caring responsibilities, for example, this would increase their needs.

In cases where assets exceed needs, the principles of compensation and sharing may be relevant. Compensation aims to '[redress] any significant prospective

[16] Marriage (Same Sex Couples) Act 2013.
[17] Civil Partnership (Opposite-sex Couples) Regulations 2019.
[18] A Sharfman and P Cobb, 'Civil Partnerships in England and Wales: 2021' (ONS, 9 December 2022) https://www.ons.gov.uk/peoplepopulationandcommunity/birthsdeathsandmarriages/marriagecohabitationandcivilpartnerships/bulletins/civilpartnershipsinenglandandwales/2021#:~:text=of%20civil%20partnerships-,There%20were%206%2C731%20civil%20partnerships%20formed%20in%20England%20and%20Wales,in%20opposite%2Dsex%20civil%20partnerships accessed 28 April 2023.
[19] *Lawrence v Gallagher* [2012] EWCA Civ 394.
[20] Matrimonial Causes Act 1973, s 23(1)(a).
[21] ibid s 23(1)(c).
[22] ibid s 24(1).
[23] ibid s 25B(4) and s 21A(1).
[24] *White v White* [2000] UKHL 54.
[25] *Miller v Miller; McFarlane v McFarlane* [2006] UKHL 24.
[26] Law Commission, *Matrimonial Property, Needs and Agreements* (Law Com No 343, 2014) x.
[27] Family Justice Council, 'Guidance on "Financial Needs" on Divorce' (FJC, 2016) 17.
[28] *S v S* [2008] EWHC 519 (Fam).

economic disparity between the parties arising from the way they have conducted their marriage'.[29] This would include the situation where one partner has sacrificed their career because of caring responsibilities. As regards sharing, in *White*,[30] the court emphasised that there should be no discrimination based on the parties' roles during the marriage: domestic and financial contributions should be valued equally.[31] This means that in cases where needs are met, any departure from an equal division of assets needs to be justified.[32]

C. Financial Claims for Children

Biological parents, whether married or cohabiting, are liable to make child support payments if their children do not live with them following separation. Parents are increasingly encouraged to make private arrangements for child support and the Child Maintenance Service, the state body in charge of child support, charges for both a calculation of the child support liability and for arranging collection.[33] Where collection takes place through the Child Maintenance Service, the level of child maintenance payable is calculated using a statutory formula based on fixed percentages of the payer's income.[34] Where a parent's income exceeds £156,000 per annum (gross) the parent with care can apply to the court for top up provision under the Children Act 1989, Schedule 1. Other situations in which Schedule 1 claims may be appropriate include claims for educational expenses or for costs attributable to disability.[35] Additionally, unlike claims for child maintenance, Schedule 1 claims can be made against a step-parent.[36]

While the purpose of Schedule 1 claims is for the financial support of a child, it is possible to include in those claims an element for a carer's allowance.[37] Such allowances are, however, relatively tightly constrained. For example, the Court of Appeal has explained:

> The literal or purposive interpretation of Schedule 1 does not permit of the concept of sharing or compensation for the benefit of the child, nor, by the back door, financial

[29] *Miller v Miller; McFarlane v McFarlane* [2006] UKHL 24 [13].

[30] *White v White* [2000] UKHL 54.

[31] Note that s 25(2)(f), one of the factors the court must consider when considering what would be a fair outcome, refers explicitly to both domestic and financial contributions. While there have been cases in which there has been a departure from equality based on a special (financial) contribution under s 25(2)(f), the courts have emphasised that such cases are exceptional: see, for example, *Work v Gray* [2017] EWCA Civ 270.

[32] *White v White* [2000] UKHL 54.

[33] Gov.uk, 'Child Maintenance Service' www.gov.uk/child-maintenance-service/payments#:~:text=You%20have%20to%20pay%20a,the%20payment)%20for%20receiving%20parents accessed 22 June 2023.

[34] Gov.uk, 'How the Child Maintenance Service Works out Child Maintenance' https://www.gov.uk/how-child-maintenance-is-worked-out accessed 28 April 2023.

[35] Child Support Act 1991, s 8.

[36] See also Matrimonial Causes Act 1973, Part II.

[37] *Re P (a child)* [2003] EWCA Civ 837.

> provision and compensation for the carer beyond that element attributable to the care of the child during his minority, or other determined duration of dependency.[38]

Thus, even where a formerly cohabiting carer might be able to bring a claim under Schedule 1, the scope for the law to respond to the financial costs of caring is limited. This is compounded by the fact that Schedule 1 claims are rarely brought in practice,[39] and tend to be seen as most appropriate in big money cases.[40]

D. Child Arrangements on Separation

Where parents are married, they both automatically have parental responsibility[41] ('all the rights, duties, powers, responsibilities and authority which by law a parent of a child has in relation to the child and his property'[42]). Where the parents are not married, the mother will automatically have parental responsibility.[43] The father will have parental responsibility if he is named on the birth certificate,[44] if the parents make a parental responsibility agreement[45] or if the court orders it.[46]

The position with respect to where the child is to live/spend time is the same for married couples and cohabitants. Arrangements concerning where a child is to live and who the child is to spend time with are governed by the best interests of the child.[47] In considering what is in the child's best interests, the court is directed to consider a list of statutory factors, known as the welfare checklist.[48] These factors include matters such as the child's wishes and feelings,[49] the child's physical, emotional and educational needs,[50] and the likely effect of any change of circumstances.[51] The court is also directed 'to presume, unless the contrary is shown, that the involvement of [both parents] in the life of the child concerned will further the child's welfare'.[52] This does not, however, demand any particular division of a child's time.[53]

[38] *Re A (A Child)* [2014] EWCA Civ 1577 [19].
[39] Law Commission, *Cohabitation: The Financial Consequences of Relationship Breakdown* (Law Com CP No 179, 2006) 4.34.
[40] See, for example, G Douglas et al, 'A Failure of Trust: Resolving Property Disputes on Cohabitation Breakdown' (2007) https://orca.cf.ac.uk/5186/1/1.pdf accessed 28 April 2023 and Law Commission, *Cohabitation: The Financial Consequences of Relationship Breakdown* (Law Com No 307, Summary, 2007).
[41] Children Act 1989, s 2(1).
[42] ibid s 3.
[43] ibid s 2(2)(a).
[44] ibid s 4(1)(a).
[45] ibid s 4(1)(b).
[46] ibid s 4(1)(c).
[47] ibid s 1.
[48] ibid s 1(3).
[49] ibid s 1(3)(a).
[50] ibid s 1(3)(b).
[51] ibid s 1(3)(c).
[52] ibid s 1(2A).
[53] ibid s 1(2B).

III. The Approach of this Book

In addition to a theoretical and doctrinal analysis of the clash between neoliberal ideas of autonomy and childcare responsibilities, this book draws throughout on the findings of original empirical research, consisting of semi-structured interviews conducted with separated parents in England and Wales. These interviews complement the theoretical and doctrinal analysis of the law by offering insights into what the law means for its subjects.

This book also draws upon the findings of comparative research looking at Sweden which formed part of the same research project. This Swedish-focused element of the research also combines doctrinal, theoretical and original empirical work; the latter element consisted of semi-structured interviews with lawyers. Given that one of the problems with neoliberal-influenced ideas of autonomy is that they assume a level of gender equality that does not currently exist in England and Wales, Sweden's position as a leader in terms of gender equality generally,[54] and in terms of family policy in particular,[55] makes it a useful and established comparator on such issues.[56] The Swedish experience offers a perspective on whether neoliberal-influenced norms of autonomy are as problematic for family law where there is state support for caring and an emphasis on both mothers and fathers being involved in care.

A. Interviews with Separated Parents

The empirical findings discussed in this book come from semi-structured interviews conducted with 18 separated parents in 2016 and 2017. All parents had been in heterosexual relationships; as will be explored, gender roles provide an important backdrop to this research and these cannot be expected to apply in the same way outside of heterosexual relationships.

In sampling, attempts were made to capture participants with a range of post-separation situations, so as to understand how the tension between

[54] The EU gender equality index, for example, bases Sweden's top position on the relative gaps in attainment between men and women in six areas: work, money, knowledge, time, power and health (the UK ranks fifth): see EIGE, 'Gender Equality Index 2019: Sweden' https://eige.europa.eu/publications/gender-equality-index-2019-sweden accessed 28 April 2023. The World Economic Forum ranked Sweden fourth globally on the basis of gender gaps in four categories: economic participation and opportunity, educational attainment, health and survival and political empowerment (the UK ranks 21st): see World Economic Forum, 'Global Gender Gap Report 2020' www3.weforum.org/docs/WEF_GGGR_2020.pdf accessed 28 April 2023.

[55] See further Chapter 4.

[56] Other examples of Sweden being used as a comparator in matters of family law and policy include: L Ma et al, 'Fathers' Uptake of Parental Leave: Forerunners and Laggards in Sweden, 1993–2010' (2020) 49 *Journal of Social Policy* 361, S Björk, 'Doing Morally Intelligible Fatherhood: Swedish Fathers' Accounts of Their Parental Part-time Work Choices' (2013) 11 *Fathering* 221, R Klinth, 'The Best of Both Worlds? Fatherhood and Gender Equality in Swedish Paternity Leave Campaigns, 1976–2006' (2008) 6 *Fathering* 20.

neoliberal-influenced ideas of autonomy and caring responsibilities might be experienced by different types of family. While this sample does not claim to be representative of the experiences of all separated families, this approach is intended to highlight some of the issues that different types of family might experience. As outlined above, the financial claims available on separation are much more extensive for married couples than for cohabitants. However, gendered patterns of caring are seen in both types of relationship.[57] For this reason, it was important to interview both married and cohabiting parents to see whether there were differences in how the tension between the increasing expectation of autonomy in family law and the realities of childcare responsibilities was navigated. The breakdown of participants by the nature of their relationship was as follows (all names used are pseudonyms):

Table 1 Research participants in England and Wales

	Formerly married	**Former cohabitants**	**Never in a relationship with the other parent**
Mothers	5 (Antonia, Elizabeth, Laura, Ruth and Emily)	4 (Sophie, Alison, Esther and Louise)	1 (Erin)
Fathers	6 (Kenneth, Matthew, David, Andrew, Michael and Gareth)	2 (Jason and Neil)	0

In addition to their different pre-separation family arrangements, participants had in place a range of post-separation child arrangements. Elizabeth and Matthew (married to each other), Jason, Andrew and Emily all described their post-separation arrangements as shared care. For Andrew and Jason this was an exactly 50:50 arrangement. For Andrew, this involved the children spending alternate weeks with each parent, although they ultimately ended up living with him. For Jason, it meant his child spending three nights with him one week and four the next, with a very precise division of time: 'if you're half an hour late I'm just going to add it on Sunday or Saturday'. For Elizabeth and Matthew, and Emily and her husband, shared care involved the children spending five nights a fortnight with their father (although Elizabeth and Matthew intended to increase this to seven nights a fortnight as their child got older). In both cases, these arrangements were flexible. Matthew, for example, talked about a change of routine to allow him to be with a family member after an operation, and Emily talked about the children coming back to hers early when her ex-husband was away for work.

[57] See, for example, M González et al, '"Just Living Together": Implications of Cohabitation for Fathers' Participation of Child Care in Western Europe' (2010) 23 *Demographic Research* 445 and C Kalenkoski et al, 'The Effect of Family Structure on Parents' Child Care Time in the United States and the United Kingdom' (2007) 5 *Review of Economics of the Household* 353.

In contrast, Michael's children spent approximately four nights a fortnight with him, and Neil's children six nights a fortnight with him, but they considered their former partners to be the children's primary carer. In Michael's case, this seemed to be because he considered himself to have been the 'primary parent' during his marriage (at least for his youngest child) and felt that without his wife's false allegations of abuse the child arrangements 'would have been the other way around'. For Neil, the way in which he saw the arrangement was perhaps shaped by the way childcare had been divided during his relationship, and the fact that his former partner continued to work part-time afterwards. In neither case was there the sort of cooperation and flexibility described by Elizabeth and Matthew or Emily. Like Neil and Michael, Kenneth and Gareth also had regular contact with their children, who lived with their former partners, but it was less extensive. Laura had no contact at all with her children at the time of interview but would very much have liked to see them.

The sample includes six parents (Antonia, Sophie, David, Ruth, Alison, Louise) who were the primary carers for their children after separation, and whose children had limited contact with their former partners. David was unique in being a male primary carer after separation; he had not been beforehand. However, Andrew, who had a shared care arrangement after separation, had been a stay-at-home father prior to separation. Antonia, Ruth, Alison and Louise would all have liked their former partners to have more contact with their children. This seemed to be both because of the value of such contact to their children and because of the pressures of being a lone parent. Esther's children had more regular contact with their father than was the case for these other primary carers. However, she also talked about trying to alter contact patterns: 'for years it was, in the weekends that he had them, it was Saturday lunchtime 'til Monday taking them to school. So more recently I've been pushing for the Friday'.

Finally, Erin had not been in a relationship with her child's father. It was felt important to capture her experiences because not all care is performed within relationships. While the centrality of care to families makes it essential for the law to be able to respond to caring responsibilities, it is also important to think beyond this.

Sampling additionally aimed to capture participants with differing financial circumstances. Although, as noted above, the gendered division of caregiving in intact families in England and Wales has gendered financial consequences on separation, those financial consequences are experienced differently for couples with different levels of wealth.[58] Whereas women and dependent children at all levels tend to see a greater drop in their income than men, 'these changes are much greater for those women and children from formerly high-income couples (although such individuals are still better off, on average, than women and children from formerly low-income couples)'.[59] This research, therefore, sought to

[58] See, for example, Brewer and Nandi (n 11) and Fisher and Low (2016) (n 11).
[59] Brewer and Nandi (n 11) 45.

recruit parents with a range of different financial circumstances to see how they experienced the tension between neoliberal-influenced ideas of autonomy and caring responsibilities.

Whilst questions were asked around participants' financial circumstances, the extent to which precise details were given varied. Money is often seen as a private subject, so this issue was not pushed if responses were not forthcoming. Thus, it is difficult to apply a categorisation to the asset base of participants. Nevertheless, from the details that were shared, a range of financial circumstances is apparent. The only participant for whom debt appeared to be a real problem was Laura, who was made bankrupt after transferring her property to her ex-husband. At the time of interview, she was still unable to apply for credit. However, her own position was made less precarious by the presence of a new partner. Thus, the insight this sample provides into the issues of people with debt is limited. This is an important area for further research, particularly considering the current cost of living crisis.

For several participants there were no real assets to divide. For example, Louise, David, Ruth and Jason were all in a position where the assets at the end of the relationship were negligible. Sophie and Gareth both received slightly more, but it was insufficient to allow either of them to buy a new property. Further, for Sophie, who had been out of work for some time, the benefits system was an essential safety net. This was also the case for Andrew, Ruth and Alison, all of whom had been primary carers for their children during their relationships. Jason was also heavily reliant on the benefits system after separation, although he described this in terms of his choice to reduce his working hours to spend more time with his child.

For other participants (Antonia, Elizabeth and Matthew, Kenneth, Neil, Michael, Esther and Emily) there were sufficient assets for both partners to be rehoused. For the primary carers in particular, this meant a much more secure position than for those without assets. Both Esther and Antonia had brought more assets into their relationships than their former partners, which gave them claims over the family home; particularly important for Esther as a cohabitant. Further, Elizabeth and Emily both had established professional careers which enabled them to support themselves after separation. Thus, it was not just the asset base but also their career position that made them financially more secure than other participants.

For Michael and Neil, there was a perception that they were perhaps less well off than their former partners (both of whom had been the primary carers for their children during the relationship). It is hard to tell to what extent this reflects reality; research in general suggests that men tend to recover in income terms more quickly than women after divorce,[60] although of course this does not reflect the position in every case. For Michael, the feeling seemed to be at least partly related to his own greater financial contribution to the assets and his perception of his wife's unreasonable litigation conduct during their divorce, which had the effect of depleting those assets. Kenneth, who like Michael and Neil was the

[60] Fisher and Low (2016) (n 11).

main breadwinner in his household, did not seem to feel this way, but this may be because he appeared to be a particularly high earner who was easily able to meet his own (and his ex-wife's) financial needs.

B. The Swedish Element

Rather than seeking to compare laws from different jurisdictions which perform the same function,[61] the aim of the comparative element of this research was to offer a perspective 'to question the received orthodoxies of the legal system'.[62] In England and Wales, neoliberal-influenced norms of autonomy, which increasingly inform family law, are incompatible with lived realities in which caring responsibilities are gendered. The aim of looking to Sweden was to see whether such norms were as problematic in a more gender equal society. Thus, the focus of the comparison is not just legal but also concerned with the social, economic and political context, all of which are closely connected to the legal system.[63]

As part of this comparative approach, seven lawyers were interviewed in Sweden; five women and two men. Their experience ranged from less than five years to more than 20 years and is summarised in the table below:

Table 2 Research participants in Sweden

Participant name (all pseudonyms)	Overview of participant's clients and experience	Years in practice
Anna	Works at a varied practice acting for business and private clients. Anna undertakes a variety of family law work: divorce, family, custody, international cases, public law children cases.	Less than 5 years
Bertil	Bertil is a consultant at a varied practice acting for business and private clients.	More than 20 years
Clara	Clara's firm specialises in private law. Most clients walk through the door. Clients are from all levels of society. Clara does not have a typical client. She undertakes lots of custody suits and financial suits pertaining to custody.	10–15 years

(continued)

[61] K Zweigert and H Kötz, *An Introduction to Comparative Law*, 3rd edn (T Weir tr, Oxford University Press, 1998) 34.

[62] P Legrand, 'Beyond Method: Comparative Law as Perspective' (1988) 36 *The American Journal of Comparative Law* 788, 789.

[63] W Kamba, 'Comparative Law: A Theoretical Framework' (1974) 23 *International and Comparative Law Quarterly* 485, 493 and O Kahn-Freund, 'On Uses and Misuses of Comparative Law' (1974) 37 *Modern Law Review* 1.

Table 2 ***(Continued)***

Participant name (all pseudonyms)	Overview of participant's clients and experience	Years in practice
Ebbe	Ebbe's firm undertakes work in business law, family law, personal injury and criminal law. She has no typical client and undertakes family and criminal law work.	15–20 years
Eric	Varied practice advising both business and private clients (not criminal law).	15–20 years
Filippa	In her previous role, Filippa undertook migration and family law work. Much of her family law work involved disputes about children and the economic consequences of separation.	Less than 5 years
Gunilde	Gunilde undertakes private law and criminal law work. When it comes to family law, Gunilde specialises in custody, contact matters and sharing of assets on separation.	More than 20 years

Attempts were made to try and achieve a more gender-balanced sample than this. However, of six male lawyers initially contacted only one was interviewed (the second male participant was, however, recommended by one of those contacted). In contrast, interviews were secured with five of seven female lawyers contacted (although, in the event, a colleague of one of these five was interviewed in her place because of an emergency court hearing).

IV. The Impact of Covid-19

Since this research was conducted, the world has changed significantly. In 2020, Covid-19 resulted in global lockdowns and facilitated shifts in working patterns. Since then, a global cost of living crisis has also impacted many families' financial positions. While these events have impacted society as a whole, the consequences have not been borne equally. In particular, women, lower income families and minority ethnic groups have suffered disproportionately, and these impacts are connected to caring responsibilities.

First, gender inequalities in the division of caring responsibilities were compounded by Covid-19, with greater numbers of parents working from home and having to balance home schooling their children. Chung and van der Lippe explain that:

> *gender matters* when it comes to understanding the consequences of flexible working. Men and women use flexible working in different ways that leads to different outcomes for wellbeing, work–life balance and work intensification. A recurring finding is that women are more likely to (or expected to) carry out more domestic responsibilities whilst working flexibly, while men are more likely to (or are expected to) prioritise and expand their work spheres. Consequently, it is women who will fear and are more likely to face negative career outcomes due to flexible working.[64]

Research suggests that even where both parents were working from home during the Covid lockdowns, caring responsibilities were not divided equally: 'Mothers working from home spend considerably more time homeschooling and caring for children than fathers working from home.'[65] Further, '[t]his relationship also holds when we control for a broad range of individual and job characteristics …'.[66] The Covid Realities project, a participatory research project with parents and carers on low incomes likewise found:

> … strong evidence of gendered inequalities made worse by the pandemic. Women were often juggling multiple and complex roles, particularly in relation to home-schooling. Women were also more likely to manage household finances, alongside caring for children and paid work.[67]

ONS data from 2020 also suggested that women's work had been more impacted than men's by the pandemic.[68] While the reopening of schools and other services may have alleviated much of this disruption, home working, whether full-time or as part of hybrid working, appears to be more common following Covid-19.[69] There is, therefore, the possibility that flexible working will continue to have gendered effects.

Second, as the Covid Realities project observed, '[f]amilies living on a low income are profoundly disadvantaged and Covid-19 has only made this worse'.[70] The key themes identified in that project were 'the struggle to get by, the inadequacy

[64] H Chung and T van der Lippe, 'Flexible Working, Work-Life Balance, and Gender Equality: Introduction' (2020) 151 *Social Indicator Research* 365, 375.

[65] A Adams-Prassl et al, 'Inequality in the Impact of the Coronavirus Shock: Evidence from Real Time Surveys' (2020) 189 *Journal of Public Economics* 1, 6. See also C Payne and G Vassilev, 'Coronavirus and How People Spent Their Time under Lockdown: 28 March to 26 April 2020' (ONS, 27 May 2020) www.ons.gov.uk/economy/nationalaccounts/satelliteaccounts/bulletins/coronavirusandhowpeoplespentthe irtimeunderrestrictions/28marchto26april2020#main-points accessed 28 April 2023.

[66] Adams-Prassl et al (ibid) 6.

[67] R Patrick et al, 'Covid Realities: Documenting Life on a Low Income during the Pandemic' (24 January 2022) https://cdn.sanity.io/files/brhp578m/production/dbb82337a5b6c6ad1fc2e524a75bb4 123c5005b6.pdf accessed 28 April 2023, 10.

[68] R Davies, 'Coronavirus and the Social Impacts on Great Britain: 17 July 2020' (ONS, 17 July 2020) www.ons.gov.uk/peoplepopulationandcommunity/healthandsocialcare/healthandwellbeing/bulletins/coronavirusandthesocialimpactsongreatbritain/17july2020#work accessed 28 April 2023.

[69] ONS, 'Is Hybrid Working Here to Stay?' (23 May 2022) www.ons.gov.uk/employmentandlabourmarket/peopleinwork/employmentandemployeetypes/articles/ishybridworkingheretostay/2022-05-23 accessed 28 April 2023.

[70] Patrick et al (n 67) 6.

of social security, the additional pressures of lockdown, and the impact of social security and poverty on parents mental health'.[71] It is clear that higher and lower income families fared differently through the pandemic. Whereas on average spending fell during the Covid-19 pandemic, lower income families and those with children were most likely to report increased spending.[72] During lockdowns and when children were at home through self-isolating, there were additional costs because of food and heating.[73] Other costs incurred by poorer families related to remote learning: IT equipment, broadband, study materials were all required and libraries, which might previously have provided these resources, were closed.[74] Further:

> the cost of certain items (most obviously food) has risen for many: promotions have been reduced and cheaper items are harder to obtain. Many families have been forced to use more proximate but expensive stores to avoid public transport or to get groceries delivered, while charity shops have been harder to access.[75]

The result of this has been that women and poorer households have disproportionately suffered 'the post-pandemic burden of financial insecurity and worsening mental health'.[76] This situation has been compounded by the cost of living crisis in which poorer households, on average, have experienced higher rates of inflation.[77]

Third, minority ethnic groups have also been disproportionately affected by Covid-19. As well as the additional health risks faced by minority ethnic groups, these groups were also at 'particular risk … from income shocks, increased precarity and poverty'.[78] Covid-19 was not the sole cause of these issues, but rather has exacerbated existing inequalities. For example, in 2009, and while there was significant diversity between the experiences of minority groups, all minority groups had higher rates of poverty than average and compared to the white majority.[79] Further, benefits changes such as the benefit cap and two-child limit mean that larger families were disproportionately affected by child poverty. Census data from 2011 illustrates that certain ethnic and religious groups are much more likely

[71] Patrick et al (n 67) 8.

[72] M Brewer and R Patrick, 'Pandemic Pressures' (January 2021) www.resolutionfoundation.org/app/uploads/2021/01/Pandemic-pressures.pdf accessed 28 April 2023.

[73] ibid.

[74] Brewer and Patrick (n 72).

[75] Brewer and Patrick (n 72) 3.

[76] Z Cheng et al, 'Working Parents, Financial Insecurity, and Childcare: Mental Health in the Time of COVID-19 in the UK' (2021) 19 *Review of Economics of the Household* 136. See also Patrick et al (n 67) 11.

[77] P Hourston, 'Cost of Living Crisis' (Institute for Government, 17 August 2022) www.institutefor-government.org.uk/explainers/cost-living-crisis accessed 28 April 2023; D Harari et al, 'Rising Cost of Living in the UK' (House of Commons Library, 20 December 2022) https://researchbriefings.files.parliament.uk/documents/CBP-9428/CBP-9428.pdf accessed 28 April 2023.

[78] Patrick et al (n 67) 10.

[79] L Platt, 'Ethnicity and Child Poverty' (Department for Work and Pensions, Research Report No 576, 2009) https://dera.ioe.ac.uk/11016/1/rrep576.pdf accessed 28 April 2023.

to have three or more children.[80] These groups are also likely to face labour market penalties relative to the white population.[81]

In all of these cases, the financial effects of caring responsibilities are important in understanding these financial impacts and this provides vital context for the discussion that follows. Nevertheless, it is important to recognise what this book can and cannot achieve. Its focus is on how family law can do more to recognise caring responsibilities when parents separate. Family law alone cannot solve these systemic problems: it can only attempt to respond to the consequences better. Therefore, and as the authors of various reports on these issues have made clear, wider policy measures are also essential.[82]

V. Chapter Outline

This book comprises four parts. Having outlined the background and context for this book in the first part, Part II considers the roles of autonomy and care in the family law framework of England and Wales. Chapter 2 considers the reasons for care's invisibility in law and society. It begins by outlining the concept of neoliberalism in more depth and explaining how neoliberal-influenced ideas of autonomy have come to dominate family law in England and Wales. The chapter goes on to consider the meaning of care and its role within the neoliberal paradigm. Against this backdrop, the chapter explains the incompatibility of neoliberal-influenced ideas of autonomy and caring responsibilities. Chapter 3 explores the legal response to caring responsibilities on separation in England and Wales in greater detail. It begins by outlining the consequences of the failure to understand caring responsibilities. The chapter then turns to the legal response in each of the four areas of the law on separation examined throughout this book (the financial claims of cohabiting couples, financial remedies on divorce, financial arrangements for children, and child arrangements) and suggests that in each case the law fails to recognise caring responsibilities.

Part III of this books turns to examine the position in Sweden. Chapter 4 explores the Swedish approach to reconciling paid work and care, in which the state provides support that allows parents to engage in paid work. Whilst this

[80] K Stewart et al, 'A Time of Need: Exploring the Changing Poverty Risk Facing Larger Families in the UK' (Centre for Analysis of Social Exclusion, 2021) https://sticerd.lse.ac.uk/dps/case/cp/casepaper224.pdf accessed 28 April 2023.

[81] ibid.

[82] See, for example, Brewer and Patrick (n 72); K Power, 'The COVID-19 Pandemic Has Increased the Care Burden of Women and Families' (2020) 16 *Sustainability: Science, Practice and Policy* 67; E Croda and S Grossbard, 'Women Pay the Price of COVID-19 More than Men' (2020) 19 *Review of Economics of the Household* 1; K Hill and R Webber, 'From Pandemic to Cost of Living Crisis: Low-income Households in Challenging Times' https://michaelharrison.org.uk/wp-content/uploads/2022/05/From-pandemic-to-cost-of-living-crisis-low-income-families-in-challenging-times-Full-report.pdf accessed 28 April 2023; Patrick et al (n 67).

approach is important in meeting the needs of a range of families, and not just wealthy nuclear families where the parents are married, it is argued in Chapter 5 that the Swedish approach does not solve the problem of care's invisibility in society. Gendered norms around parenthood are persistent, and pervasive narratives of equality in Sweden serve to disguise this fact. Neither does the Swedish approach tackle the problem of 'privileged irresponsibility',[83] whereby those who do not care benefit financially on separation. Family law in Sweden does not seek to address the financial consequences of caring responsibilities on separation because of the emphasis on gender equality in society. Thus, while state support is an important aspect of supporting care, the Swedish approach does not offer a complete solution. A new approach is needed.

Part IV outlines a proposed new approach to family law which would aim to place care at its centre. Chapter 6 outlines the key principles of the proposed new approach. It begins by drawing together the lessons from the first five chapters to explain why a new approach is needed and why that approach is grounded in family law, rather than family policy. The chapter suggests two different mechanisms for placing care at the heart of family law. The first, a framework for embedding an understanding of care in family law decisions, is explored in Chapter 6. The second, substantive reforms to family law to better recognise care, is outlined in Chapter 7. Chapter 7 considers each of the four areas of family law on separation (the financial claims of cohabiting couples, financial remedies on divorce, financial arrangements for children, and child arrangements) in turn, and considers whether, and if so how, the law might be reformed. In each case, the chapter considers whether substantive law reform is appropriate.

Taken together, these chapters will make a case for reforming family law to better recognise the caring relationships which are at the heart of family life. They will also suggest how such reform might be achieved.

[83] J Tronto, *Moral Boundaries: A Political Argument for an Ethic of Care* (Routledge, 1993) 121.

PART II

Autonomy, Care and Family Law in England and Wales

2

The Clash between Autonomy and Care in the Neoliberal Paradigm

> **Michael**: … [Given the primary carer's relatively limited earning potential in the scenario being discussed] I don't feel she's … entitled to a greater claim … based on her lack of earnings. Indeed, you could easily argue the case that she's had a wonderful, a wonderful twelve years looking after the … children and not having to go to the daily grind. What's … that worth? Shouldn't she be … compensating him for having to, to allow her to do that? What would … I have given, to be allowed to do that? I would have loved that … so I, I don't think there's any argument for that. Unless you're saying, it's a burden looking after children and not going to work. And I would really, really disagree. I would love to do that.

Michael, one of the parents interviewed for this research, outlines here three important themes that illustrate how caring is understood in a context where family law and policy are dominated by neoliberal-influenced ideas of autonomy. These themes will be explored in this chapter and Chapter 3. First, Michael raises the idea of choice, commenting on the restrictions on his ability to choose to care for his children. Ideas of choice are central to understandings of autonomy.[1] However, as Michael's statement reveals, choices are far from straightforward. When it comes to caring for children, the expected roles of different parents are different, and shape the choices open to them. In Michael's case, for example, there appear to have been constraints on his ability to choose to care.

The second significant feature of Michael's words is his suggestion of an idealised conception of care: care is viewed as a positive experience that contrasts favourably with the 'daily grind' of paid work. Michael rejects the idea that care is a 'burden'. However, this understanding contrasts with some of the descriptions of childcare given by primary carer participants to this research. Antonia, for example, said that '[b]eing a mother is really boring … It's a really tedious, boring job.' Sophie commented several times on how difficult it was to be a single parent and to balance work with caring responsibilities: '[I]t's incredibly hard, to be honest.' Emily explained how much she valued the time the children spent

[1] M Fineman, *The Autonomy Myth* (The New Press, 2004); A Heenan, 'Neoliberal Autonomy and Financial Remedy Reform: Lessons from Sweden' (2020) 3 *Child and Family Law Quarterly* 263; A Heenan, 'Neoliberalism, Family Law, and the Devaluation of Care' (2021) 48 *Journal of Law and Society* 386; K Lynch, *Care and Capitalism* (Polity, 2022).

with their father: 'when you're a single parent on your own with two really young children, those weekends off, hard as though they might be to begin with, they became really precious time to me'.[2] Michael's understanding of care is perhaps reflective of a wider societal lack of engagement with the question of what it means to care. As Chapter 1 explained, caring can carry financial costs. This chapter and Chapter 3 will explore societal understandings of care and how they often fail to understand this.

The third feature of Michael's statement, which is closely connected to the second, is the idea that caring alone does not justify financial compensation. As explained in Chapter 1, the legal response at the end of a relationship differs depending on whether a couple are married or not. Chapter 3 will consider the legal framework in greater detail, and explore how that legal framework reflects, or perhaps fails to reflect, the costs of care.

This chapter begins by outlining the concept of neoliberalism, which is central to the theoretical framework for this book. It outlines how neoliberal-influenced ideas, such as norms of individual responsibility and the freedom of choice suggested by Michael, increasingly underpin family law and policy. Against this backdrop, the chapter goes on to consider the role of care in a neoliberal-influenced society and the gendered, raced and classed ways in which expectations of care are set. This analysis reveals the incompatibility between the work involved in care and neoliberal-influenced ideas of autonomy.

I. The Influence of Neoliberal Ideas in Family Law and Policy

A. Understanding Neoliberalism

Central to understanding the broader context in which family law and policy operate is an understanding of neoliberalism. At the core of neoliberalism is the imposition of market rationality upon political and social life. As Brown explains '[t]hat is, more than simply facilitating the economy, the state itself must construct and construe itself in market terms, as well as develop policies and promulgate a political culture that figures citizens exhaustively as rational economic actors in every sphere of life'.[3] Several consequences flow from this. First, as regards the state, this drive to marketisation underscores a preference for a minimalist state.[4] Relatedly, as Larner explains, '[i]n conjunction with

[2] See also Lynch on the time-consuming nature of 'hands on caring': Lynch (n 1) 79.

[3] W Brown, 'American Nightmare: Neoliberalism, Neoconservatism, and De-Democratization' (2006) 34 *Political Theory* 690, 694.

[4] W Larner, 'Neo-liberalism: Policy, Ideology, Governmentality' (2000) 63 *Studies in Political Economy* 5; Lynch (n 1) 2.

this general shift towards the neo-liberal tenet of "more market," deregulation and privatization have become central themes in debates over welfare state restructuring'.[5] So not only is the role of the state reduced, but its operation is increasingly influenced by market ideals.

The second important consequence of this understanding of neoliberalism is what it means for the individuals who live in a world shaped by neoliberal-influenced policies. Brown's description above highlights the neoliberal understanding of individuals as rational economic actors.[6] Neoliberalism, however, goes further than this, entailing 'a host of policies that figure and produce citizens as individual entrepreneurs and consumers whose moral autonomy is measured by their capacity for "self-care" – their ability to provide for their own needs and service their own ambitions'.[7] This encouragement for citizens to be financially independent of the state[8] is also evident in how families are understood: they 'are essentially expected to be both self-governing and self-sufficient, rather than relying on state support'.[9] Kaganas further suggests that policies influenced by neoliberalism understand citizens through the lenses of individual responsibility and autonomy.[10] Thus, policies influenced by neoliberalism take as their starting point actors who are economically rational, financially independent, responsible and autonomous. These overarching understandings of the nature of neoliberal subjects have consequences for how they are expected to behave. For example, because choices are deemed to be freely made, those who make them are held responsible for the costs.[11]

B. Neoliberal-influenced Ideas of Autonomy and Family Law

In family law, a vision of autonomy underpinned by neoliberal understandings has become increasingly dominant. Diduck argues that individual autonomy has become almost the essence of justice in family law.[12] She suggests that this is expressed in two connected ways:

> The first expression is structural and procedural. It relates to the creation of an autonomous system of dispute resolution that is separate from and runs parallel with the formal justice system. The second expression is conceptual and relates to assumptions

[5] Larner (ibid) 5. See also Brown (n 3) 694.

[6] Brown (n 3) 694. See also T Harman, 'Neoliberalism, Governmentality, and Ethics' (2009) 6 *Foucault Studies* 37 and T Lemke, '"The Birth of Bio-Politics": Michel Foucault's Lecture at the Collège de France on Neo-Liberal Governmentality' (2001) 30 *Economy and Society* 190, 201.

[7] Brown (n 3) 694.

[8] See, for example, Fineman (n 1) and J Herring, *Relational Autonomy* (Springer, 2014).

[9] L Buckley, 'Relational Theory and Choice Rhetoric in the Supreme Court of Canada' (2015) 29 *Canadian Journal of Family Law* 251, 258.

[10] F Kaganas, 'Justifying the LASPO Act: Authenticity, Necessity, Suitability, Responsibility and Autonomy' (2017) 39 *Journal of Social Welfare and Family Law* 168.

[11] Lemke (n 6) 201.

[12] A Diduck, 'Autonomy and Family Justice' (2016) 28 *Child and Family Law Quarterly* 133.

> about a particular kind of individual autonomy that must be activated and allowed to flourish in family justice.[13]

The structural and procedural aspect of autonomy underpins moves to encourage private ordering in the Family Justice System. Private ordering, the idea that individuals should be free to create recognised legal obligations outside of the formal court system,[14] has always been influential in family law.[15] However, recent developments have resulted in it becoming the default expectation for the resolution of family law disputes. First, and most significantly, the Legal Aid, Sentencing and Punishment of Offenders Act 2012 (LASPO 2012) removed legal aid funding for private family law matters, with the exception of cases involving evidence of domestic abuse.[16] Thus, for very many people the only options available to them are to represent themselves in court, reach a private settlement or take no action at all. More recently, a Court of Appeal decision[17] expressly promoted family law arbitration as a solution to court backlogs, normalising a move away from the court system for those who can afford it.[18] These developments are connected to the wider neoliberal goal of a smaller state where functions are privatised.[19] This facet of autonomy is supported by an assumption that the individuals resolving disputes outside of the court system have equal bargaining power.[20] This assumption is misplaced in the family context, where there can be significant inequalities of bargaining power.[21]

More central to this book is Diduck's conceptual aspect of autonomy, which focuses on the kind of autonomy promoted by the Family Justice System. This can be explored from two connected perspectives. The first relates to the way in which the Family Justice System understands the legal subject and how he behaves. The neoliberal norms of individuals outlined above connect to several of the themes raised by Michael's words at the outset of this chapter. Consistently with neoliberal understandings of individuals and the decisions they make, Michael talks about care as if it is a choice. However, the idea of caring as a choice fails to recognise the realities of making decisions around care. Decisions about who should care for children are complex and, as later sections of this chapter will discuss, may be influenced by factors such as gender, race, and class. The idea of choice becomes even more difficult after separation when decisions around care are informed by

[13] ibid 134.

[14] B Bix, 'Private Ordering and Family Law' (2010) 23 *Journal of the American Academy of Matrimonial Lawyers* 249; S Cretney, 'Private Ordering and Divorce – How Far Can We Go?' [2003] *Family Law* 399.

[15] A Heenan, 'Haley v Haley: Family Law Arbitration and the New Frontier of Private Ordering' (2021) 84 *Modern Law Review* 1385.

[16] LASPO 2012, s 9 and Sch 1, para 12.

[17] *Haley v Haley* [2020] EWCA Civ 1369.

[18] Heenan (n 15).

[19] Larner (n 4).

[20] Heenan (2021) (n 1); S Thompson, *Prenuptial Agreements and the Presumption of Free Choice* (Hart Publishing, 2015).

[21] See, for example, Heenan (2021) (n 1); Thompson (ibid).

pre-separation norms[22] and may be limited by a partner's actions.[23] Further, and consistently with Lemke's suggestion that individuals are considered responsible for the costs of their choices in the neoliberal paradigm,[24] Michael suggests that caring should not be financially compensated. As will be discussed in Chapter 3, this is not the position the law takes. Instead, at least where a couple are married, there is some recognition that caring generates what Fineman describes as 'derivative dependency',[25] which recognises that 'those who care for others are themselves dependant on resources to undertake that care'.[26]

The second aspect of Diduck's conceptual dimension of autonomy concerns the ways in which neoliberal-influenced understandings of autonomy have shaped the substantive law. The impact of neoliberal-influenced ideas of autonomy is particularly evident in the law dealing with the financial consequences of divorce and the examples that follow are drawn from that area of law. However, as Chapter 3 will explore, neoliberal influences can be seen more widely in family law. The first, and perhaps most obvious, example of neoliberal-influenced ideas of autonomy influencing the law is the growth of pre-nuptial agreements. While pre-nuptial agreements are not binding in English and Welsh law, they are persuasive. This changed legal approach was explained by the Supreme Court as follows:

> The reason why the court should give weight to a nuptial agreement is that there should be respect for individual autonomy. The court should accord respect to the decision of a married couple as to the manner in which their financial affairs should be regulated. It would be paternalistic and patronising to override their agreement simply on the basis that the court knows best.[27]

The concept of autonomy to which respect is accorded here is consistent with neoliberal understandings. In line with ideas of choice discussed above, this extract from the judgment in *Radmacher* places importance on respecting the decision of a married couple. It does not, however, consider the issues of power at play in such decisions[28] or recognise that members of a couple may have different interests. A second notable feature of this extract from the majority judgment in *Radmacher* is that the decision being respected is one about the couple's financial affairs. This makes sense in the neoliberal paradigm where economic rationality is prized and expected. However, it fails to understand that family decisions may be motivated by the needs of the family as a whole, even if collective interests conflict with the interests of individual family members. For example, a decision that one parent

[22] Heenan (2021) (n 1); C Lacroix, 'Freedom, Desire and Power: Gender Processes and Presumptions of Shared Care and Responsibility after Parental Separation' (2006) 29 *Women's Studies International Forum* 184.

[23] R Treloar, 'High-conflict Divorce Involving Children: Parents' Meaning-making and Agency' (2018) 40 *Journal of Social Welfare and Family Law* 340.

[24] Lemke (n 6) 201.

[25] Fineman (n 1) 35.

[26] ibid 36.

[27] *Radmacher (formerly Granatino) v Granatino* [2010] UKSC 42 [75].

[28] Thompson (n 20).

performs more childcare and the other works more may suit the needs of the family as a whole, but have long-term financial consequences for the carer's earning capacity. The breadwinner may also suffer disadvantages, for example the loss of a deeper relationship with his or her children through not being able to care.

A second, and related, area of the law in which neoliberal-influenced understandings of autonomy are evident is the broader law of financial provision on divorce. Consistently with the norms of financial independence and individual responsibility outlined above, financial clean breaks, meaning that there are no ongoing financial ties between the adults,[29] are the norm on divorce: recent research looking at 400 court files found that ongoing spousal support was only paid in 16 per cent of cases.[30] This links to several of the themes outlined above that shape the neoliberal paradigm. For example, if individuals are financially independent and behave economically rationally then the absence of support from a spouse should not be problematic. However, this fails to recognise the realities of family life in the same way as the law's view of prenuptial agreements does.

Thus, the Family Justice System is increasingly dominated by neoliberal-influenced understandings of autonomy. Autonomy influences how disputes are resolved. It informs the way in which we think about the legal subject and has even come to shape the law that is applied. However, these norms fail to capture the realities of family life. Crucially, neoliberal-influenced conceptions of autonomy fail to account for the impact of caring responsibilities on the ability to be autonomous.

II. The Role of Care

Having explored the concept of neoliberalism and the centrality of autonomy within the neoliberal framework, it is important to think about care. This section begins by briefly explaining the choice to use the language of care. It goes on to think about what it means to care, and the role of the state in supporting care. It then explores how this fits with the neoliberal paradigm outlined above. It is suggested that at the same time as assuming that individuals are autonomous, the neoliberal paradigm relies on unpaid care work. However, that work is not openly acknowledged. For example, whilst unpaid care is indispensable to society, it does not form part of economic measures such as gross domestic product (GDP).[31] Further, even ONS attempts to calculate unpaid care relative to GDP[32] base that

[29] It is not possible to have a clean break as regards financial obligations for children.

[30] E Hitchings and J Miles, 'Financial Remedies on Divorce: the Need for Evidence-based Reform' (2018) www.nuffieldfoundation.org/sites/default/files/files/briefing%20paper%20Jun%202018%20FINAL.pdf accessed 28 April 2023.

[31] C Payne and G Vassilev, 'Household Satellite Account, UK: 2015 and 2016' (ONS, 2 October 2018) www.ons.gov.uk/economy/nationalaccounts/satelliteaccounts/articles/householdsatelliteaccounts/2015and2016estimates#focus-on-childcare accessed 28 April 2023.

[32] See, for example, ibid.

value on the market value of child minder services[33] which are 'sex-segregated or sex-stereotyped jobs, which are filled by women and lower paid'.[34] The result is that the importance and value of care is hidden.

A. Why 'Care' and the Role of an Ethic of Care

The topic of this book has overlaps with other areas of study, most notably social reproduction theory and literature on an ethic of care. Turning first to social reproduction theory, in explaining her preference for that terminology, rather than the language of care, Bhattacharya explains that:

> If, as we propose, the spatial distinction between production (public) and reproduction (private) is a historical form of appearance, then the labor that is dispensed in both spheres must be theorized integratively.[35]

Thus, social reproduction theory is about challenging the separation between the public and the private and recognising the private work that goes into producing the public worker. This is an important project, and relevant to the discussions in this book, but not the purpose of this book. This book focuses on private family law and considers how care can be placed at its centre. It is, therefore, primarily focused on private relationships. This does not mean that the role of the state is unimportant: state interventions, such as affordable childcare, might allow carers to engage in paid work to a greater extent so that the financial disadvantage they suffer on separation is reduced. However, the state is not the primary focus. This will be explored in greater detail in Chapter 6, but for clarity at this stage this private focus is the reason for the choice to use the language of 'care'.

In relation to an 'ethic of care',[36] while my analysis is informed by some of those writing in an 'ethic of care' tradition,[37] my aim here is to consider the question of how to make care more visible within a private family law framework, rather than to contribute to the ethic of care literature per se. In taking this approach, I do not reject the possibility that an ethic of care could be utilised in achieving a more holistic approach to dealing with the role of care in society, although not all

[33] D Webber and C Payne, 'Chapter 10: Methodological Annex' (ONS, 7 April 2016) www.ons.gov.uk/economy/nationalaccounts/satelliteaccounts/compendium/householdsatelliteaccounts/2005to2014/chapter10methodologicalannex#annex-1-methodology-for-all-the-activities accessed 28 April 2023.

[34] M Waring, *Counting for Nothing*, 2nd edn (University of Toronto Press, 2004) 227.

[35] T Bhattacharya, 'Introduction: Mapping Social Reproduction Theory' in T Bhattacharya (ed), *Social Reproduction Theory* (Pluto Press, 2017) 9.

[36] Gilligan, whose work is often credited with the development of care ethics as a moral theory, suggests that an ethic of care conceives of morality as 'concerned with the activity of care' and 'centers moral development around the understanding of responsibility and relationships': see C Gilligan, *In a Different Voice* (Harvard University Press, 2003) 19.

[37] For example, my analysis draws upon critiques of neoliberal capitalism put forward by Lynch: Lynch (n 1) and Tronto (J Tronto, *Caring Democracy* (New York University Press, 2013) and J Tronto, *Moral Boundaries: A Political Argument for an Ethic of Care* (Routledge, 1993)) and uses Tronto's understanding of the practice of care: Tronto (1993) ibid, 106–108.

advocates of an ethic of care accept the utility of such an approach in the law.[38] However, assessing the feasibility of doing so is beyond the scope of this book and there are dangers of seeking to apply an overarching moral theory to a defined legal issue like this in isolation: without considering the connections to other areas of law and other domains of life holistically, there is a risk of unintended consequences.

B. What Does It Mean To Care?

Attempts to find a universal definition of care have been criticised for inattention to context and, in particular, a focus on the global North.[39] Even when the focus of care is narrower, and a universal description is not sought, there can be a failure to recognise difference based on race,[40] class[41] or the intersection of these and other factors.[42] Constructions of care often focus on motherhood as experienced by middle- and upper-class white women. Not only does this result in a conception of good parenting that is gendered, raced, and classed,[43] but it fails to understand the different work that parenting involves in different contexts. For example, it has been suggested that a focus on the experiences of white mothers ignores the work done by Black mothers in 'trying to foster a meaningful racial identity in children within a society that denigrates people of color'[44] and 'teach[ing] their children to deal with the unjust racialised world outside'.[45]

Given these challenges, this book does not propose a universal definition of care. Rather, its objective is to think more critically about what childcare involves in the family context, something that is not systematically considered in family law and policy, or indeed society more generally. Thus, the care that this book is primarily focused upon takes place within what Herring describes as 'caring relationships'.[46] He explains his preference for this concept over 'care' as follows:

[38] See, for example, V Held, *The Ethics of Care* (Oxford University Press, 2006). For an argument in favour of such an approach, see J Herring, *Caring and the Law* (Hart Publishing, 2013) 84–85.

[39] P Raghuram, 'Care Ethics beyond the Global North' (2016) 15 *ACME: An International Journal for Critical Geographies* 511; P Raghuram, 'Race and Feminist Care Ethics: Intersectionality as Method' (2019) 26 *Gender, Place and Culture* 613.

[40] Raghuram (2019) (ibid).

[41] For example, in Sweden it has been suggested that it is easier for middle-class than working-class fathers to work part-time for childcare reasons: see J Larsson and S Björk, 'Swedish Fathers Choosing Part-time Work' (2017) 2 *Community, Work & Family* 142.

[42] O Hankivsky, 'Rethinking Care Ethics: on the Promise and Potential of an Intersectional Analysis' (2014) 108 *American Political Science Review* 252.

[43] P Hamilton, 'The "Good" Attached Mother: An Analysis of Postmaternal and Postracial Thinking in Birth and Breastfeeding Policy in Neoliberal Britain' (2016) 31 *Australian Feminist Studies* 410.

[44] P Hill Collins, 'Shifting the Center: Race, Class, and Feminist Theorising about Motherhood' in E Nakano Glenn et al (eds), *Mothering: Ideology, Experience, and Agency* (Routledge, 2016).

[45] Raghuram (2019) (n 39).

[46] Herring (n 38) and J Herring, 'Ethics of Care and Disability Rights: Complementary or Contradictory?' in L Gelsthorpe et al (eds), *Spaces of Care* (Hart Publishing, 2020).

> My hope was that in using this terminology the contributions of both parties would be recognised. We should recognise that traditional division between carer and cared for fails to capture the dynamic of a caring relationship. We are all givers and receivers of care. What we do is not understood as an 'activity' but as a part of a relationship. The relationship gives what is done meaning and value. It is important, too, to realise that most caring is 'embedded in long-term dyadic relationships' such as partner, parent or child (Larkin and Milne 2014: 26). These are relationships marked by a shared life course and history. They are fluid and complex and need to be understood in their relational context.[47]

The sort of care that family law often deals with is the care performed within families. A relational aspect is, therefore, key. A good example of this relational element can be seen in the observations of several participants to this research who noted that their children's needs varied.[48] In some cases, this change was temporal: Antonia's children asked her to cut back on work when she divorced.[49] In other cases, it was noted that different children had different needs: for example, Sophie's children had different relationships with their father because they had been different ages at the time of separation and Gareth noted the different dynamics between each of his children and their parents.[50] Herring's idea of caring relationships means recognising these aspects of care. However, it also means recognising that care is not a one-dimensional activity; caring relationships are also a source of meaning and value for carers.

Care is not, however, only relational. Duffy distinguishes nurturant and nonnurturant care work.[51] Whereas the former is concerned with the relational aspects of care that aim to improve the wellbeing of another person,[52] nonnurturant care refers to those who are involved in reproductive labour more broadly but whose work is not necessarily relational.[53] Examples of the latter would include hospital cleaners or cafeteria workers.[54] Both of these aspects of care are important, but the performance of these different types of work 'is one of the major axes of racial-ethnic and class stratification within reproductive labor'[55] with 'some of the most significant concentrations of racial-ethnic workers … in the jobs that I call nonnurturant'.[56] Ignoring this bigger picture, therefore, overlooks and devalues important aspects of care.

The distinction between nurturant and nonnurturant work is particularly important when it comes to thinking about things like public forms of care.[57] Public

[47] Herring (2020) (n 46) 173.
[48] Heenan (2021) (n 1) 400.
[49] ibid.
[50] ibid.
[51] M Duffy, *Making Care Count* (Rutgers University Press, 2011).
[52] ibid 9.
[53] ibid 18.
[54] ibid.
[55] ibid.
[56] ibid.
[57] Tronto (2013) (n 37) 20.

support for care is a concern of this book, which explores the role of the state as well as the role of the law. Chapters 4 and 5 will consider the Swedish approach in which the state plays an important role in performing care, through heavily subsidised state childcare, and in supporting parental care, through generous parental leave provision. Where care is provided by the state it is not necessarily relational in the same way as the care performed within families. The distinction between nurturant and nonnurturant care is, therefore, important to remember. It is also useful in starting to think about the range of care performed within families. Duffy suggests that there is a distinction between spiritual and menial labour that largely maps on to the distinction between nurturant and nonnurturant care.[58] This could equally apply to care performed within the family; for example, comforting a child and cleaning up after them when they have been ill are very different aspects of care, both of which are vital, and it is important to be able to capture this.

While this book does not seek to achieve a universal definition of care, it is important to have a framework for thinking about care within the family more systematically. This work takes Tronto's four phases of care as a starting point.[59] These are:

1. caring about – recognising the need for care;
2. taking care of – assuming some responsibility for the need and determining how to respond to it;
3. caregiving – the direct meeting of needs for care;
4 care receiving – the final phase of caring, which focuses on the experiences of the recipient of care as a way of assessing how adequately care is provided.[60]

The advantage of Tronto's approach is that it forces us to think more deeply about what is involved in care. Recognising that 'care' captures a range of different activities can help to illuminate differences in the care performed by different actors. This approach also provides a way of interrogating the consequences of different forms of care and recognising that not all phases carry the same consequences. For example, caregiving may require those performing care to restructure their working patterns in a way that those who provide financial support for care (taking care of) are not required to do. This may have long-term financial consequences for the caregiver. Recognising this does not detract from the idea that caregiving has a value to the carer. It simply recognises that not all those who care are impacted in the same ways and that different forms of care have different consequences.

It is also important to think about differences between caregivers. Giving up work, or reducing working hours, to look after children can have long-term financial consequences for the caregiver. However, very diverse circumstances can underpin

[58] Duffy (n 51) 18.
[59] Tronto (1993) (n 37) 106–108.
[60] One of the examples Tronto gives is a person with limited mobility who may prefer to feed him or herself, even though it would be quicker for a caregiver to feed him or her: see further Tronto (1993) (n 37) 108.

these decisions. For example, a caregiver may be able to decide not to work because their partner works in a highly paid job and provides financial support. This sort of choice is not open to all caregivers. Conversely, in abusive relationships, not being able to work may be an aspect of the control exerted over the caregiver by their partner. Further, expectations around care are not universal, meaning that norms around whether and how to care impact individuals differently.

Focusing only on performing the physical acts of care may not, therefore, capture all of the work performed by caregivers and its impact. Tronto's discussion of privileged irresponsibility provides a way of capturing a broader cohort of people with the responsibility for care. She describes this idea as follows:

> Dividing up responsibility privileges those who are excused by not needing to provide care; thus the privileged avoid responding directly to the actual processes of care and the meeting of basic needs.[61]

The idea of responsibility is illuminating here. Whether a child's primary carer works full-time, part-time or not at all, a key feature in all cases is the idea of responsibility. The idea of the 'mental load', explained by Chung as being in charge of 'worrying about the family'[62] has been observed by feminist writers[63] and is a vital part of caring that is often overlooked. Lynch's description of the mental element of 'love labour' captures the work involved in this mental load:

> … it involves holding the persons and their interests in mind, keeping them 'present' in mental planning, and anticipating and prioritizing their needs and interests. It involves listening, affirming, supporting and challenging, as well as identifying with people at times of distress.[64]

Tronto suggests that attentiveness and responsibility, which would seem to be connected to the idea of the mental load, are ethical dimensions of care which follow on from the four phases outlined above.[65] However, for my purposes here, which are to use these four phases of care as a lens through which to critique private family law, it makes more sense to understand the mental load as an integral part of those phases. This does not mean that the mental load is unimportant or should be assumed to be present in any of Tronto's four phases of care. Rather, it is an element that needs to be thought about in analysing caring activity. For example, when thinking about caregiving it will be important to include the work involved in planning caring activities as well as in performing them.

[61] Tronto (1993) (n 37) 121.

[62] H Chung, 'Return of the 1950s Housewife? How to Stop Coronavirus Lockdown Reinforcing Sexist Gender Roles' (*The Conversation*, 30 March 2022) https://theconversation.com/return-of-the-1950s-housewife-how-to-stop-coronavirus-lockdown-reinforcing-sexist-gender-roles-134851 accessed 28 April 2023.

[63] See, for example, Emma, 'The Gender Wars of Household Chores: A Feminist Comic' (*The Guardian*, 26 May 2017) www.theguardian.com/world/2017/may/26/gender-wars-household-chores-comic accessed 28 April 2023.

[64] Lynch (n 1) 70.

[65] Tronto (1993) (n 37) 127.

C. Who Should Be Responsible for Care?

The previous section noted that performing care may carry financial costs, for example there may be long-term financial penalties for career sacrifice. This raises the question of who should bear those costs. Miles[66] suggests that there are three levels of responsibility: local responsibility for yourself, the horizontal responsibility of individuals who are (or were) in a relationship, and the vertical responsibility of the state. As Hale explains, these different levels of responsibility are connected: '[t]he more the private family can look after its own, the less the State will have to do'.[67]

Recognising the diversity of caring practices means recognising that the answer to the question of who should bear responsibility for the costs of caring has different implications for different families. For example, if horizontal responsibility is prioritised then this is only a realistic option for financial support where a partner has resources; in many cases there are only debts. It also assumes the presence of a partner. Further, the availability and extent of horizontal support for the costs of childcare is currently shaped by the nature of the parents' relationship; cohabiting couples have fewer claims available to them than married couples.

While it would be possible to extend the scope of financial remedies on divorce to cover parents in a wider range of situations, this is not a perfect solution either if we truly want to support carers. First, most parents have debts rather than assets, so the presence of financial claims would make little practical difference. Second, there is a concern about power imbalances if a caregiver is rendered financially dependent on their child's other parent, particularly in abusive relationships.[68] Thus, there are important reasons to think beyond intra-partner responsibility when thinking about care. As Chapters 4 and 5 will discuss, in Sweden, the state plays a far more proactive role in supporting care. Thinking about care from this perspective too is vital if caregiving is to be supported in all families and not just families where the parents are married and have assets (and where the ability to realise such claims is not limited by factors such as domestic abuse). While it is beyond the scope of this book to address the state response comprehensively, Chapter 6 reflects on the role of the state and its intersection with family law.

The need for the state to play a role does not, however, exclude the need for an intra-partner dimension. Family law needs to be able to look at individual situations and consider what is fair as between a particular couple. This will reproduce broader level societal inequalities: those caregivers in wealthy families will do better financially on separation than those living in poverty prior

[66] J Miles, 'Responsibility in Family Finance and Property Law' in J Bridgeman et al (eds), *Regulating Family Responsibilities* (Ashgate, 2011).

[67] B Hale, 'Equality and Autonomy in Family Law' (2011) *Journal of Social Welfare and Family Law* 3, 4.

[68] Heenan (2021) (n 1).

to separation. While this reinforces the need for a broader societal approach to responsibility for caregiving, it does not preclude the need to consider the financial arrangements made in these cases. The alternative is to reward privileged irresponsibility: those parents who choose not to perform the physical work of care benefit financially from these decisions on divorce. This will be explored further in Chapter 6.

D. The Role of Care in the Neoliberal Paradigm

Having explored the role of care, it is important to consider how this relates to the neoliberal paradigm outlined above, and in particular how it fits with the emphasis on individual autonomy. Unpaid care work is central to neoliberalism. As Chelliah explains:

> Neoliberal ideologues claim individuals must work out their own problems within the sphere of the nuclear family because it is too expensive for the government to provide provision for the wellbeing of people. Thus, a mother's unpaid work of caregiving becomes integral to the functioning of the neoliberal state.[69]

Unpaid care, therefore, fills the gaps left by the decline of the welfare state. To use the language of levels of responsibility, local (individual) or horizontal (intra-partner) responsibility come to fill the void left by an absence of vertical (state) responsibility. This centrality of care, however, raises two questions that are connected to the themes raised by Michael.

First is the question of who performs this care. Chelliah suggests that this is the responsibility of mothers, something that is consistent with Michael's assertion that the choice to care was not one that was open to him. While it is the case that care is gendered, as the next section will explore, other factors such as race and class are also crucial in understanding care within the neoliberal paradigm.

A second question raised by this understanding of the role of care in the neoliberal order is how caring responsibilities fit with the neoliberal-influenced understandings of autonomy explored in the preceding section. As Vandenbeld Giles explains, 'inherent within neoliberalism is a morality that places mothers at its very core. And yet, while neoliberal philosophy prioritizes the role of mothers, it contradictorily recognizes only individual market actors'.[70] Section II.F below will explore this dilemma. It suggests that the incompatibility between neoliberal-influenced understandings of autonomy and care result in a position whereby care is generally invisible in society, which may help to explain Michael's understanding of it as a positive experience that does not justify a financial claim.

[69] J Chelliah, 'Austerity and Gender Neutrality' in M Vandenbeld Giles (ed), *Mothering in the Age of Neoliberalism* (Demeter Press, 2014) 190.

[70] M Vandenbeld Giles, 'Introduction' in Vandenbeld Giles (n 69) 3.

E. Who Cares in the Neoliberal Paradigm?

The central role of mothers in providing care in the neoliberal paradigm is reinforced by 'an intensive mothering ideology promoting overwhelming devotion to one's child'.[71] Crowley explains this ideology as follows:

> The philosophy inherent in intensive mothering requires that all mothers put forth as much energy as possible into nurturing their children at the expense of any other interests or activities that they may desire in their own personal lives. More specifically, this ideology demands that all mothers expend enormous emotional, physical and financial resources on their children; they also must rely heavily on experts and other professionals to guide them into producing the best possible developmental outcomes for their sons and daughters.[72]

As will be discussed in the next section, these norms are incompatible with the neoliberal-influenced understandings of autonomy outlined above; Vandenbeld Giles notes 'the inconsistency of a neoliberal paradigm necessitating economic actors yet demanding full-time motherhood'.[73] Before going on to consider that clash in more detail, however, it is vital to unpick these norms of intensive mothering and consider to whom they apply.

At a basic level, 'intensive mothering' is gendered: mothers, not fathers, are expected to perform this sort of care. This norm is reflected in societal attitudes as captured by British Social Attitudes data. In the 2019 British Social Attitudes survey, 51 per cent of respondents believed that a woman should stay at home (19 per cent) or work part-time (32 per cent), with the father working full-time, where there is a child under school age.[74] The first of these figures marks a reduction from the 2018 report, when the figures were 33 per cent and 38 per cent respectively,[75] figures which at that time had shown very little change from 2012.[76] However, this reduction in the proportion of people favouring a stay at home mother did not translate into an increase in support for parental sharing of paid work and care:[77] in the 2019 survey only 6 per cent favour both parents working full-time and 9 per cent favour both parents working part-time. Instead, the proportion of respondents who could not choose an option increased from

[71] L Rodriguez Castro et al, 'Negotiating "Ideal Worker" and Intensive Mothering Ideologies: Australian Mothers' Emotional Geographies during Their Commutes' (2020) *Social and Cultural Geography* 1, 4.

[72] JE Crowley, 'Staying at Home or Working for Pay? Attachment to Modern Mothering Identities' (2014) 34 *Sociological Spectrum* 114, 116.

[73] Vandenbeld Giles (n 70) 9.

[74] J Curtice et al (eds), *British Social Attitudes 36* (The National Centre for Social Research, 2019) www.bsa.natcen.ac.uk/media/39363/bsa_36.pdf accessed 28 April 2023.

[75] E Attar Taylor and J Scott 'Gender' in D Phillips et al (eds), *British Social Attitudes: The 35th Report* (The National Centre for Social Research, 2018) www.bsa.natcen.ac.uk/latest-report/british-social-attitudes-35/gender.aspx accessed 28 April 2023.

[76] Attar Taylor and Scott (n 75).

[77] Curtice et al (n 74).

19 per cent to 30 per cent. The 2019 report does not include attitudes in relation to the position when the youngest child has started school. In the 2018 report, 49 per cent suggested that a woman should work part-time at this stage.[78]

The findings of my research echo this wider gendered picture, but also reveal the complexity of ideas around gender equality. Participants to my research were asked about two scenario questions, one involving a female carer and one involving a male carer. There were two different versions of each scenario, with half of the participants receiving one and half receiving another, in which the genders were reversed. After they had commented on the scenarios, participants were asked whether it would have made a difference to their answer if the genders were reversed. All participants said that gender should not make a difference in these scenarios, albeit that three[79] suggested that assumptions about gender were pervasive and that in reality it was hard to be sure about whether inherent biases would have made a difference to their answers. Nevertheless, some participants seemed to feel there were inherent differences between men and women which impacted the care they performed. This was most obvious in the interviews with some of the married parents who, either during their relationships or afterwards, had arrangements in which one parent did most of the care:

> **Antonia**: … as a rule women are a bit more emotionally involved with the children. Um, and the men are more the fun disciplinarian.
>
> **Laura**: … I think children ought, this is my personal belief, I personally believe that children ought to be with the mother. Because, you know, if the mother is compos mentis and is financially able, then the children ought to be with their mother because the mother gives them birth.
>
> **Ruth**: Maybe the younger generation maybe a bit different but the, obviously, the generation I'm in, um, I don't think [clears throat] many, a lot of men that I know anyway would want to do that. Even though they might, the thought of it might sound quite good being home and everything else. But yeah, I think it's the breadwinning, sort of caveman sort of attitude [laughs].
>
> **David**: Men, men do want to be out at work. Um, they know. Men aren't stu … well most men are stupid. But I know men who aren't stupid who know that it's harder work at home.

Antonia, Laura and Ruth had all been primary carers during their relationships. For Antonia and Ruth, the gendered division of labour continued after separation, and both expressed a desire for greater involvement by their ex-husbands. Following separation, both Laura and David's roles were atypical of their gender. David became the primary caregiver for his children and Laura lost contact with hers. It seems that in all cases, their statements about the differences between men

[78] Attar Taylor and Scott (n 75).
[79] Erin, David and Elizabeth.

and women are related to their own experiences. For Antonia and Ruth, their ideas of traditional gender roles reflect their own experience. Laura's statement about the role of mothers can perhaps be understood in the context of her grief at not seeing her children; she is trying to underline the importance of her role in their lives. Elsewhere in her interview, she seemed to recognise the importance of both parents playing a role and she expressed support for shared care. Likewise, David was 'the only boy' in his club of single parents in the early 1990s, reinforcing his experience as unusual, and he experienced difficulties in his encounters with the Child Support Agency:

> **David**: Um, and they'd say, 'Right, I'll get your papers,' so you'd hear dur-dur-dur, and they'd go, 'Right, so um I see you haven't been making your payments,' or, 'When's the next payment due?' Um … by default, I was the absent parent and I'd have to tell them. And, and every single time they'd go, 'Oh, uh, hang on, we have to reset everything.' I said, 'Surely you don't. You, you have an absent parent and a parent with care. One is the payee and one is the payer.' It's, it's black and … isn't it? 'Yeah, but you're Mr [Surname].' 'Yes, I am. And I I'm, I'm the payee, I'm the parent with care.' 'Give me a minute, I need to uh, I need to tap away …' You don't. You don't, honestly, just take gender out of the equation. There are two parties, yeah, and they couldn't get it. It was so bizarre.

Gendered expectations around care like these are reflected in societal working patterns. In England and Wales, the most common working arrangements for parents with children aged between three and four is a full-time working father and part-time working mother.[80] Data from 2019 suggest that there are also gender differences in whether mothers and fathers change their employment patterns for childcare reasons (56.2 per cent of mothers had, compared with 22.4 per cent of fathers)[81] and the nature of those changes (whereas 3 in 10 mothers reduced their working hours for childcare reasons only 1 in 20 fathers had done so).[82] This appears to be the case even where the mother was the higher earner prior to children being born.[83] As outlined in Chapter 1, these trends were exacerbated during the coronavirus pandemic.

Caring patterns are similarly gendered. In 2012, a British Social Attitudes survey found that on average women undertook 13 hours of housework and 23 hours of caring for the family compared with 8 and 10 hours respectively for

[80] R Murphy et al, 'Families and the Labour Market, UK: 2021' (ONS, 22 July 2022) www.ons.gov.uk/employmentandlabourmarket/peopleinwork/employmentandemployeetypes/articles/familiesandthelabourmarketengland/2021#employment-rates-for-parents-in-the-uk accessed 28 April 2023. Note, however, that whereas until 2020 the most common working arrangement for families where both parents worked was for the father to work full-time and the mother to work part-time, since 2020 the most common working arrangement has been for both parents to work full-time: Murphy et al (ibid).

[81] T Vizard, 'Families and the Labour Market, UK: 2019' (ONS, 4 October 2019) www.ons.gov.uk/employmentandlabourmarket/peopleinwork/employmentandemployeetypes/articles/familiesandthelabourmarketengland/2019#balancing-work-and-family-life accessed 28 April 2023.

[82] ibid.

[83] A Andrew et al, 'The Careers and Time Use of Mothers and Fathers' (12 March 2021) https://ifs.org.uk/publications/careers-and-time-use-mothers-and-fathers accessed 28 April 2023.

men.[84] ONS data from 2016 suggests a similar split: women's unpaid work totalled 25.54 hours per week as compared to 15.99 hours for men, with women undertaking 4.67 hours of childcare for men's 1.89 hours per week.[85] ONS data from 2021 also shows gendered differences in unpaid childcare and housework, with men spending around 56 minutes per day on this compared with women's 85 minutes per day.[86]

When it comes to paid work, women are more likely to work part-time. Around 42 per cent of women work part-time as compared with 12 per cent of men.[87] Further, 2011 census data suggest that where individuals do not work at all, for men this is most commonly because they are students (37 per cent)[88] or sick and disabled (27 per cent)[89] whereas women are most commonly economically inactive because they are looking after the family and home (31 per cent).[90] These wider societal attitudes to and practices around care may, therefore, be one reason why Michael felt the choice to care was not open to him.

The experiences of participants to this research illustrate what decisions around care may look like on an individual level. Importantly, where such choices were actively made, they appear to be constrained by factors like the ability to reconcile paid work and care and gendered understandings of parenting. Antonia, for example, decided to re-train ahead of having children. She explained:

> **Antonia**: … when I got to my late twenties and I [was in a professional career] and I thought I can't carry on – I'd like a family at some point and I can't carry on doing this type of work with a family, it doesn't work. So I actually picked the part [of my job that I enjoyed most] and I retrained in that because I knew it was something I could do around the children.

In other cases, where more active choices were made around the division of caring responsibilities, gender norms appear to have been important:

> **Gareth**: Um, yeah. It was definitely discussed. So it was largely discussed in terms of, uh … girls, girls get pregnant, they have babies then you have a year off maternity leave and

[84] J Scott and E Clery, 'Gender roles' in A Park et al (eds), *British Social Attitudes 30* (The National Centre for Social Research, 2013) www.bsa.natcen.ac.uk/media/38723/bsa30_full_report_final.pdf accessed 28 April 2023.

[85] ONS, 'Women Shoulder the Responsibility of Unpaid Work' (ONS Digital, 10 November 2016) http://visual.ons.gov.uk/the-value-of-your-unpaid-work/ accessed 28 April 2023.

[86] Murphy et al (n 80).

[87] ONS, 'Women in the Labour Market: 2013' (25 September 2013) www.ons.gov.uk/employmentandlabourmarket/peopleinwork/employmentandemployeetypes/articles/womeninthelabourmarket/2013-09-25 accessed 28 April 2023. The House of Commons Library suggests more recent figures of 38% and 13% respectively, but does not link to the source of the ONS data it references. See S Irvine et al, 'Women and the UK Economy' (House of Commons Library, 4 March 2022) https://commonslibrary.parliament.uk/research-briefings/sn06838/#:~:text=Most%20part%2Dtime%20employment%20was,compared%20to%2013%25%20of%20men accessed 10 January 2023.

[88] ONS, '2011 Census analysis: Ethnicity and the Labour Market, England and Wales' (13 November 2014) www.ons.gov.uk/peoplepopulationandcommunity/culturalidentity/ethnicity/articles/ethnicityandthelabourmarket2011censusenglandandwales/2014-11-13 accessed 28 April 2023.

[89] ibid.

[90] ibid.

it's all lovely and you look after the baby and you go and have coffee with friends and you, um, make the home nice. And that's what my friends have done and other people have done and that's what we'll do. So it's kind of like, I don't know, a tradition and it's something that the, the women have wanted to do. And it's seen as that's something, like, I dunno, it's almost like you get married, you get a big white dress, you have your big day, and that's, that's the accepted, and that's what I'm looking forward to. Um, so it's kind of more, uh, a picture of what is gonna happen is painted, rather than actually all the details are looked at and scrutinised and poured over.

Alison: So [ex partner's] approach was very much … oh, you're a mum now. You should stay home, give up your job, don't need to work. And I kind of believed that as well myself. I believed that, initially, the best person to care for the baby is one of the parents.

However, not all parents made active choices around work and care. As Emily explained, 'it was just something that kind of just evolved. As we went along.' The deciding factor in discussions was often economic:

Andrew: … after we'd been going out for a little while it kind of looked like this thing was going somewhere and we were talking about children … And we were both quite, kind of, keen that, that one of us would stay at home. Um, and economically it made more sense for me to do that because of her earning potential.

Esther: I think, its just taken for granted that the lower paid, if you're working … um …. You know … my ex used to say to me, well you go out and earn the money I earn. And I'd go, well I can't, you know, I can't – I'm not clever enough or, you know, sort of – and it's like well, therefore, you know, yeah you need to do all the, if they're sick the doctors appointments, the dentists, the opticians, the … um shoe fittings and, you know.

Michael: She … got into an argument with [her boss]. Uh, resigned in a huff and he then blackballed her so she was unable to get another job. So, she was unable to work, and we had children come along and it was a natural, natural thing to do [for her to stay at home].

These economic decisions make sense in view of the significant cost of childcare in England and Wales. The OECD estimates that the UK has the second highest net childcare costs among leading economies.[91] A 2022 TUC poll suggests that 32 per cent of working parents spend more than a third of their wages on child-care, 18 per cent of those whose children are not yet in school spend between a third and a half of their wages on childcare and 15 per cent spend more than half of their wages on childcare.[92] For BME and disabled parents, these figures are even higher.[93] Further, a 2022 poll of 26,962 parents by Pregnant Then Screwed and Mumsnet suggests that 62 per cent were spending the same or more on childcare

[91] OECD, 'Net Childcare Costs' (2021) https://data.oecd.org/benwage/net-childcare-costs.htm 28 April 2023.

[92] TUC, 'TUC Poll: 1 in 3 Parents with Pre-school Children Spend More Than a Third of Their Pay on Childcare' (17 March 2022) www.tuc.org.uk/news/tuc-poll-1-3-parents-pre-school-children-spend-more-third-their-pay-childcare accessed 28 April 2023.

[93] ibid.

as on their rent or mortgage.[94] In the same poll, 43 per cent of mothers said that the cost of childcare had made them consider leaving their job and 40 per cent said they worked fewer hours than they would like to as a result.[95] These costs can have even more severe consequences for young and single parents, who were most likely to have cut down on expenses like food, heating or clothing to afford childcare, with 13 per cent of single parents saying that increased childcare costs had pushed them to use a foodbank.[96] Economic decisions are not gender neutral given the presence of the gender pay gap and these wider norms around who should care.

Gender is not, however, the only factor that influences caring patterns. The gendered division of labour described above is more pronounced within certain ethnic groups. For example, 2011 Census data[97] suggests '[w]omen who were Bangladeshi (54 per cent), Pakistani (52 per cent), Gypsy or Irish Traveller (45 per cent) and Arab (39 per cent) had the highest economic inactivity because of looking after the family or home'.[98] Bangladeshi, Pakistani and Gypsy or Irish Traveller women were also most likely to work part-time.[99] ONS analysis suggests that socioeconomic and cultural factors may contribute to differences between ethnic groups.[100] These differences are important because they suggest that norms of motherhood are not universal and that different women experience them differently. However, without more information there is a limit to how far these norms can be unravelled from this data.

It has been suggested that the norms of intensive motherhood apply primarily to middle class and upper class white women.[101] For working class, minority Black and ethnic women and immigrant women, there instead seems to be an expectation of paid work.[102] As Bloch and Taylor explain:

> [w]hile women with race and class privilege are encouraged to focus almost solely on self-sacrificial caregiving and are assumed to be wed mothers, the ideology of intensive mothering (that children are a full-time 'investment') does not apply to marginalized women who are expected to be unwed, single parents who have made selfish, poor choices if they are not actively involved in the labour market.[103]

This reinforces the idea that mothering norms are diverse and underlines the difficulty of trying to trace the interplay between those norms and caring patterns. It

[94] Pregnant Then Screwed, 'Press Release – 1 in 4 Parents Have Had to Cut Down on Heat, Food & Clothing to Pay for Childcare' (25 March 2022) https://pregnantthenscrewed.com/one-in-four-parents-say-that-they-have-had-to-cut-down-on-heat-food-clothing-to-pay-for-childcare/ accessed 28 April 2023.
[95] ibid.
[96] ibid.
[97] At the time of writing, similar analysis is not yet available for the 2021 Census.
[98] ONS (n 88).
[99] ibid.
[100] ibid.
[101] Lynch (n 1) 63.
[102] JA Sutherland, 'Mothering, Guilt and Shame' (2010) *Sociology Compass* 310; Duffy (n 51) 18.
[103] K Bloch and T Taylor, 'Welfare Queens and Anchor Babies' in Vandenbeld Giles (n 69) 200.

is notable that the Census data discussed above does not appear to differentiate between recent immigrants and those who were born in the UK. Data from Sweden suggests that fathers' use of parental leave increases with time spent in Sweden 'indicating an adaptation to the leave-use pattern of Swedish-born fathers'.[104] It is, therefore, possible that these broader patterns of care across ethnic groups disguise differences within them.

Reinforcing the importance of thinking beyond gender, Hamilton suggests that the contradiction between ideas of intensive parenting and neoliberal expectations of continued economic productivity are racialised in two ways. First, norms of intensive mothering are a consequence of the 'neoliberal decimation of state support for child-rearing',[105] norms which are in themselves underpinned by '[t]he discursive construction and cultural deployment of racialised figures such as the "welfare mother"… or the "baby mother"… operate as justification for the enactment of neoliberal policies'.[106] The second way in which the neoliberal incompatibility between autonomy and care is racialised is that 'through the elision of race as a reasonable explanation for inequality, women of colour's inability to meet the standards of intensive mothering is framed as a result of their individual failings rather than a consequence of the withdrawal of state support and the ongoing effects of structural, gendered racism'.[107] Thus, at the same time as race is actively drawn upon as a justification for neoliberal policies, the reality of racism is denied by those policies, stigmatising those who are not able to meet their demands.

While it is, therefore, the case that norms of intensive motherhood are focused on married white middle- and upper-class women, their impact applies more widely: the encouragement for some mothers to engage in 'privatized self-sacrificing motherhood'[108] perpetuates a system in which '[s]tate responsibility to provide resources for *all* mothers is thus alleviated'.[109] The impacts of this are most keenly felt by those who cannot perform the sort of motherhood demanded by neoliberal conceptions.[110] For those who are unable to choose not to engage in paid work, the responsibility for care does not go away. As discussed above, the mental load (the opposite of the privileged irresponsibility described by Tronto[111]) remains.

[104] E Mussino et al, 'Does Time Count? Immigrant Fathers' Use of Parental Leave for a First Child in Sweden' (2018) 73 *Population* 363, 375.

[105] Hamilton (n 43) 415.

[106] ibid.

[107] ibid.

[108] Bloch and Taylor (n 103) 200.

[109] ibid.

[110] ibid and Vandenbeld Giles (n 70) 10; Lynch (n 1) 63.

[111] Tronto (1993) (n 37) 121.

F. The Invisibility of Care in the Neoliberal Paradigm

Despite the norms of intensive mothering outlined above, Michael's account suggests an idealised conception of caregiving that contrasts sharply with the 'daily grind' of paid work. In my data, this sort of attitude was most common among those who had been the main breadwinner during a relationship and spent significant portions of time with their children after separation but outside of school times. Thus, one explanation for Michael's perception of care may be that the aspects of care not performed by him were less visible. Nevertheless, Michael's understanding of care is sited within a wider context where care is invisible and devalued. Exploring the competing neoliberal norms surrounding autonomy and care, and who they apply to, may help to explain this.

There is a clear contradiction between the ideals of intensive motherhood and the market-driven norms of neoliberalism. Neoliberal-inspired policies as they relate to the workplace are cast in terms of formal equality and gender neutrality.[112] Rodriguez Castro et al, for example, describe an '"ideal work" ideology, that promotes the idea that good workers should exhibit an all-encompassing devotion to the labour market'.[113] This tension is not, however, experienced equally. As explored in the previous section, expectations around who should care and the responsibility for performing that care affect different people differently.

In addition to the impact of gender on the question of who should care, research indicates that gender impacts understandings of how those people should care. In contrast to the understandings of intensive motherhood described above, understandings of fatherhood appear to prioritise a different type of care, which may be more compatible with neoliberal norms of the ideal worker. Dermott suggests that:

> The aspects of parenting the fathers viewed as most significant indicated that 'caring about' was more important than "caring for"; fathers concentrated on the aspects of parenting that were least "work-like" and downplayed the requirement to perform regular child maintenance activities.[114]

Demott notes that these elements were valued because of their role in developing and facilitating 'a strong parent-child relationship'.[115] In this research, there were similar, subtle, suggestions about the different expectations of fathers. For example, several participants referred to the idea of fathers being 'hands on' or 'involved':

> **Antonia:** … so he often would do, you know, school drop offs and pick ups and um take them out or, um, yes spend time with them. He played games with them, like board games and things. So yeah, he, he was a pretty hands-on dad.

[112] Buckley (n 9) 258.
[113] Rodriguez Castro et al (n 71) 4.
[114] E Dermott, *Intimate Fatherhood A Sociological Analysis* (Routledge, 2008) 62.
[115] ibid.

> **Emily:** Um, I think one of the big things for me was that because he was, um, pretty hands on anyway I never worried, about them when they were with him.
>
> **Kenneth:** … at the weekends I was a very hands on dad, and as I said, I'd done the night feeds and I'd, you know, I'd done all of the night feeds for number two and I'd done one of the two or three night feeds for number one.

These examples help to illustrate some of the differences in what is expected of mothers and fathers. The level of caregiving required to be considered an involved or 'hands on' father was relatively low. Antonia, for example, talks about playing games with children and Kenneth talked about being involved at the weekends. Emily said this of her ex-husband's role during their relationship:

> I was very much the person who made the decisions and he'd go along with them. So even when they were tiny, you know, when you're trying to get them into routines and things like that, it was very much, follow my lead. Um, yeah, although he was quite hands on. So he would, you know, he would do, uh, I mean, I, I said, so, but he would do express feeds and, um, they, we had little routines, so he would do all the washing of all the bottles and all of that sort of stuff. And he was never a dad who didn't change nappies or, you know, spend time with them.

Where fathers are expected to be breadwinners, the desire to prioritise relationship building activities is understandable. The point is not to criticise this desire, but rather to illuminate the difference between understandings of the care fathers should perform and the care involved in ideals of intensive motherhood. In particular, the former does not necessarily carry the same penalties for ongoing earning capacity, although it is important to recognise there may be other penalties, such as being less able to spend time with one's child. Given the increasing drive in family law and policy for parents to achieve financial independence on separation, this has the potential to leave those performing intensive mothering and those performing other aspects of care in different financial positions.

Another perspective on the differences between the burden of the care performed by mothers and fathers can be seen in the different priorities attached to paid work and care. Amongst my participants, all primary carers had either given up work or reduced their hours during their relationship. Only one breadwinner had done this while his children were young. More common for fathers was to have access to a degree of 'schedule control', meaning 'the ability to alter their schedule. This includes flexitime; control over the starting and ending times of work and working-time autonomy (the ability to determine work hours and schedules)'.[116] Schedule control tended to be the product of seniority in a professional job and it is, therefore, possible that it carries less in the way of financial penalties than changing one's working hours altogether. It appears from the interviews with some

[116] H Chun, '"Women's Work Penalty" in Access to Flexible Working Arrangements across Europe' (2019) 25 *European Journal of Industrial Relations* 23, 24. As participants in this study were interviewed post-separation, it is difficult to be sure of the extent to which schedule control was utilised to perform care before separation as opposed to being used to increase the share of care performed afterwards.

of those who used flexible working that it allowed for caring responsibilities in a way that was compatible with their jobs:

> **Matthew**: [M]y employer [is] … very understanding in that … if I need to leave at short notice, … it's not a problem. … I think it's easier in my position, being a manager, in that … I'm responsible for my own diary, my own time, … I'm not doing the kind of work that needs me to be … sat at a desk … for 35 hours a week and … there's a bit more flexibility … , so, ultimately, as long as I'm kind of delivering what I need to do, it's not too much of a problem.
>
> **Kenneth**: I've got the sort of job where you're never really not working. … [S]o I will either work very late, sometimes I will work from home, sometimes, whatever … [T]he flip side of that is I have some flexibility …

Here, both Matthew and Kenneth suggest that flexible working allowed them to continue to deliver around caring. These options are not available to everyone; not everyone can work remotely or flexibly. It is also important to think about the question of responsibility for care in these situations. For example, what happens where it is no longer possible to reconcile paid work and care even when working flexibly? Which parent needs to take time off if the children are sick, for example? Neil's interview seems to suggest that being able to care is conditional on flexibility: if he had not been able to work in this way then he would not have been able to care:

> **Neil**: I could probably think of a dozen men that I know who are in a similar situation to me, but who don't enjoy the flexibility of employer, … so … they've just defaulted very, very quickly into being the sorts of fathers that … see their children once every fortnight … [M]y point is that … the employer flexibility thing … is absolutely crucial in this. … I couldn't possibly do what I do if I was working for an employer that wasn't prepared to do that.

Again, this can be understood in the context of societally gendered scripts of parenthood: fathers are not expected to be primary carers and are expected to work so the choices about whether to care are constrained by working patterns.

III. The Problem of Parental Separation

Having identified the incompatibility between neoliberal-influenced ideas of autonomy and caring responsibilities, it is important to identify why this is such a problem on parental separation before going on to consider the legal response in Chapter 3. In intact families, this incompatibility between financial independence and the demands of caring can be reconciled by the unit as a whole. For example, one parent may work more and the other may care more, allowing the family as a whole to achieve some degree of financial independence from the state. This is, of course, a simplified picture – not all intact families are able to achieve this balance and not all parenting begins in the context of an intact family – but it helps to explain the existence of norms around intensive mothering in the neoliberal paradigm.

Even for those families who can achieve some version of this balance, however, separation creates problems because this balance is unravelled. Somehow two new units need to be created, and those units are each expected to be financially independent. This is far less achievable for a partner who has done more caring, and explains the neoliberal emphasis on paid work. As McRobbie outlines:

> … With the high rate of divorce, having a career does not just provide women with an income and independence, it also reduces the cost of welfare to government. It thus makes sense for government to champion women who will enter the labour market and stay in it.[117]

This is, however, incompatible with norms of intensive motherhood and the more general realities of caring responsibilities. Chapter 3 will explore how this general invisibility of care impacts the lives of separating parents. It will consider the real world consequences for carers, their children and those who are prevented from caring. It will also consider the way in which the law approaches this conundrum and identify the shortcomings of the legal response to care on separation.

[117] A McRobbie, 'Neoliberalism, the Family and the New "Mediated" Maternalism' (2013) 80 *New Formations* 119, 121.

3

Parental Separation and the Invisibility of Care in England and Wales

I. Why Does the Invisibility of Care Matter?

Caring responsibilities carry indirect financial costs; what Fineman refers to as 'derivative dependency'.[1] Women's income suffers more on separation and divorce than men's[2] because of decisions made around work and care during relationships.[3] Chapter 2 discussed gendered patterns of childcare in society, which have been exacerbated by the Covid-19 pandemic; women are more likely to care than men and more likely to adapt their working patterns, for example by working part-time. These patterns have financial consequences. First, women from every ethnic group, with the exception of white Irish women, experience a gender pay gap when compared with white British men.[4] Similarly, in terms of full-time work, women of almost every ethnic group (the exceptions are Black Caribbean women and white Irish women) experience a gender pay gap as compared with men from the same ethnic group.[5] Whilst not the only explanation for the gap, the need to balance caring responsibilities is something that is a greater problem for women than men. For example, within the EU only 72.2 per cent of women with children work as compared with 90 per cent of men.[6] This explanation is also supported by the fact that the gender pay gap in England and Wales is greatest from age 40 upwards which the

[1] M Fineman, *The Autonomy Myth* (The New Press, 2004) 35.

[2] H Fisher and H Low, 'Who Wins, Who Loses and Who Recovers from Divorce?' in J Miles and R Probert (eds), *Sharing Lives, Dividing Assets* (Hart Publishing, 2009); M Brewer and A Nandi, 'Partnership Dissolution: How Does it Affect Income, Employment and Well-being? (Institute for Social & Economic Research, September 2014) www.econstor.eu/bitstream/10419/126462/1/79669074X.pdf accessed 10 January 2023.

[3] Fisher and Low (ibid).

[4] A Breach and Y Li, 'Gender Pay Gap by Ethnicity in Britain – Briefing' (Fawcett Society and University of Manchester, March 2017) www.fawcettsociety.org.uk/gender-pay-by-ethnicity-britain accessed 28 April 2023.

[5] ibid.

[6] Eurostat, 'Higher employment rate for men with children' https://ec.europa.eu/eurostat/web/products-eurostat-news/-/ddn-20210809-1 accessed 22 June 2023.

ONS suggest is 'likely to be connected to women taking time out of the labour market to have children'.[7]

Further, part-time and flexible working may have consequences for career progression. For example, a recent study suggests that working parents, and mothers in particular, often sacrificed 'desirable aspects of a job, like pay and opportunities for career progression' for flexible working.[8] This is consistent with the findings of a 2014 YouGov Survey for the Department for Culture, Media and Sport,[9] which found that 43 per cent of respondents felt people in flexible working arrangements did not have the same opportunities for career progression as those who were not (29 per cent felt that they did).[10] Further, only 24 per cent of respondents thought that those who took a career break and returned to work had the same opportunities as those who worked continuously, with women more likely to disagree than men (57 per cent compared to 48 per cent).[11] It is, therefore, perhaps unsurprising that research using data from the British Household Panel Survey and Understanding Society has concluded that gendered patterns in part-time work were an important explanation for differences in men and women's hourly rates of pay, particularly for college graduates 'because they affect the amount and type of labour market experience that men and women build up, and this experience affects the hourly wage levels they can command'.[12] The authors of the study also note that it is not only taking time out of paid work but also working part-time that affects women's wages, 'because extra experience in full-time work leads to higher hourly wages, whereas extra experience in part-time work does not'.[13]

These costs matter because of the increasing impact of neoliberal-influenced ideas of autonomy, which underpin the emphasis upon financial independence where couples separate. This chapter explores the legal framework in England and Wales and suggests that it fails to recognise and address the costs of caring responsibilities.

[7] ONS, 'What is the Gender Pay Gap?' (ONS Digital, 12 February 2016) http://visual.ons.gov.uk/what-is-the-gender-pay-gap/ accessed 28 April 2023.

[8] Global Institute of Women's Leadership, King's College London, Working Families and University of East Anglia, 'Working Parents, Flexibility and Job Quality: What Are the Trade-offs?' (2021) https://workingfamilies.org.uk/wp-content/uploads/2021/11/Working-parents-flexibility-and-job-quality-what-are-the-trade-offs.pdf accessed 28 April 2023.

[9] Department for Culture Media & Sport, 'Attitudes towards Equality: Findings from the YouGov Survey' (June 2014) https://assets.publishing.service.gov.uk/government/uploads/system/uploads/attachment_data/file/316290/Attitudes_towards_Equality.pdf accessed 28 April 2023.

[10] ibid.

[11] ibid.

[12] M Costa Dias et al, 'The Gender Pay Gap in the UK: Children and Experience in Work' (IFS, February 2018) https://ifs.org.uk/publications/gender-pay-gap-uk-children-and-experience-work accessed 28 April 2023, 22.

[13] ibid 23.

II. How Does the Law in England and Wales Respond to the Costs of Care?

A. The Financial Consequences of Cohabitation

The law views unmarried couples through the lens of neoliberal-influenced visions of autonomy. As Diduck explains, cohabitants are:

> … deemed to have chosen not to marry/register their partnership and [so they] must therefore live with the consequences of that choice, regardless of the disadvantage it may confer upon them. This position is justified by the claim that it would be violation of their autonomy and therefore unfair to subject them to a regime which they had chosen to avoid.[14]

This understanding of cohabitants draws on several of the themes which underpin neoliberal-inspired conceptions of the legal subject. For example, it draws on the idea that this relationship status is a free choice for which the individuals who have made it must accept the consequences.[15] However, such an understanding of cohabitation is not consistent with research evidence about the reasons why couples cohabit rather than marry, which suggests that cohabitants with an ideological opposition to marriage form only one sub-set of cohabiting couples.[16] Other couples (the 'romantics') see cohabitation as a step towards marriage, or make decisions based upon legal or financial grounds (the 'pragmatists') or may be in a situation where one partner wants to marry and the other does not, or where one partner is more committed ('uneven couples').[17]

Nevertheless, consistently with a neoliberal approach which prioritises market ideology, the law that applies to cohabitants on separation is restrictive and makes few concessions to the nature of the couple's relationship. In cases where a property is registered in joint names, there is a presumption that the beneficial interest is also equally shared and this is hard to rebut.[18] While this may offer some protection to a cohabiting partner who has contributed less financially because of childcare or other responsibilities, this would only be the case if the property is registered in joint names. This is less likely in some types of cohabiting relationship (eg uneven couples).

In cases where a property is registered in one partner's sole name and a court is assessing whether the other has a financial interest in the family home, the court

[14] A Diduck, 'Autonomy and Vulnerability in Family Law: the Missing Link' in J Wallbank and J Herring (eds), *Vulnerability, Care and Family Law* (Routledge, 2013) 105.

[15] T Lemke, '"The Birth of Bio-Politics": Michel Foucault's Lecture at the Collège de France on Neo-Liberal Governmentality' (2001) 30 *Economy and Society* 190, 201.

[16] A Barlow and J Smithson, 'Legal Assumptions, Cohabitants' Talk and the Rocky Road to Reform' (2010) 22 *Child and Family Law Quarterly* 328.

[17] ibid.

[18] *Stack v Dowden* [2007] UKHL 17.

must consider the law of constructive trusts,[19] under which a beneficial interest in property can be established through the combination of a common intention that a party should have a beneficial interest in the property and detrimental reliance by that party on the common intention. While, as outlined in the introduction, this marks a slight relaxation of the position that applies to other co-owners of land (whose interests are determined purely based on financial contributions under the law of resulting trusts), and while there seems to have been some relaxation[20] of the orthodox approach under which it was 'extremely doubtful' that anything less than a direct contribution to the purchase price or mortgage would do,[21] it is clear that care and domestic contributions more generally cannot be the foundation for such an interest. In the recent case of *Dobson v Griffey*, which echoes the approach of the House of Lords in *Lloyds Bank v Rosset*,[22] the judge said this in dismissing the female cohabitant's claim:

> Her labour and commitment were understandable in the context of their relationship and their intended long-term future together with children. This was to be her home, and that of her children. It is unnecessary to suppose some quasi-commercial bargain between them to explain it.[23]

Underpinning this judicial pronouncement are unarticulated, gendered, assumptions about the nature of family life. This gender dimension can be seen more starkly in Lord Bridge's comment in *Rosset* that 'it would seem the most natural thing in the world for any wife,[24] in the absence of her husband abroad, to spend all the time she could spare and to employ any skills she might have … to accelerate progress of the work quite irrespective of any expectation she might have of enjoying a beneficial interest in the property'.[25] In contrast to the neoliberal-influenced ideas of autonomy articulated above, which prioritise economic rationality, the female partners here are assumed to be motivated by the wellbeing of the family. This is consistent with suggestions that decision-making in intact families is grounded in ideals of solidarity[26] or interdependence.[27] It also resonates with norms of intensive motherhood which suggest prioritising everything for one's children. However, the result of the legal framework outlined above is to leave that partner in a financially precarious position on separation.

[19] ibid.

[20] See, for example, *Slater v Condappa* [2012] EWCA Civ 1506; *Curran v Collins* [2015] EWCA Civ 404; *Graham-York v York* [2015] EWCA Civ 72.

[21] *Lloyds Bank plc v Rosset and Another* [1990] 1 AC 107.

[22] *Lloyds Bank plc v Rosset and Another* [1990] 1 AC 107.

[23] *Dobson v Griffey* [2018] EWHC 1117 (Ch) [84].

[24] While this case involved a married couple, the law it considers applies to cohabiting couples. The framework for financial provision on divorce for married couples is different.

[25] *Lloyds Bank plc v Rosset and Another* [1990] 1 AC 107, 131E.

[26] A Barlow, 'Solidarity, Autonomy and Equality: Mixed Messages for the Family?' (2015) 27(3) *Child and Family Law Quarterly* 223.

[27] A Heenan, 'Causal and Temporal Connections in Financial Remedy Cases: the Meaning of Marriage' (2018) 30(1) *Child and Family Law Quarterly* 75.

The failure of the legal framework to recognise the value of care in this context is exacerbated by the increasing drive towards private ordering in the Family Justice System, which means that couples are increasingly left to make arrangements themselves without legal advice. Smart has suggested that 'caring for' (which broadly corresponds to caregiving in Tronto's definition) is often 'invisible to all but those who do it (and sometimes even to them)'.[28] In my research, this sort of invisibility was most apparent amongst fathers who had reached arrangements on separation whereby their children spent a relatively large percentage of time with them, but not necessarily during the working week. Both Gareth and Michael had arrangements in place for their children whereby the children spent a large proportion of time with them, but the majority of that time tended to take place during periods when the children were not at school. For example, Gareth's children spent time with him every other weekend and during the school holidays. Similarly, Michael's children spent every other weekend with him, one night in the week and half of school holidays. Similarly to Michael's views on the value of care which were outlined in Chapter 2, Gareth said this about his and his ex-wife's respective positions:

> **Gareth**: … the second time round I was pretty galled that I'd worked my arse off to save up a load of money for the family and then to kind of have it, half of it taken away. Um, when, it was like equally plausible that she could have worked her arse off and I could have looked after the kids but I didn't have the same opportunities. It was just, like, yeah, looking after the kids was something she wanted to do whereas it's something I wanted to do as well …

This contrast between looking after children and working your 'arse off', echoes Michael's words cited at the outset of Chapter 2, and envisages caring as a wholly enjoyable experience. Part of the reason for Michael and Gareth's feelings on the matter may be that they would both have liked to spend more time with their children than they did. Thus, caring was denied to them; a theme explored further below. It is, however, important to recognise that the sort of care involved on weekends and school holidays, when routines and so on are less important, is different to that involved during the school week. It may be that this difference is also partly responsible for the invisibility of some of the burdens of caregiving in these accounts. The danger of this, however, is that when it comes to making financial arrangements at the end of a relationship this invisibility of care may create inequalities of bargaining position between carers and breadwinners, with the result that carers do worse financially.

The perceived undervaluation of caring responsibilities was most common among female cohabitants who had been the primary carer during a relationship. Alison, for example, felt that whilst the legal profession recognised the value of caring, her ex-partner did not. Her own financial position was precarious.

[28] C Smart, 'The Legal and Moral Ordering of Child Custody' (1991) 18 *Journal of Law and Society* 485, 489.

She had limited claims as a former cohabitant and, in particular, no claim for spousal maintenance. Esther likewise felt that caregiving was not given the same value as breadwinning 'particularly from a male point of view'. Esther was less clear than Alison about whether these different roles were equally valuable. One explanation for this might be that Alison had legal advice directly on the point, whereas Esther saw a solicitor 'just for the free half an hour advice'.

These examples illustrate the dangers of care being undervalued in a system shaped by ideas of autonomy; for cohabiting couples this lack of value can be seen in the legal framework as well as wider societal understandings of care. Without a formal legal entitlement, cohabitant carers are dependent on the goodwill of a former partner or the ever-reducing safety net of the state. These issues are not unique to cohabiting couples; reductions in legal aid availability may mean that spouses who have legal entitlements are unaware of this fact. Nevertheless, the fact remains that, at least theoretically, for spouses the law is better able to respond to the costs of care.

B. Financial Provision on Divorce or Dissolution

Married couples have a greater range of financial claims available to them than cohabiting couples, that go some way to meeting the costs of care. However, neoliberal-influenced ideas of autonomy are increasingly apparent in this context too. As outlined in Chapter 1, in deciding what combination of orders to make, the judge is directed to consider a statutory list of factors[29] to determine what would be a fair result on the particular facts.[30] The statutory factors include the spouses' 'income, earning capacity, property and other financial resources',[31] their 'financial needs, obligations and responsibilities',[32] their standard of living,[33] their ages and the length of the marriage,[34] as well as other factors such as any disability suffered by either party[35] and their conduct.[36]

Particularly significant when it comes to taking account of caring responsibilities is the 'contribution factor'. The statute directs the court to consider 'the contributions which each of the parties has made or is likely in the foreseeable future to make to the welfare of the family, including any contribution by looking after the home or caring for the family'.[37] In contrast to the historical position whereby a homemaker would be awarded enough to meet his or her 'reasonable

[29] Matrimonial Causes Act 1973, s 25.
[30] *White v White* [2000] UKHL 54.
[31] Matrimonial Causes Act 1973, s 25(2)(a).
[32] ibid s 25(2)(b).
[33] ibid s 25(2)(c).
[34] ibid s 25(2)(d).
[35] ibid s 25(2)(e).
[36] ibid s 25(2)(g).
[37] ibid s 25(2)(f).

requirements' with the breadwinner retaining the rest, case law now makes clear that '[t]here should be no bias in favour of the money-earner and against the home-maker and the child-carer'.[38] Caring responsibilities and other non-financial contributions are, therefore, considered to have a value by the law of financial remedies on divorce. However, that value is fixed by reference to the value of financial contributions; rather than care and other non-financial contributions being attributed a value of their own, they are generally considered equal to the value of the financial contributions in a particular case.

The extent to which contributions, or indeed any of the other statutory factors, affect the outcome in a given case depends in large part on the level of assets involved. In most cases, the assets (or debts), when divided, are insufficient to meet both spouses' needs. Meeting needs is, therefore, the court's focus when seeking to achieve 'fairness'.[39] In this sort of undertaking, 'needs' can include needs generated by caring responsibilities – Fineman's idea of derivative dependency discussed above.[40] While this is not strictly compensation for caring, the legal framework does in this way recognise that care may carry financial costs.

The position is different in cases where the assets exceed needs. In these cases, two other principles, compensation and sharing, are relevant to the court's determination of what is a fair result.[41] Turning first to the sharing principle, in *White*,[42] the court emphasised that there should be no discrimination based on the parties' roles during the marriage: domestic and financial contributions should be valued equally.[43] Much like the idea of needs, care has an implicit value here by being equated with financial contributions. The idea of non-discrimination falls into difficulty, however, when it comes to the doctrine of special contribution: the idea that one party has made a contribution to the welfare of the family that is unmatched by the other and which, 'for the purpose of the sharing principle, should lead to a departure from equality'.[44]

Cases where special contribution arguments succeed are rare,[45] but the doctrine remains a useful illustration of the differences in the ways in which financial and non-financial contributions are weighted. While, theoretically, the concept of special contribution is not limited to financial contributions, there have been no reported cases where a domestic contribution has been sufficient. This is perhaps unsurprising given that non-financial contributions are not valued per se, but rather simply equated with a financial contribution in any given case. There is no obvious way

[38] *White v White* [2000] UKHL 54.

[39] *Miller v Miller; McFarlane v McFarlane* [2006] UKHL 24 and *Charman v Charman* [2007] EWCA Civ 503.

[40] Fineman (n 1) 35.

[41] *Miller v Miller; McFarlane v McFarlane* [2006] UKHL 24 and *Charman v Charman* [2007] EWCA Civ 503.

[42] *White v White* [2000] UKHL 54.

[43] Note that s 25(2)(f), one of the factors the court must consider when considering what would be a fair outcome, refers explicitly to both domestic and financial contributions.

[44] *Charman v Charman* [2007] EWCA Civ 503 [79].

[45] See, for example, *Work v Gray* [2017] EWCA Civ 270 and *WM v HM* [2017] EWFC 25.

to evidence the inherent value of a non-financial contribution and show that it is greater than a financial one. Further, as was explained in the case of *Charman*:

> in practice, and for a self-evident reason, the claim to have made a special contribution seems so far to have arisen only in cases of substantial wealth generated by a party's success in business during the marriage. The self-evident reason is that in such cases there is substantial property over the distribution of which it is worthwhile to argue.[46]

This approach to quantifying the value of non-financial contributions such as caring responsibilities makes sense from a practical perspective. If the value of the parties' respective contributions were separately weighed in any given case, this would be a lengthy and costly undertaking. Further, if marriage is seen as 'partnership of equals',[47] this sort of undertaking seems unnecessary: both parties should be assumed to have contributed what they can in their own ways to that partnership. The notion of special contribution undermines this. However, if it is possible for a financial contribution to be so exceptional that it trumps the value of a non-financial contribution, then there must be some way of determining the value of the non-financial contribution in its own right. The fact that there is not, is indicative of the tension between neoliberal-influenced understandings of autonomy and care. Whereas neoliberalism valorises intensive motherhood, the only system of value in the neoliberal framework is that derived from the paid work undertaken by the economically rational, financially independent, responsible and autonomous neoliberal individual.

Also relevant when considering how the law understands and values care is the compensation principle, which Lord Nicholls in *Miller; McFarlane* described as follows:

> This is aimed at redressing any significant prospective economic disparity between the parties arising from the way they conducted their marriage. For instance, the parties may have arranged their affairs in a way which has greatly advantaged the husband in terms of his earning capacity but left the wife severely handicapped so far as her own earning capacity is concerned. Then the wife suffers a double loss: a diminution in her earning capacity and the loss of a share in her husband's enhanced income.[48]

Baroness Hale (as she then was) explained the principle in this way:

> A second rationale, which is closely related to need, is compensation for relationship-generated disadvantage. Indeed, some consider that provision for need is compensation for relationship-generated disadvantage. But the economic disadvantage generated by the relationship may go beyond need, however generously interpreted. The best example is a wife, like Mrs McFarlane, who has given up what would very probably have been a lucrative and successful career. If the other party, who has been the beneficiary of the choices made during the marriage, is a high earner with a substantial surplus over what

[46] *Charman v Charman* [2007] EWCA Civ 503 [80].
[47] *Miller v Miller; McFarlane v McFarlane* [2006] UKHL 24 [16] (Lord Nicholls), [141] (Lady Hale).
[48] ibid [13] (Lord Nicholls).

> is required to meet both parties' needs, then a premium above needs can reflect that relationship-generated disadvantage.[49]

Lord Nicholls' understanding of the principle appears to be tied to the economic disparity between partners: a claim arises because the claimant's own earning capacity is 'handicapped' by decisions made during the marriage (such as the decision to care for children) and because the claimant's spouse has benefited from these same decisions. However, subsequent case law has made clear that compensation is based on the disadvantage suffered by the claimant: 'I appreciate that it is based in part on the other party's career having benefited but I regard that as an assumption rather than an evidential issue which has to be determined, in part because of the difficulty of undertaking any such exercise.'[50]

Baroness Hale's understanding of the compensation principle seems to be similar to Lord Nicholls', but she adds the requirements that the claimant spouse has given up 'what would very probably have been a lucrative and successful career' and the breadwinning spouse 'is a high earner with a substantial surplus over what is required to meet both parties' needs'. These requirements describe well the position of Mrs McFarlane who received compensation in that case, but serve to restrict the operation of the doctrine to a small selection of very high earners.

Interestingly, while rejecting the idea of compensation purely for losses caused by caring, Michael (quoted at the outset of Chapter 2) suggested that compensation might be justified where there had been a benefit to the breadwinner's career in not caring for children. Below is a relatively lengthy section from his interview in which he considered the issue of compensation at some length. The quote at the start of Chapter 2 forms part of this discussion and seeing it in context is important. It puts a different emphasis on Michael's words; in wider context they are not as harsh as they appear in an isolated quotation. Michael's seeming dismissal of care is a part of a larger argument about when compensation should be payable: he is not simply diminishing its importance in isolation. Nevertheless, this casual dismissal serves to demonstrate the invisibility of care in society; Michael's words make sense within a neoliberal framework where care is sidelined:

> **Michael:** … So I'm, I'm, I'm curious as to – one important factor here is how much, uh, not being focused on the children, how much has that enabled him to advance his career.
>
> 'Cause if he was already earning the equivalent of hundred thousand, a hundred and fifty thousand a year in bonuses, then, obviously that's not, hasn't benefitted him at all.
>
> **Interviewer:** So i-it, so really what it depends, you know, if he was earning that level before then the, sort of, her giving up work is not necessarily the same as if he'd been earning a lot less. Is that, is that what you're saying there?

[49] ibid [140] (Lady Hale).
[50] *Waggott v Waggott* [2018] EWCA Civ 727 [139].

Michael: I am. Uh, in, in my own case, uh, despite not being the par- the stay-at-home parent I was spending so much time in childcare and housework that my real-term earnings decreased.

So, uh, if my real-term, my, uh, if my earnings had doubled, then obviously things would have been a bit different.

Interviewer: Mm. So what I'm, I guess, um, what I'm trying to think through is what the implications of that are. So, for example, um, would it make a difference in terms of the way you divided assets up or would it be in terms of things like maintenance or possibly both?

Michael: Um … both. If, if her taking the hit has enabled him to increase his earnings by 50 per cent then clearly she's entitled to a share in that.

On the other hand, if her taking the hit hasn't enabled him to increase his earnings by 50 per cent then she's entitled to, just entitled to a share of what there is right now.

And not his future earnings.

Interviewer: Ok

Does she get in that, so we were sort of talking before about potentially some compensation for having giving up her job – would she still get that, it's just that she wouldn't necessarily get the share in the future earnings?

Michael: Well, in this particular scenario, uh, if you're working in an administrative role, that's, that's not something which is going to take off and … that's not, there's not much of a career path there.

So she hasn't actually sacrificed a great deal. She's – If the, if the situation had been reversed, he'd sacrificed his job, she'd still be on the equivalent of thirty thousand a year, she wouldn't be earning two hundred and fifty thousand a year.

Interviewer: Ok, so it's her potential rather than the sort of –

Michael: Exactly.

There wasn't, there wasn't the potential there. So, uh … so with that in mind, uh, I don't feel she's earn- she's entitled to a greater claim, based on … uh, based on her lack of earnings. Indeed, you could easily argue the case that she's had a wonderful, a wonderful twelve years looking after the, looking after the children and not having to go to the daily grind. What's, what's that worth? Shouldn't she be, shouldn't she be compensating him for having to, to allow her to do that?

What would, what would I have given, to be allowed to do that? I would have loved that. I … Uh so, so I, I don't think there's any argument for that. Unless you're saying, it's a burden looking after children and not going to work. And I would really, really disagree. I would love to do that.

So, uh, the sole question of compensation here does hinge on, how much has her looking after the children enabled him to advance his career to this point …

In contrast to the case law, which stresses detriment to the claimant, this understanding of compensation seems to focus primarily on the benefit to the breadwinner: what has he gained in not having to care? While Michael's understanding of compensation seems to leave open the possibility of a claim where the claimant spouse had a high earning potential, this is not clear in this discussion.

Further, like the legal approach to compensation, the claimant's earnings are seen as fixed. The fact that caring prevents other opportunities, such as the opportunity to retrain, is ignored.[51] Care then does not have a value of its own, except to the person performing it who is freed from the monotony of paid work. Further, care is not seen as something that the breadwinner also has a duty to perform for their child, and which they have been freed from. In this way, privileged irresponsibility[52] is perpetuated.

C. Financial Support for Children

The claims discussed so far are for the benefit of the adults in a relationship. Financial claims also exist for the benefit of their children. Parents are financially responsible for their biological children on separation. Consistently with Diduck's[53] structural and procedural aspects of autonomy, outlined in Chapter 2, parents are encouraged to make private arrangements concerning the financial support of their children.[54] While a statutory formula based on fixed percentages of the payer's income is available, and is used where parents cannot reach an agreement, it is not clear to what extent those making private arrangements refer to it. Where collection does take place through the Child Maintenance Service, the state body in charge of child support, charges are made for both a calculation of the child support liability and for arranging collection. Where a parent's income exceeds £156,000 per annum (gross) the parent with care can apply to the court for top up provision above the amount due under the statutory formula.[55] It is also possible for step-parents to be ordered to provide financial support (both income and capital claims are available) in some circumstances.[56] Such claims are rarely brought in practice,[57] and tend to be seen as most appropriate in big money cases.[58]

The legal approach to child maintenance, renders the costs of care invisible in important ways. First, the child support formula is based on the division of a child's time. This does not necessarily mirror the way in which care is divided. Esther's situation provides a good illustration of this. She explained:

[51] Heenan (n 27).

[52] J Tronto, *Moral Boundaries: A Political Argument for an Ethic of Care* (Routledge, 1993) 121.

[53] A Diduck, 'Autonomy and Family Justice' (2016) 28 *Child and Family Law Quarterly* 133, 134.

[54] See, for example, Gov.uk, 'Child Maintenance Service' www.gov.uk/child-maintenance-service/payments#:~:text=You%20have%20to%20pay%20a,the%20payment)%20for%20receiving%20parents accessed 22 June 2023.

[55] Children Act 1989, Schedule 1.

[56] Matrimonial Causes Act 1973, Part II and Children Act 1989, Schedule 1.

[57] Law Commission, *Cohabitation: The Financial Consequences of Relationship Breakdown* (Law Com CP No 179, 2006) 4.34.

[58] See, for example, G Douglas et al, 'A Failure of Trust: Resolving Property Disputes on Cohabitation Breakdown' (2007) https://orca.cf.ac.uk/5186/1/1.pdf accessed 28 April 2023 and Law Commission *Cohabitation: The Financial Consequences of Relationship Breakdown* (Law Com No 307, Summary, 2007)

> **Esther**: I pick them up from school. Um, feed them. Um … take them to – they go to, you know, clubs, beavers, you know, that type of thing. Yeah, I do all the running around and then he collects them after work. And literally just time, just sort of like half an hour before bed, huh, clearly.

This is a particularly extreme example, but there were other examples in which shared time arrangements for children on separation did not necessarily translate into an equal division of caregiving responsibilities. For Andrew, for example, separation did result in more dual responsibility insofar as his ex-wife would take the children to the doctor or dentist if an appointment fell in the week that they were with her. However, he remained primarily responsible for making those appointments in the first place. This experience was shared by other parents who had adopted a shared care arrangement:

> **Elizabeth:** … the um, the doctors and dentists and things I tend, I tend to deal with that. Um, I dealt with it when we were together. I have no doubt if we were still together that I would be the one dealing with it. Um, that said, and I mean I obviously keep [their] dad in the loop so [their] dad knows if [they've] got a doctor's appointment or anything like that and if I can't take [them] [their] dad takes [them].
>
> **Interviewer:** Um I was, I was just, uh, sort of wondering about, sort of, um, practicalities and things. So, uh, things like doctors, dentists, all the kind of mundane, everyday stuff. How does that all work?
>
> **Emily:** They happen here [laugh]. Yeah, so I do all of that. With them. Unless of course there was an emergency when they were with their Dad. In which case he would do it. Yeah. Yeah.

These examples are important from a financial perspective because they demonstrate the extent to which the financial consequences of caregiving can be shared unequally even where time is shared equally. In Esther's case, albeit not involving a shared care arrangement, her ex-partner's overnight contact during the week relied upon her being in a job which allowed her to finish early to collect the children. In contrast, her partner did not need to make any adjustments to his own working patterns. Thus, his salary and future career prospects remained unaffected. Notwithstanding this, his overnight contact would serve to reduce his child support liability. Esther's ex-partner in fact continued to make child maintenance payments at a level that enabled her to continue making mortgage payments. However, this had consequences in terms of the power dynamics within the relationship, with her feeling 'beholdened [*sic*]' to him.

A second way in which the legal approach to child maintenance renders the costs of care invisible is through the emphasis on private ordering. Where care is invisible in society the danger is that the fact that it costs money to care may be hidden from those who are not performing that care (ie the payers of child maintenance).[59] Research demonstrates gendered spending patterns within intact

[59] See also K Lynch, *Care and Capitalism* (Polity, 2022) 48.

families. In particular, women are more likely to pay for children's expenses and for childcare than men.[60] Nyman's Swedish research accordingly suggests that this results in different insights into household expenses:

> All of the women in this study claim that they have a better feel for what needs to be bought on a regular basis, from food items, to children's clothes, because it is they who have had this responsibility at least from the time their first child arrived. This gives them a unique insight into the daily needs and costs of the household, insight that their husbands often do not have. This insight into the family's daily needs, and the special knowledge that these women have of how much is needed for food each week, how much a pair of new shoes for one of the children costs, or which of the children's friends will be having birthday parties and be expecting birthday presents also means that the women feel economic pressures and therefore also limitations in a more detailed, acute and close-to-home way than most of their husbands do.[61]

This suggests that unequal sharing of these aspects of care means that some of the costs of care are hidden to the person not performing them. There is some evidence of this phenomenon from this research, both during the course of relationships and after separation. First, some participants described how their partners challenged their spending during their relationships. Alison, for example, explained that she disliked asking for money from her partner when she was at home caring for the children. She explained that this was partly because she liked 'standing on my own two feet'. Additionally:

> **Alison:** Um … And … also there was the kind of like … well, you've been to the Co-op three times today, you know, what's that all about? 'Cause obviously he could see it on our joint account 'cause that was my real only money was coming out of the joint account. And, um, I used to, you know, I, um, I used to try and make my money last as much as possible. But [sigh] yeah, no, nightmare. Nightmare.

Louise likewise described how her partner would question her spending:

> **Louise**: … he would suddenly go out and buy a golf club. One golf club for a hundred pounds. But then the next week, he would look at the shopping list and go mental at me because I'd spent three pounds on a bottle of shampoo and said, you know, what's wrong with Asda's own or … So it was a bit, a bit one-sided financially really.

At the time, she was receiving sickness benefits and so 'we didn't have much money'. While they did 'throw money into the pot' which was used for rent and food, she suggested that 'all of his money was his [laughs] um … yeah. I mean, pretty much'. Pahl's research, which resonates with Nyman's findings outlined above, suggests that men and women have different spending patterns, with

[60] J Pahl, 'The Gendering of Spending within Households' (2000) 75 *Radical Statistics* 38 www.radstats.org.uk/no075/pahl.htm accessed 28 April 2023, J Pahl, 'Individualisation in Couple Finances: Who Pays for the Children' (2005) 4 *Social Policy and Society* 381, C Nyman, 'Gender Equality in "The Most Equal Country in the World"? Money and Marriage in Sweden' (1999) 47 *The Sociological Review* 766.

[61] Nyman (ibid).

women tending to be responsible for greater numbers of smaller purchases.[62] Thus, one reason for these enquiries about spending may be that these women's partners simply did not spend in the same way, or on the same things, and so did not understand their spending patterns.

Similar examples can be seen in post-separation experiences around child maintenance. Emily and Louise both explained that their partners (in Emily's case an ex-husband and in Louise's case a former cohabitant) seemed to perceive child maintenance as being for their benefit rather than being for the children.

> **Emily**: …'cause a lot of his pay is based on bonuses, depending on performance and things like that. Um, and I've had to really fight to get those out of him. So, um, that has caused a bit of tension. I think, I sense of bit of resentment from him that he thinks he's paying me money. I think that's quite common. Um, he doesn't really like paying me money [Laughs]. Um, and I'm not sure he reminds himself it's not really for me.
>
> **Louise**: … every time I spoke about money it would end up in a huge argument where he would call me a money grabbing … whatever. Um, you know, I just want, you know, I wanted to get as much money out of him as I could. He, he could never see that, actually, I was doing it for the children.

This perception may also explain the fact that rather than pursuing regular child maintenance, Alison asked for contributions for 'definite things rather than anything he could say, "Oh, that's for you"'. These experiences suggest a difference in how these mothers and their partners understood children's needs. Alison's approach can be understood as a reaction to this; in asking for specific items, she avoided any accusation that she was profiting from the payments. The danger with this approach, however, is that sometimes children's needs are not so easily separated out. For example, food, heating, travel and other basic necessities form part and parcel of the carer's household expenses and it is not easy to portion out those elements that relate to the children as opposed to the person caring for them. Further, this sort of approach may mean that the payer becomes the sole arbiter of what children need. An example of what this might look like can be seen in Gareth's interview. Before exploring this, it is important to note that Gareth did pay regular child maintenance, so his discussion relates solely to paying additional amounts over and above this. Thus, his ex-wives were not in the position of not receiving regular maintenance. However, his discussion about the sorts of factors he would take into account in deciding whether to make extra payments illustrates the pitfalls of a situation where child maintenance is paid sporadically for distinct items. Gareth explained:

> **Gareth**: And in terms of finances like I pay, I dunno, I, I, I keep getting told that they can't, like they need more money and they need to, need to pay for things and I kind of trust that that's the case, and will pay for extra things. And like stuff that the kids like doing that I like doing. Like football club and things like that, then I'll pay for.

[62] Pahl (2000) (n 60).

> That's like other stuff that's not really my cup of tea then they tend to pay for it and finance it and it kind of – the kind of extra payments on top of the, uh, of what we have agreed each month.
>
> Um, and just like, yeah. If they want me to get some shoes or something then I'll buy shoes and it's not really a, it's not really a big drama. And we tend to, like, go halves on big Christmas and birthday presents and things like that.

Here, Gareth suggests a greater willingness to pay extra amounts of child maintenance for activities that he and the children have in common, whereas he is less inclined to support other activities that he does not have an interest in. He also indicates a willingness to pay for items like shoes, which may perhaps be understood as essential. This is not necessarily problematic where regular child maintenance is being paid. Where it becomes potentially concerning is for those in Alison's situation where all financial support for children is negotiated in this way. The danger is that if expenses are not perceived as reasonable then children may go without.

A different perspective on child maintenance is offered by some of the fathers who were payers. Gareth and Neil both suggested that the money they paid was not just used for children, but also went towards their former partner's living expenses:

> **Neil:** It is my view, that the money that I pay is for the, um, the maintenance of the children. Um, a-as previously mentioned, I'm starting to feel that that might not be the case because, um, I don't really think, um, 8-8 year old children don't really need hand-made sofas to sit on while they watch, um, bloody Top Gear or whatever it is they're gonna watch. Um, but, you know, that's a sort of slightly facetious example but you see my point. Um, I – so, and that was the approach in trying to work out how much money and for what I was going to pay was absolutely based on the premise that I'm, I'm paying for the children, you know, um, my partner is, my former partner is, a young and able woman who's quite capable of supporting herself. Um, she has, chosen to work part-time, um … I, it, it, the point could have spun differently, it could be me that was working part-time and, that, that wouldn't be too much of an issue for me 'cause, you know, a-as demonstrated by the fact that I've already done it. Um, so, no I, I think that – u-unless there are compelling reasons not to, I, I think, I think maintenance is for the maintenance of the children only. Um, and, yeah. That, that's not gonna change in my mind I don't think.

Gareth explained that he had recently had his children for longer periods of time, but had not reduced his child maintenance payments: 'Cause I feel like the – It's not like they're suddenly working more and earning more money. I feel like I'm more paying towards their household running rather than like, this is how much money I'm paying and it needs to go into clothes and food for the children.' However, he suggested that 'actually the kids don't cost really anything to feed at all. It purely is the fact that they take up a lot of, uh, organisational and, productive time'. I sought to explore this point further:

> **Interviewer:** So it's more about the impact of the kids on the ability of, of their mums to work, than it is about the sort of direct cost of the kids itself?

> **Gareth:** It kind of, it kind of is. 'Cause I mean [older two] are at school every day, for I mean, um, so, so [first wife] could work every day, um, she could work full time and earn [inaudible] she could do it, it works, there's like after school clubs and things like that. I mean it's not impossible but I get that she doesn't want to and I think that, whatever it is that she's actually doing she will make of success of within her own time so that's fine. I'm kind of, I'm not worried about her. [Second wife]. She does the same job as me so she has the problems with the nursery. Um, but she had chosen to work part-time because she wants to spend more days with [youngest] while [they're] young. Um. So she could actually. She could work full-time as well. I'm glad that she doesn't, 'cause I think it's nice for [them] to spend time with [their] mum.

It is, of course, impossible to know the realities of these different situations and the respective financial positions of these participants and their former partners. What these extracts do, however, is suggest that there may be differences in perspectives about what are acceptable costs for children. Alison explained how this played out in her relationship:

> Um, and this, this can be a huge source of disagreement because there can be disagreement about, um, the, the cost of running the children. So, you know, even my mum or, even [ex-partner] they kind of like, they don't get, 'cause they're, you know, the children like horse riding and that's what [child], my disabled [child], does. It's seventy quid. Seventy quid! That's [inaudible] loads of money. And then all the other things. And, and the attitude is but they – why are they doing that? They don't have to do that. It's like, well they've gotta do something. We haven't got a garden for them to run riot in so we need to, you know, do other things. Um … And yeah, kind of like … there's different, like, how much money do you spend on the kids. I spend quite a lot so they … they take the bulk of my money. Definitely.

These extracts suggest that it is possible that payers are more likely to see children's needs as being acceptable if they relate to immediate costs such as food and clothing. However, payees may take a broader view of what children's needs entail. This resonates with Treloar's research, which suggests gendered perspectives on financial support.[63] Whereas mothers understood financial responsibility 'as an aspect of care for children',[64] fathers were more likely to see 'financial autonomy as an aspect of individual identity' and to seek a 'rebalancing of financial responsibilities and child care' on separation.[65]

The invisibility of care in this regard may be problematic if the result is that carers and their children receive less than is required to meet their financial needs. Further, Treloar's research found that '[w]hen collecting child support proved difficult, most mothers gave up on that avenue and struggled on, therefore exercising a form of agency'.[66] There were similar examples in this research. Andrew,

[63] R Treloar, 'High-conflict Divorce Involving Children: Parents' Meaning-making and Agency' (2018) 40 *Journal of Social Welfare and Family Law* 340.

[64] ibid 346.

[65] ibid 346.

[66] ibid 346.

for example, explained that his reaction towards his ex-wife's attempts to end her child support liability was '"Sod ya, I'm gonna get through this in spite of you"'. Louise had a similar experience: her ex-partner threatened that if she pursued the increase in child maintenance that she was due he would never see the children again. She explained her reaction as follows: 'I s'pose probably for the last few years – probably five, six years – I've just never asked for anything. Never. … If I haven't been able to afford it, they don't have it. But I wouldn't, I just will not ask him for anything.' There are, therefore, very real financial consequences to care being invisible.

D. The Arrangements for Children

Child arrangements on separation provide a different perspective on the treatment of care within the legal system. Whereas the previous sections considered the third of the themes raised by Michael in Chapter 2 – that care does not warrant financial compensation – the law dealing with child arrangements provides a perspective on the second theme; how care is viewed. It is suggested that the law in this area echoes the wider invisibility of care in the neoliberal paradigm.

In England and Wales, a child's welfare is the court's paramount consideration when considering where a child should live or who they should spend time with.[67] A court is also directed to consider a statutory checklist of factors, known as the welfare checklist.[68] These are important matters when it comes to thinking about care. For example, the need to consider the child's 'wishes and feelings'[69] is consistent with Tronto's suggestion that listening to the experiences of care receivers is an important aspect of caring well.[70] Further, it seems logical that an important part of caring well is to respond to the child's 'physical emotional and educational needs',[71] their 'age, sex, background'[72] and other relevant characteristics and 'any harm'[73] the child has suffered or is at risk of suffering. It is also reasonable that ensuring good care requires considering the ability of parents and other relevant people to meet those needs.[74] In practice, however, it appears that care is rendered invisible in these sorts of decisions.

Consistently with the position in relation to child support, child arrangements tend to focus on the time children spend with their parents. In research looking at County Court approaches to child arrangement orders, Newnham and Harding suggested that this focus on time, rather than 'the benefits of care for children',

[67] Children Act 1989, s 1(1).
[68] ibid s 1(3).
[69] ibid s 1(3)(a).
[70] Tronto (n 52) 107–108.
[71] Children Act 1989, s 1(3)(b).
[72] ibid s 1(3)(d).
[73] ibid s 1(3)(e).
[74] ibid s 1(3)(f).

meant that the courts tended to 'understate the significance of caring and particularly the pre-separation primary carer's role'.[75] One example of this sidelining of care could be seen in highly litigated cases, where shared residence was imposed. Newnham and Harding suggest that in such cases 'children's experiences of care were often secondary to the goals of reducing conflict and resolving adult disputes about status'.[76] A further example, was in the 'comparatively uncritical tendency actively to promote as much contact as possible as long as this did not put the child in physical or emotional danger'.[77] In such cases, '[c]ontact became a goal in itself, rather than a means of promoting the child's best interests. The nature and quality of care was rarely discussed'.[78] Thus, despite the directives in the statute to focus on what is best for the child and to consider particular aspects of the child's experience, there appears to be a heavy focus on adult interests.

This is not to say that care is entirely absent in these cases. In addition to the factors above, the welfare checklist also directs the court to consider the 'likely effect [on the child] of any change in his circumstances'.[79] Giving weight to the status quo suggests that past care may be recognised as having a value. Nevertheless, as Newnham and Harding observe, in practice that value is often hidden:

> The courts' reluctance to upset the status quo could be seen as an implicit acknowledgement of the importance of care. However, recommendations against moves were generally justified in the case files in terms of the harm associated with upsetting routines or uprooting children rather than an express examination of the quality of care being provided. Where child welfare related accusations were made against both non-resident and resident parents the court would respond, for example, by asking Cafcass or Children's Services to investigate, but unless there was evidence of a serious problem such allegations were not taken further. Understandably, courts appeared unwilling to impede progress towards a compromise by going beyond the initial assumption that both parents were equally capable of caring for their children into forensic enquiries into who did what, and when. While parenting was not questioned unless there was evidence of very serious problems, particularly good quality of care provided was rarely acknowledged. The social and legal construction of mothering in terms of natural, instinctive self-sacrifice means the daily efforts involved in raising children largely go unremarked.[80]

In contrast, in those cases where residence was changed, care became more visible:

> The topic of care became visible in this group, possibly because the facts of these cases went against the prevailing, gendered cultural pattern of parenting, but more likely

[75] A Newnham and M Harding, 'Sharing as Caring? Contact and Residence Disputes between Parents' (2016) 28 *Child and Family Law Quarterly* 175, 176.
[76] ibid.
[77] ibid.
[78] ibid.
[79] Children Act 1989, s 1(3)(c).
[80] Newnham and Harding (n 75) 178–79.

> because the mothers' caring practices could not be taken for granted. The issue of care had to be confronted and investigated. The court's reliance on social workers' assessments of parents' caring skills made this a highly visible, important topic.
>
> In this group of cases, fathers were valued as substitute care givers and also often praised for the positive impact their good quality care was having on the children.[81]

The experiences of participants to my research highlight that children's needs can be diverse and complex and that meeting them may require a more nuanced approach than simply agreeing a particular division of time. Erin, for example, had not been in a relationship with her child's father, and he lived in a different city from her. At the time of interview their child was under the age of two so it was difficult for Erin to travel regularly with them to see their father. Further, because she was living with her own parents it was not feasible for her child's father to visit as often as she would have liked him to be able to. Nevertheless, Erin explained the importance of prioritising this relationship:

> Um, but 'cause he's, 'cause he's also, like, he's of Caribbean, um, descent, kind of Indo-Caribbean descent I also felt that, like, being on the birth certificate and [child] having my name and his name and things like that was really important so that, you know, it's not trying to like wipe out all of his side so that, um, so [child] had kind of access to whatever [child] decides [their] identity is as [they] grows up.

Another important aspect of care could be differences between children and their needs. Sophie, for example, explained that her eldest child had 'quite a strong relationship with [their] father' whereas her younger child, who was much younger when she and her ex-partner split, felt that her new partner was their Dad. One consequence of this was that her older child had regular telephone contact with their father which her younger child did not. Gareth outlined at some length the complexity of responding to these sorts of differing needs in practice:

> So … each of my kids are different. So sometimes I will … have just [oldest]. So [oldest] and [second child] have completely different personalities and sometimes [second child] just needs some time with [their] mum. Sometimes [oldest] just needs some time with [their] mum. … [I]t's not just, 'Right, here's the kids, here's their coats, bring them back on Sunday'. … [W]e do change it around a bit and actually the dynamics between [oldest] and [youngest] and [second child] and [youngest] and the three of them are such that you do tend to … shift things around, pay attention to what they're saying. … [A]nd also … the kids tend to play their parents in completely different ways, … so a lot of [oldest's] behavioural issues aren't behavioural issues when [they are] with me, and a lot of [second child's] behavioural issues with me aren't behavioural issues [with mum]. So … as much as we have … cross words to say to each other, … we have to keep talking about all of this stuff 'cause otherwise we can have phantom problems with the children.

Additionally, some participants discussed the way that their children's needs changed over time. Antonia, for example, explained that after her divorce her

[81] ibid 181.

children had asked her to cut back on work, which she thought was because they needed more reassurance from her. Alison talked about creating opportunities for her older children to develop independence as they made the transition to secondary school. Likewise, Louise explained how her elder child had become much less willing to go and stay with their father, who lived some distance away, as they got older:

> **Louise**: … my eldest [child], [they] can't be both-, can't be bothered, it sounds awful, my eldest [child] really can't be bothered to go and see him. That's partly because, you know, [they're] sixteen and [they've] got quite a good social life and [they] works, and they [play sports] and they've got a [partner] …. I think, what I'm trying to say is I think the fact that [their] father now obviously lives so far away, when they were younger it wasn't such an issue because they were quite happy to go down there for the weekend, but now it cuts into their social life. And because he's so far away they can't just, you know, he can't just sort of take them out for Sunday lunch or take them out for tea or take them out to the cinema. Um, and it's quite a big chunk of their time, to go and spend a whole weekend. So, they will do it but they do it out of a sense of duty.

Similarly, when I discussed Emily's shared care arrangement with her, she explained that 'it's all about what's, what works best for [the children]. So that's always been at the front':

> **Emily**: … so there is responsiveness within the pattern that we've got. Yes. And actually though I can see it becoming more tricky as they get older. Because they're starting sometimes to want to be here, rather than there. 'Cause he lives half an hour's drive from me. So it's near enough. Um, it's near enough. He does bring them back for parties and he drops them off at friends' houses and things like that, so if he wasn't doing those things, I think it would be more of an issue. But he's quite good at doing that stuff.

These nuances are not straightforward to incorporate into the legal framework; by their nature they require a level of flexibility that would be difficult to provide for or enforce in a court order. However, these discussions demonstrate how important aspects of care are absent from social and legal understandings. They also highlight the disconnect between pre- and post-separation positions. Whereas Chapter 2 explored the drivers for gendered caring patterns within intact families, the legal framework on separation is consistent with neoliberal ideas of autonomy, which assume gender equality in such matters.

III. The Costs of Not Caring

The previous sections make it clear that ignoring care can have important consequences for carers and their children which are frequently overlooked by the family law and policy framework. The financial costs of caring are particularly important to recognise given the prevailing neoliberal order which emphasises economic independence: care interferes with the ability to achieve this. Nevertheless, and without undermining the need to recognise these costs, it is also important to recognise that caring can have a value to the carer and that not being able to care can have consequences too.

Chapter 2 considered at some length extracts from Michael's interview, in which he commented, '[w]hat would, what would I have given, to be allowed to [stay at home and look after my children]? I would have loved that'. Likewise, Gareth observed:

> So it's pretty much geared up that somebody takes a year off to look after the children. Um, then it kind of creates this precedent where the guy's off working and earning the money. But in actual fact that's because the girl can take a year off, get paid, and look after the child, whereas the guy can't. You get like 8 weeks or something.
>
> So I mean it's not like. I would have chosen to have a year's paternity leave personally. And turn the tables. But I don't have that option.

Other breadwinner fathers restructured their working lives following separation to allow them to spend greater time with their children. Jason decided to reduce his working hours after agreeing a shared care arrangement with his former partner:

> I guess most sane adults would say, right, ok, put my [child] into childcare, then I could do more hours to pay for the childcare. But what I realised was … I'm going to – I don't get this time back with [them], you know, and there's no refunds on parenting. So, I was, I wanted to put as much as I can into the time with [them]. Because also that could give [their] mum justification – well, you're not with [them] anyway, you're putting [them] into childcare, [they] might as well be with me. So I wasn't willing to compromise my time with [them]. So that means – meant I couldn't work as many hours.

This extract suggests two complementary motivations for Jason's decision. The first, that 'I don't get this time back with [them]', recognises that care has a value. In fact, care is so valuable that he is prepared to go against what he thinks 'sane adults' would do and cut down his working hours to be able to care. This perception that his choice is not a sane one resonates with the sort of neoliberal ideology outlined in Chapter 2: individuals are expected to work and to actively choose not to do so in favour of caring is seen as irrational. This extract from Jason's interview also suggests a second motivation for the decision to cut down his working hours: improving his bargaining position with respect to his former partner. While this motivation is not necessarily connected to the first, the context here suggests that it is likely and highlights a related difficulty for those who were not caregivers during their relationships: not living with your children means that you do not get to experience the regular daily aspects of care. Louise's interview captures this well in describing the position of her new partner, who had children from a previous relationship:

> Um, and he's found it difficult, you know. You know, things like he wasn't, he wasn't there to put [his children] to bed at night, and, when they were there to wake up and he missed all of that. So that was a different, so that was something different that I never even thought about. I took that for granted but I never thought that [my children's] dad would have actually missed out on all of that.

In a similar vein to Jason, Gareth decided to work as a contractor, rather than an employee, so that he had control over his hours and was able to see his children regularly, something that wouldn't have been possible with his previous rota. However, in doing this he suffered some of the financial consequences that caregivers often experienced:

> **Gareth**: So now I work fixed Monday to Thursday so I always have my Friday and weekends free for the kids. Which is great, but they're trying their best to stop people contracting … uh, so I've kind of – And I don't get sick pay, I don't get a pension and I'm constantly stressed I'm not gonna be able to find any work. So I don't have any real job security and, um. I mean the benefit is that I earn more but I mean, that's, that's great, but I mean I could do with some security to be perfectly honest.

While these examples are from breadwinner fathers, it is important to remember that not being able to care may be an issue for a far wider range of parents. Chapter 2 discussed the expectations of working class and Black and minority ethnic mothers, who are often expected to prioritise paid work. The position of mothers who cannot perform the physical aspects of care to the extent expected by norms of intensive mothering is not necessarily the same as that of a former breadwinner father who wants to care more post-separation. They may, for example, continue to carry the mental load of caring, which may not be the case for those who have been primary breadwinners, and they may additionally suffer guilt at not being able to fulfil the neoliberal expectations around caregiving that were outlined in Chapter 2. However, it is important that their experience is also considered when thinking about the importance of making care visible. There is, therefore, a case for making care visible from the perspective of caregivers (whether working full-time or not), those who are cared for and those who perform other aspects of care such as caring about or taking care of.

IV. Can Ideas of Autonomy and Caring Responsibilities Be Reconciled in Family Law and Policy?

Chapters 2 and 3 have explored the very real tension between understandings of autonomy and the demands of caring responsibilities within a neoliberal framework. This incompatibility creates a particular tension on separation where parents, understandably, seek a level of autonomy to start again but caring responsibilities are ongoing. Chapter 4 looks to Sweden as a lens through which to assess the role of the state in this dilemma. As explained in Chapter 1, Sweden is a leader in policies that facilitate gender equality. It, therefore, takes a very different approach from England and Wales in providing state support for caring. The next two chapters will evaluate that approach and consider whether there are lessons that can be learned that will help to make care more visible and valued in England and Wales.

PART III

The Swedish Approach

4

The Swedish Approach: State Support for Autonomy

> **Bertil:** … between the lines, in very much of the Swedish legislation, uh, since the sixties I should say that, um, both men and women should get out and work. It's um, it's a political decision that is, um, that has affect [*sic*] very many laws.

In Sweden, the state is seen as central in facilitating autonomy, something that is accompanied by a strong focus on gender equality in society. Bertil, a Swedish lawyer interviewed for this research, explained that family law in Sweden needed to be understood in this wider context. Looking at the provisions of Swedish family law alone might suggest that they are less generous than those in England and Wales. However, to look at family law in isolation, without considering the role of the state, presents a misleading picture. This chapter will, therefore, explore both the Swedish legal provisions and the wider societal context.

The Swedish vision of autonomy overlaps with, but is different from, the neoliberal-inspired visions of autonomy that dominate in England and Wales. Two key arguments will be made in this chapter. The first is that if autonomy is considered a worthwhile goal, then the Swedish approach to autonomy, which recognises the incompatibility between the aspirations of economic independence and choice, and recognises the necessity of state intervention to facilitate economic independence, is superior to neoliberal conceptions. The second argument is that, regardless of whether some form of autonomy is the ultimate goal, there is a role for the state in supporting carers. Further, it is vital for the state to play this role if all carers, and not just the relatively privileged who are able to make financial remedies claims on divorce, are to care effectively. Nevertheless, Chapter 5 will argue that the Swedish approach continues to overlook the work involved in, and the value of, care. As a result, a new approach is needed, albeit one that, like the Swedish one, envisages a role for the state in supporting care.

This chapter begins by exploring the concept of 'statist individualism', the idea that in Sweden an alliance between the state and individual facilitates individual autonomy.[1] This concept is compared with neoliberal understandings of autonomy, revealing that the Swedish approach better allows caring responsibilities

[1] L Trägårdh, 'Statist Individualism: The Swedish Theory of Love and its Lutheran Imprint' in J Halldorf and F Wenell (eds), *Between the State and the Eurcharist* (Pickwick, 2014) 27.

and autonomy to be reconciled, albeit that it too has limitations. The chapter then considers how statist individualism fits with the emphasis on gender equality in Swedish society more generally. Against this backdrop, the chapter will outline the Swedish legal framework and consider what this reveals about understandings of autonomy in that context. The discussion concludes with a reflection on how the sort of state support provided in Sweden might inform state approaches to supporting care in England and Wales.

I. Swedish Statist Individualism

The idea of statist individualism,[2] and its implications for individual autonomy, is explained in Booth's summary of an interview with Henrik Beggren:[3]

> Sweden's 'statist individualism', as he terms it, enables the very purest form of wholly independent love to blossom between two people. Wives don't stick around because their husband keeps the joint bank account pin code locked in a drawer in his desk, and husbands don't hold their tongues because their wife's father owns the mill … '… The main objective is not to be dependent on your family, the wife shouldn't be dependent on the husband, the children should be autonomous when they are eighteen, old people should not be dependent on their children taking care of them, and therefore to a large extent the state steps in and provides these things …'[4]

This idea, that the state is responsible for dependency, is an example of the vertical dimension of responsibility discussed in Chapter 2. Trägårdh suggests that the objective in Sweden is to 'liberate the individual citizen from all forms of subordination and dependency within the family and in civil society'.[5] This differs from the neoliberal-inspired conception of the state in England and Wales in several ways. First, the Swedish approach favours state support over charitable or family support. Trägårdh suggests that in Sweden social and political movements sought to 'eradicate the need for charity and civil society and family-based social services by establishing state guaranteed social rights based on citizenship in the form of a universalist welfare state'.[6] In contrast, 'the (neo)liberal vision of civil society … centers on the idea that family- and civil society-based provision of social services through charities and local communities is preferable given the overarching aim to keep the state at arm's length'.[7] Thus, in Sweden, the state is seen as a positive force rather than a cause for concern.

A second difference between the Swedish vision and neoliberal understandings of autonomy is that, whereas in the neoliberal paradigm individuals are

[2] See Trägårdh (n 1) 27.
[3] A Swedish Historian and journalist.
[4] M Booth, *The Almost Nearly Perfect People* (Random House, 2014) 360.
[5] Trägårdh (n 1) 22.
[6] Trägårdh (n 1) 30.
[7] ibid.

assumed to be autonomous, statist individualism recognises that they are not. Instead, statist individualism envisages autonomy as an aspiration, which the state is there to facilitate. A good example of how the state endeavours to do this can be seen in Swedish childcare policy.[8] Preschool costs are heavily subsidised and are capped at SEK 1,572 (circa £142) for a child per month.[9] Subsidised childcare allows both parents to undertake paid work, thereby helping to prevent, or at least reducing, intra-partner dependence. Thus, autonomy in the Swedish context is also strongly connected to economic independence, but a role for the state is assumed in achieving this.

Relatedly, a third difference between the Swedish vision of autonomy and neoliberal-inspired conceptions concerns the idea of choice. As was explained in Chapter 2, choice is central to neoliberal-inspired ideas of autonomy.[10] In Sweden, choice appears to be a less important aspect of autonomy. As Bertil observed in the words at the start of this chapter, there is a strong emphasis on paid work in Sweden. This is supported by an individualised welfare policy and income tax regime; Sundström explains that '[w]ithin Swedish welfare policies the individual right to self-sufficiency is emphasized and the social security system is consequently based on the individual's rights rather than on the needs of the family'.[11] As a result, '[l]abour market participation is expected from both men and women independent of family situation …'.[12] The Swedish individual income tax regime, introduced in 1971,[13] underpins this model of the individual worker. As Gunnarsson explains, '[i]ndividual obligations via income tax, and individual social rights based on earnings-related social security schemes are measures that, as one of several objectives, aim to increase economic autonomy for married women'.[14] The corollary of this is that, as Lewis and Åström observed in the 1990s, 'it is still not clear that women are in a position to make a genuine choice between paid and unpaid work'.[15] Paid work is expected of all adults.

The dilemma of choice in the Swedish context is perhaps best illustrated by the controversy around cash for care schemes, which are described by Giuliani

[8] Trägårdh (n 1).

[9] Stockholms Stad, 'Fees for Preschool' https://translate.google.com/translate?hl=en&sl=sv&u=https://forskola.stockholm/avgifter/&prev=search&pto=aue accessed 28 April 2023 (page translated using Google translate).

[10] M Fineman, *The Autonomy Myth* (The New Press, 2004); A Heenan, 'Neoliberal Autonomy and Financial Remedy Reform: Lessons from Sweden' (2020) 3 *Child and Family Law Quarterly* 263; A Heenan, 'Neoliberalism, Family Law, and the Devaluation of Care' (2021) 48 *Journal of Law and Society* 386; K Lynch, *Care and Capitalism* (Polity, 2022) 2.

[11] E Sundström, 'Should Mothers Work? Age and Attitudes in Germany, Italy and Sweden' (1999) 8 *International Journal of Social Welfare* 193, 197.

[12] ibid 197.

[13] Å Gunnarsson, 'Introducing Independent Income Taxation in Sweden in 1971' (2016) FairTax Working Paper Series No 2, Forum for Studies on Law and Society https://umu.diva-portal.org/smash/get/diva2:930244/FULLTEXT01.pdf accessed 28 April 2023.

[14] ibid 5.

[15] J Lewis and G Åström, 'Equality, Difference and State Welfare: Labor Market and Family Policies in Sweden' (1992) 18 *Feminist Studies* 59, 61.

and Duvander as 'a subsidy for parents whose children are between the ages of one and three and who are not using publicly subsidised childcare'.[16] A cash for care scheme was initially introduced in Sweden in 1994, and was abolished a year later.[17] A second scheme, which ran between 2008 and 2016, drew explicitly on ideas of choice, suggesting that it would enable parents' flexibility in combining paid work and care.[18] This scheme was, however, controversial because of the recognition that these sorts of choices may conflict with societal goals of gender equality.[19] While defenders of the scheme suggested that it served to value 'the unpaid work women do at home and contributing to making women who do not work outside the home equal to their working husbands and to working women',[20] not all women made use of the scheme equally. Ellingsaeter explains that:

> … 17 per cent of applicants had only primary education (9 years or less), compared to 11 per cent in the total population … It is estimated that almost 50 per cent of the women who receive the benefit are economically dependent on their partners … The likelihood of taking the benefit declined with increasing income and education ….[21]

This discussion reveals the tensions inherent in neoliberal understandings of individuals. Individuals within the neoliberal paradigm are assumed to have freedom of choice. However, as the discussion of cash for care schemes illustrates, choices can interfere with the ability to be financially independent, another key assumption of neoliberal individuals. Further, individuals are held to be responsible for their choices. This is connected to the idea that those choices are informed by economic rationality, but this is far from straightforward when thinking about caring responsibilities. First, as Chapter 2 explored, within the neoliberal paradigm caring responsibilities are not understood within the same framework of economic rationality. Second, while it is possible that economic rationality plays a role in choices around caring, it is important to consider whose choice we are thinking about and the other factors that influence that choice. For example, in England and Wales, factors such as the gender pay gap and the cost of childcare may make it economically rational for a family as a whole to have one parent (often the mother) who works part-time. The same decision may not be economically rational for the mother herself, or indeed for a single mother. Given the extent to which childcare is subsidised in Sweden, it may be harder to see cash for care as a purely economic decision, although the fact that those likely to be earning less were most likely to make use of it

[16] G Giuliani and AZ Duvander, 'Cash-for-care Policy in Sweden: An Appraisal of Its Consequences in Female Employment' (2017) 26 *International Journal of Social Welfare* 49.

[17] AL Ellingsaeter, 'Cash for Childcare: Experiences from Finland, Norway and Sweden' (Friedrich Ebert Stiftung, April 2012) http://library.fes.de/pdf-files/id/09079.pdf accessed 28 April 2023.

[18] AZ Duvander and AL Ellingsaeter, 'Cash for Childcare Schemes in the Nordic Welfare States: Diverse Paths, Diverse Outcomes' (2016) 18 *European Societies* 70, 76.

[19] See, for example, NIKK, 'Increased Parental Choice Can Lead to Reduced Gender Equality' (Nordic Information on Gender, first published in (2007) 2 *NIKK*) and Ellingsaeter (n 17).

[20] NIKK (ibid).

[21] Ellingsaeter (n 17) 6.

suggests that there may be an economic dimension. In both contexts, however, it is important to consider societal norms around care.

Chapter 5 will explore the importance in Sweden, like England and Wales, of societal norms of care, which are influenced by factors like gender, race and class. Nevertheless, it is important to note when thinking about the differences between the Swedish idea of statist individualism and neoliberal-inspired ideas of individual autonomy that statist individualism recognises the impact of these norms, cash for care schemes aside, insofar as it does not seek to prioritise choice where that would conflict with the goal of financial independence. Thus if, as seems to be the case, financial independence is the most important goal of family law in England and Wales, a Swedish understanding of autonomy, which recognises constraints on choice and a role for state support, would better facilitate this.

II. Gender Equality and Family Policy in Sweden

Alongside, but connected to, the Swedish vision of state supported autonomy, gender equality is an important goal in Sweden. In trying to understand the meaning of gender equality in Sweden, a useful starting point is the Official Website of Sweden, which describes the 'Swedish approach to gender equality' as follows:

> The overarching Swedish principle is that everyone, regardless of gender, has the right to work and support themselves, to balance career and family life, and to live without the fear of abuse or violence.
>
> Gender equality implies not only equal distribution between men and women in all domains of society. It is also about the qualitative aspects, ensuring that the knowledge and experience of both men and women are used to promote progress in all aspects of society.[22]

Gender equality in Sweden started with efforts to get women into work on more equal terms to men.[23] However, the Swedish approach has been described by Lewis and Åström as 'significantly different from the "equal to men" formulation'.[24] The idea of women having dual roles,[25] as mother and worker, has been influential and:

> the Swedish equal opportunities strategy has involved, first, defining all adults as workers and providing incentives to ensure that women enter the labour market and,

[22] The Official Site of Sweden, 'Gender Equality' (last updated 18 November 2022) https://sweden.se/society/gender-equality-in-sweden/ accessed 28 April 2023.

[23] L Martinsson et al, 'Introduction' in L Martinsson et al (eds), *Challenging the Myth of Gender Equality in Sweden* (Polity Press, 2016) 9.

[24] Lewis and Åström (n 15) 65.

[25] Lewis and Åström (n 15) and J Bussemaker, 'Recent Changes in European Welfare State Services: A Comparison of Child Care Politics in the United Kingdom, Sweden, Germany and the Netherlands' 1997 Program for the Study of Germany and Europe 7.6 http://aei.pitt.edu/63647/ accessed 28 April 2023.

> second, providing compensation to women and men for lost earnings with generous recognition of the needs of parents.[26]

This dual approach is reflected in two key measures of family policy in Sweden: state childcare and parental leave. Whereas universal state childcare is intended to allow all adults to work, parental leave policies were designed to ensure the sharing of care more equally between parents. As this chapter and Chapter 5 will highlight, their success in achieving this has been mixed, but they nevertheless offer lessons when thinking about how the state could play a greater role in supporting care in England and Wales.

In exploring each of these policies in turn, this chapter will attempt to consider their implications for women in different circumstances. This is not straightforward in a context where gender equality is, and has been, so central to the political agenda; de los Reyes highlights that 'traditional perspectives on gender equality in Sweden commonly refer to women as a collective entity with common interests, needs, and problems'.[27] The analysis in this chapter does not claim to be exhaustive, but it attempts to move beyond an analysis that views all women's circumstances as being the same.

A. State Childcare

Subsidised childcare is connected both to ideas of statist individualism and gender equality. As childcare is more commonly performed by women, state childcare facilitates gender equality by allowing women to work. This, in turn, helps to avoid carers being financially dependent on their partners; an example of statist individualism. Universal childcare also has a wider objective in Sweden. It has been suggested that the 'strong feeling of communal responsibility for universal child care' in Sweden[28] is connected to achieving social equality. The 2001 National Childcare goals, for example, stated that:

> [t]he importance of activities in contributing towards compensation for difference in the growing-up conditions for children from different parts of the population and in creating places of interaction for children from different ethnical, cultural and social backgrounds has been emphasised.[29]

Strandbrink and Pestoff observe that this goal means that state childcare arrangements may differ in different parts of the country. For example, in areas with a

[26] Lewis and Åström (n 15) 72.
[27] P de los Reyes, 'Working Life Inequalities: Do We Need Intersectionality' (2017) 8 *Society, Health and Vulnerability* 14, 15.
[28] Bussemaker (n 25) 9.
[29] National Childcare Goals (Ds 2001:57; *Barnafödandet i fokus. Från befolkningspolitik till barnvänligt samhälle*, 57) quoted (and translated) in P Strandbrink and V Pestoff, *Small-scale Welfare on a Large Scale: Social Cohesion and the Politics of Swedish Childcare* (Södertörns högskola, 2006) 42.

'relatively large proportion of refugees and newly arrived Swedes in the ward; i.e. groups who generally have higher levels of unemployment and make more extensive use of social insurance systems', 'the childcare system becomes an important tool to assess and strengthen the bonds of social solidarity. It provides the local polity with a direct means to reach (out to) families with little or no footing at all in Swedish society. The emphasis on language development is a prominent aspect of this.'[30]

These dual rationales for childcare policy – gender equality and social equality – were important drivers of social policy after the Second World War. Eldén and Anving explain that whereas the former aimed to create equal opportunities for all children, the latter 'questioned the male breadwinner model and the "double role" women faced when entering the labour market while still being primarily responsible for care at home'.[31] These dual rationales relate to two different concepts of equality in Sweden. Svensson and Gunnarsson explain that '*Jämställdhet* should be translated as either sex or gender equality, but has different connotations depending on context. In essence it embraces the specific equality between men and women, and no other form of equality such as that between social classes.'[32] The other concept of equality is '*jämlikhet*', which is used 'to refer to the aim of achieving social justice for the working class'.[33]

Despite aiming to achieve both gender equality and a measure of social justice, it seems that class increasingly plays a role in both the childcare that children from different backgrounds receive, and the way in which their parents conceptualise what good care involves. Thus, increasingly, there are parallels with the neoliberal understandings of care that were discussed in Chapter 2. Eldén and Anving suggest that political initiatives increasingly support privatised childcare options.[34] For some upper-middle class families, nannies or au pairs play a role in childcare, to address two particular needs. The first, is '*to solve the "jigsaw puzzle of life"* as they call it: to make the everyday life of managing a home, family and job possible'. Second:

> hiring a nanny/au pair is also justified by discourses of what is *good for children*, with reference to the quality of care that can be offered, both through the kind of parenting that is made possible when a nanny/au pair is present, and through the additional 'care value' that the nanny/au pair can bring.[35]

[30] Strandbrink and Pestoff (ibid) 185.

[31] S Eldén and T Anving, 'New Ways of Doing the "Good" and Gender Equal Family: Parents Employing Nannies and Au Pairs in Sweden' (2016) 21 *Sociological Research Online* www.socresonline.org.uk/21/4/2.html accessed 28 April 2023.

[32] EM Svensson and A Gunnarsson, 'Gender Equality in the Swedish Welfare State' (2012) 2 *Feminists@Law* http://journals.kent.ac.uk/index.php/feministsatlaw/article/view/51/160 accessed 28 April 2023.

[33] ibid.

[34] Eldén and Anving (n 31).

[35] ibid 5.1.

Turning first to the idea of private childcare to meet the challenges of everyday life, while this shows some similarity to the challenges of resolving the conflict between neoliberal-inspired ideas of autonomy and caring responsibilities outlined in Chapter 2, in that privatised solutions allow different groups of parents to better reconcile these competing demands, the Swedish experience is different. A nanny or au pair is not an alternative to day care in Sweden but an additional form of childcare: for example, someone to pick a child up from day care.[36] Not only does this allow those parents who can employ a nanny to conform to norms of good parenthood by limiting the number of hours a child spends in day care,[37] but it also allows women to pursue careers.[38] This latter aspect, which Eldén and Anving relate to men's failure to share care and housework,[39] will be discussed in Chapter 5 when considering the invisibility of care in the Swedish model.

Increasing support for private childcare through tax deductions, therefore, allows wealthier women to enjoy a very different position from other women. This increased privatisation of care also has consequences for the women who perform it; de los Reyes explains the particular impact on migrant women, for example:

> The creation of low paid, unqualified jobs in a gender and ethnically-segregated labour market has historically been accompanied by the characterisation of migrant women as less competent and qualified than other women and also in less need of welfare reforms such as child-care provision or part-time working. A clear example of this is when employment opportunities within the tax-subsidised domestic service sector are presented as an integration strategy for migrant women. Additionally, the class and ethnical dimensions of this strategy become evident when it is argued that a market for care work can help to achieve gender equality goals, since it allows (wealthy) women to solve work life imbalances by buying care work and other reproductive work.[40]

Thus, while some women are privileged by support for private childcare, others are disadvantaged by the same strategies. This underscores the need to think beyond gender as a single category of analysis. It also suggests that if the state is to provide support for all carers, there is a need to understand their different experiences and the extent to which state childcare alone genuinely facilitates engagement in paid work. This may mean, for example, recognising that different types of work have different working hours. The existence of state childcare that is available to, and affordable for, all is a critical measure in supporting all carers. Unlike strategies that try and rely on sharing care more equally between parents, universal childcare also caters to those like single parents who cannot rely on sharing care with a partner.

[36] ibid 6.2.
[37] ibid 7.2.
[38] ibid 6.3.
[39] ibid 6.3.
[40] P de los Reyes, 'Practising Intersectionality, Challenging Power' in K Dalborg and M Löfgren (eds), *Perspectives on Cultural Leadership. The Fika Project* https://europeanculturalleadershipdotorg.files.wordpress.com/2015/10/perspectives_web.pdf accessed 28 April 2023, 227.

B. Parental Leave

Whereas state childcare focuses on parents' positions as paid workers, Swedish policy around parental leave is focused on their role as carers. Swedish parents are entitled to 480 days of paid parental leave, which can be taken until a child is 8.[41] Although this leave is notionally divided between the parents, only 90 days are reserved to each parent,[42] meaning that the leave is lost if it is not taken.[43] In practice, this means that the reserved months tend to be referred to as 'daddy months',[44] with mothers taking the majority of the leave.[45] In addition to parental leave, parents are entitled to up to 120 days of temporary parental leave so that they can take time off work when children under 12 are sick.[46]

When, in 1974, Sweden became the first country to introduce paid parental leave for fathers[47] and a gender-neutral parental leave replaced maternity allowance,[48] the moves were explicitly linked to efforts to promote gender equality. Björnberg explains:

> The political discourse at the time [that policies relating to parental leave and childcare were introduced] also stressed that equality between men and women was important to the reform. Individual and mutual responsibility for family subsistence was seen as necessary for gender equality to be accomplished. Both parents were regarded as responsible for the care of children and for domestic work.[49]

This recognises that achieving gender equality requires a division of unpaid as well as paid work. This recognition was also behind the introduction of reserved months of parental leave. The introduction of the first of these reserved months in 1995 was explicitly couched in the language of gender equality:

> It is important that fathers take parental leave. An increased use of parental leave by fathers should contribute to a change in attitudes among managers; they will view parental leave as something natural to consider when planning and organizing the work. This change in attitudes is necessary for both men and women to dare to take parental leave

[41] The Official Site of Sweden, 'Children in Sweden' https://sweden.se/life/society/children-in-sweden accessed 28 April 2023.

[42] The Official Site of Sweden, 'Work-life balance' https://sweden.se/life/society/work-life-balance accessed 28 April 2023.

[43] ibid.

[44] See, for example, J Ekberg et al, 'Parental Leave – A Policy Evaluation of the Swedish "Daddy-Month" Reform' (2013) 97 *Journal of Public Economics* 131, E Mussino et al, 'Does Time Count? Immigrant Fathers' Use of Parental Leave for a First Child in Sweden' (2018) 73 *Population* 363.

[45] The Official Site of Sweden (n 41). See also Chapter 5.

[46] Statistics Sweden, 'Women and Men in Sweden: Facts and Figures 2022' www.scb.se/contentassets/1fbf4f9815374356a786278faca6a7f0/le0201_2021b22_x10br2202.pdf accessed 28 April 2023.

[47] AZ Duvander et al, 'Swedish Parental Leave and Gender Equality – Achievements and Reform Challenges in a European Perspective (Institute for Future Studies, 2005) www.iffs.se/media/1118/20051201134956filU8YIJLRAaC7u4FV7gUmy.pdf 28 April 2023.

[48] ibid.

[49] U Björnberg, 'Ideology and Choice between Work and Care: Swedish Family Policy for Working Parents' (2002) 22 *Critical Social Policy* 33, 35.

> without a feeling of jeopardizing their career or development opportunities at work. Another reason for increasing fathers' use of parental leave is that women's prospects of achieving equal opportunities to men in the labor market will be limited, as long as women are responsible for practical housework and children. A shared responsibility for the practical care of children would mean a more even distribution of interruptions in work between women and men, and women would thereby gain better opportunities of development and making a career in their profession.[50]

There are two justifications for encouraging fathers to take parental leave in this passage. The first appears implicitly to recognise the value of care. It is considered important that both parents can take this leave without fear of jeopardising their careers. By implication, parental leave is important. Nevertheless, even in this context the primary concern is about paid work: parents should feel their careers are safe if they take leave. The second justification is framed more clearly in terms of paid work: sharing childcare is necessary for women to be able to work. The relative importance placed upon paid work is also illustrated by restrictions placed on parental leave applied to immigrant families. In 2010, the government suggested that restricting the parental leave entitlement of such families was important 'to improve the chances of newly arrived foreign-born women to get a job'.[51] The issue was explained more fully by the committee considering the new rules:

> … the provisions regarding parental benefit mean that when parents come to Sweden with older children, they may be entitled to the same amount of parental benefit for the older child that is normally paid out in connection with a child's birth … The regulations are currently designed in such a way that overcompensation arises in relation to the needs of parents with older children for parental leave and benefit. This results in an opportunity to take long-term leave from work, job-seeking, education or other activities that are aimed at bringing parents closer to the labour market. For some people coming to Sweden, getting established on the labour market becomes a long and drawn-out process.
>
> Overcompensation leads to the parents, primarily women, using a relatively high number of days of parental benefit for older children.[52]

These discussions, and the measures which resulted from them, help to demonstrate the importance placed upon paid work in the Swedish context: adults are understood primarily as workers, albeit that there are policy measures which allow them to reconcile a period of caring with this role. These discussions also serve to highlight a wider point around gender and its interplay with other factors. The perceived problem here is specifically migrant women, who are considered

[50] Government Bill 1993/94: 147 Gender Equality Policy: Shared Power – Shared Responsibility. Translation from Ekberg et al (n 44) 132.

[51] Swedish Government (2010). Government declaration (18 September 2010). Stockholm: Swedish Government. Cited in M Nygård and AZ Duvander, 'Social Inclusion or Gender Equality? Political Discourses on Parental Leave in Finland and Sweden' (2021) 9 *Social Inclusion* 300, 307.

[52] Statens Offentliga Utredningar, 'Begränsningar i föräldrapenningen för föräldrar som kommer till Sverige med barn' (SOU 2016:73).

to hold different attitudes to paid work from Swedish women. This is important. Chapter 2 outlined the way in which in the neoliberal paradigm expectations of mothers differ: for example, working class and Black and minority ethnic mothers are expected to engage in paid work, whereas for upper and middle class white mothers the norms are different. This is not necessarily the same in the Swedish context where the norm of paid work is pervasive for all adults, although the discussion of cash for care schemes above suggests that perhaps it is seen as more problematic where women with lower levels of income or education choose to care rather than to work. The second way in which this discussion is important is that it suggests that traditional norms of motherhood are a particular problem for migrant women. However, as Chapter 5 will explore, such norms continue to be pervasive in Swedish society, despite the emphasis on paid work.

There is a clear link between parental leave and ideals of gender equality. Additionally, and while perhaps less obvious than the link between state childcare and statist individualism, there are connections between parental leave provisions and the idea of statist individualism. In encouraging parents to share care work between them, there is an attempt to disrupt gendered patterns of dependency. Perhaps more significantly, from the perspective of statist individualism, rights to parental leave are individual and not familial, and so not affected by relationship breakdown.[53] The parental leave policy, therefore, recognises the need to share unpaid as well as paid work if the financial independence that is seen as so important for autonomy is to be recognised. This offers important lessons for England and Wales in thinking about how state support could help facilitate care and change gendered attitudes to caring. Nevertheless, as will be discussed in Chapter 5, parental leave uptake differs by gender and income in Sweden as well as in England and Wales.

III. The Swedish Family Law Framework

Against this backdrop of statist individualism and gender equality, as Bertil suggested at the outset of this chapter, Swedish family law makes sense. While it would be inaccurate to describe Swedish family law as neoliberal, some of its key provisions are consistent with neoliberal ideas. For example, as will be discussed below, the Swedish approach to dealing with property at the end of a relationship has much in common with a Private Members Bill (the 'Divorce (Financial Provision) Bill')[54] that seeks to reform the law of financial provision on divorce in England and Wales. This Bill, which has been introduced into the House of Lords

[53] AZ Duvander and N Korsell, 'Whose Days are Left? Separated Parents' Use of Parental Leave in Sweden' in R Nieuwenhuis and LC Maldonado (eds), *The Triple Bind of Single-parent Families* (Policy Press, 2018) 263–64.

[54] The Divorce (Financial Provision) HL Bill (2019–21).

repeatedly, proposes three main changes to the law in England and Wales. First, it seeks to limit the division of assets on divorce to matrimonial property, meaning property that was acquired during a marriage other than by gift or inheritance. Currently, all property belonging to a couple falls within the courts' powers under Matrimonial Causes Act 1973, section 25, and in cases where the parties' needs exceed their assets, there may need to be recourse to non-matrimonial property. Second, the Bill seeks to make pre-nuptial agreements binding; they are currently persuasive but not binding. Finally, the Bill seeks to limit the term of periodical payments to five years, unless the claimant can establish serious financial hardship; currently the courts have a wide discretion to make periodical payments for any period, including until one of the spouses dies if this is required by the circumstances of the case.

Understanding the Swedish legal approach in its wider context provides a further perspective on the difficulties of a neoliberal approach, which does not allow for state support, in reconciling paid work and care. It is also serves to demonstrate the interplay between family law and policy, which is important in thinking about how to support care for all carers, and not just those who are able to make financial remedies claims on divorce. This section will focus on five aspects of the law on separation: private ordering, deferred community of property, spousal maintenance, pensions, child support and the law on child arrangements.

A. Private Ordering

As in England and Wales, private ordering is an important aspect of autonomy in Swedish family law. Chapter 2 outlined the increasing role of private ordering in the Family Justice System in England and Wales and explained the assumption of equal bargaining power which accompanies this.[55] The Swedish approach of statist individualism aims to avoid dependency. Although this does not necessarily eliminate all power imbalances, for example those linked to domestic abuse, this strategy may serve to reduce the potential for power imbalances linked to unequal financial positions.[56] Against this backdrop, it is perhaps unsurprising that private ordering seems to be well accepted in Sweden. In particular, the deferred community of property regime is seen as a private matter.[57] Deferred community will be discussed in the next section, but in brief it is the set of rules

[55] S Thompson, *Prenuptial Agreements and the Presumption of Free Choice* (Hart Publishing, 2015) and Heenan (2021) (n 10).

[56] For discussion of the link between power imbalances and economic positions see, for example, Heenan (2021) (n 10); J Kelly, 'Power Imbalance in Divorce and Interpersonal Mediation: Assessment and Intervention' (1995) 13 *Mediation* Quarterly 85, J Pahl, *Money & Marriage* (Palgrave, 1989) and Thompson (ibid).

[57] M Jänterä-Jareborg, 'Marital Agreements and Private Autonomy in Sweden' in J Scherpe (ed), *Marital Agreements and Private Autonomy in Comparative Perspective* (Hart Publishing, 2012) 376.

that deal with the division of property at the end of a relationship. Where a couple are married, these rules provide that each spouse owns his or her own property and is responsible for his or her own debts, but each spouse also has a right to claim half of the marital property's net value at the end of the marriage.[58] For cohabitants, there is a more limited form of community of property.

Research suggests that private ordering without legal advice is common in family situations.[59] The simplicity of the regime is seen as an important element in making this possible. As Brattström explains:

> In Sweden, simplicity has also been an important reason for the comprehensive set of rules concerning division of property: by dividing up everything, one avoids the problem – among others – of proving ownership of what is to be shared.[60]

It is, therefore, perhaps unsurprising that the lawyers interviewed for my research were broadly supportive of the default position. For example, Ebbe felt that the basic rule of a 50:50 decision was a good one because it provided a starting point: 'if you don't want it, you can change it'. For Clara, because the 'basic assumption is that, you're supposed to work' and that is was 'very rare' that one party did not, 'normally the pure partition of goods, ensure that the one person gets to live quite comfortably anyway'. However, if couples are to make these sorts of arrangements privately it might be expected that they would have knowledge of the regime. My participants suggested that this was not the case:

> **Anna**: … I think most people maybe [aren't] aware that all, like, everything, will be divided if you separate, uh, or if you get divorced. Um, like maybe when you … are, uh, not married and just cohabiting. I don't think people understand that if you buy like an apartment together, uh, and then you separate, that if you … buy this apartment to, uh, live together in it, that's, uh, a property that can be divided …
>
> **Eric**: The ignorance of what the law actually does and doesn't is quite, it's increasing … And especially by the young people. They don't have a clue what they're doing when they [become] cohabitants … or if they go into marriage …
>
> **Gunilde**: [People wrongly think that the position for cohabitants and spouses is the same]. It is and it isn't. But I think … we are telling so much about it in, in the media and, uh, everywhere … I find it very odd that they … can think so … but people do.

The fact that people do not understand the financial implications of their relationships when they enter them does not necessarily detract from the idea that simple rules facilitate private ordering on separation. However, Eric and Anna suggested that the growth in asset values in recent years may have increased the role of

[58] M Jänterä-Jareborg et al, 'National Report: Sweden' (CEFL, October 2008) http://ceflonline.net/wp-content/uploads/Sweden-Property.pdf accessed 26 June 2023.

[59] M Brattström, 'Bodelning mellan makar – verklighetens betydelse för framtidens regelutformning' (Särtryck från Tidskrift for Familierett, Arverett og Barnevernsrettslige Spørsmål (FAB), 2011) (translated using Google translate).

[60] M Brattström, 'Spouses' Pension Rights & Financial Settlement after Divorce', *Scandinavian Studies in Law* (Social Private Law, Volume 50) 334.

lawyers in financial arrangements on separation.[61] The data from my research also lend some support to the idea that the real benefit of the rules may lie not so much in people's ability to apply them for themselves as in the avoidance of conflict. For example, Clara said of the rules on spousal maintenance (discussed below) 'I do think we do avoid a lot of angry, uh, going to court'. Likewise, when discussing a scenario question relating to cohabitants, Ebbe explained that she would advise clients not to bother about assets that did not form part of the community: 'So don't fight about those things because it's not worth fighting for. Because it's not included in the dividing. Of assets.'

Much like private ordering, this idea of conflict avoidance is unproblematic when dealing with two individuals who are equals. However, where there is a significant difference in the financial position of two parties, it is the stronger party who benefits from the maintenance of the status quo. If these features of private ordering and conflict avoidance are present, which is the case in England and Wales with its emphasis on dispute resolution outside of court, then the Swedish approach is preferable. Unlike the position in England and Wales, in Sweden the state attempts to level the playing field by avoiding individual responsibility for dependency. There is also an accepted role for the state in meeting hardship where needs are not met. Nevertheless, as Chapter 5 will explore, Sweden has not succeeded in eliminating these inequalities.

B. Community of Property

Given the general emphasis on individualism in Swedish family law and policy, the community of property regime is perhaps unusual because of its focus on partnership. Cooke et al explain that '[i]n its most basic form, community of property originates in the ideology of the community of persons created through the marriage union'.[62] England and Wales does not have a matrimonial property regime.[63] Instead, income, capital and pensions are dealt with together, and the different aspects can be offset against one another. For example, one partner might receive a greater share of capital in return for not claiming spousal maintenance. In contrast, in Sweden, a set of rules provide for what is to happen to property at the end of a relationship. These are separate from the provisions relating to spousal maintenance or pensions, albeit that the share of property that a spouse receives may affect their need for spousal maintenance. Under the deferred community of property regime, each spouse retains their own property and debts, but has a right to claim half of the marital property's net value at

[61] Eric referred to this phenomenon specifically in the context of the division of community property, whereas Anna made the suggestion in the context of conveyancing transactions.

[62] E Cooke et al, 'Community of Property A Regime for England and Wales?' (The Nuffield Foundation 2006) 3.

[63] S Cretney et al, *Principles of Family Law*, 7th edn (Sweet & Maxwell, 2002) 102.

the end of the marriage.[64] Marital property comprises all property that is not separate (as defined in section 7:2 of the Marriage Code).[65] For cohabitants, a more limited form of community of property exists than for married couples, comprising any home that has been acquired for mutual use and the household goods.[66]

The community of property regime in Sweden originated in the Marriage Code of 1920, at a time when achieving equality between spouses meant recognising a traditional, gendered, division of labour.[67] The regime granted wives, who would not generally be working outside the home and who would therefore have limited property of their own, an equal share in the marital property. As Sörgjerd explains, this recognised the fact that 'the housewives shouldering of the necessary work in the joint household made the husband's career possible'.[68] The protective purpose of the deferred community regime and the idea of marriage as a mutual project is accordingly an important limitation on statist individualism in Sweden. Further, given the emphasis on private ordering and conflict avoidance described in the previous section, this sort of default entitlement provides a counter to the power imbalances that may otherwise exist.

There have been some moves away from the default position, albeit that these seem to make little difference in practice. The Marriage Code of 1987 allowed the courts a discretion to allow for an unequal division of property where the usual rule would be unfair to the wealthier spouse. Carlson explains that:

> To the extent it is unfair, taking into consideration particularly the length of the marriage but also the financial circumstances of the spouses, that one spouse in the estate division is to transfer property to the other in accordance with chapter eleven [of the Marriage Code], the division of the estate can be made instead so that the first spouse can retain more of his or her marital goods.[69]

The Marriage Code therefore provides the courts with a discretion to adjust the division of assets in some cases. The legislative preparatory works refer to a period of five years, after which the expectation is that marital property is equally divided.[70] Prior to that, as Bradley explains, 'it is recommended that a one year marriage should give a one-fifth entitlement with pro rata allocation thereafter'.[71] Participants to my research did, however, see an equal division of marital assets as the norm. This ability to depart from an equal division of assets is underpinned by a concern to protect those who bring assets into marriages. This was reflected to some extent in participant concerns with the community of property system:

[64] National Report: Sweden (n 58).
[65] L Carlson, *Fundamentals of Swedish Law*, 2nd edn (studentlitteratur Ab, 2012) 207.
[66] ibid 211.
[67] C Sörgjerd, *Reconstructing Marriage* (Intersentia, 2012) 76.
[68] ibid.
[69] Carlson (n 65) 210.
[70] ibid.
[71] D Bradley, *Family Law and Political Culture* (Sweet & Maxwell, 1996) 78.

> **Filippa**: But in one way I think … in the light of the community today where people won't … live together for their whole lives any more, then I think that maybe it's too generous in one way … So, it would be good with a more flexible system maybe. But then we have the problem that that would probably lead to more disputes.

The concern that an equal division may be unfair in these circumstances reflects the expectation in Sweden, consistent with the preceding discussion and central to the rules on spousal maintenance discussed below, that all adults should work outside the home.[72] It is consistent with a view of marriage where spouses are seen as autonomous individuals, responsible for their own support. This vision is made possible by the greater role of the state in Swedish society. In contrast, despite moves to introduce a similar legal framework in England and Wales, no such state support exists. Thus, there are advantages to the Swedish approach. Chapter 5 will, however, reveal the extent to which inequalities continue to exist in Sweden as a result of caring responsibilities. It is, therefore, worth reflecting here on what the community regime means in cases where a couple are in unequal positions resulting from caring responsibilities. Importantly, an equal share of marital property may not meet the carer's needs. While the state provides a safety net in such cases, it does not attempt to redress inequalities arising from the different roles performed by parents during their relationships.

Participants in this research were asked to consider two scenario questions. The first involved a cohabiting couple with three children (2, 4 and 6). As cohabitants, the only property available for division would be their shared home worth SEK 2,500,000, meaning that each would receive around SEK 1,250,000 (circa £125,000 at the time of interview).[73] However, the male cohabitant, who had been the children's primary caretaker, was earning only SEK 80,000 (circa £8,000 at the time of interview) per annum. In contrast, his partner was working full-time and earning SEK 300,000 (circa £30,000 at the time of interview) per annum. On these facts, it is possible that the male cohabitant and three children could struggle to find rented accommodation, whereas the female cohabitant might be able to purchase a new property by herself. The result would be similar in Sweden if the couple were married. This tended to be recognised by participants without concern. For example, Bertil explained, 'Yes. Uh, the Swedish courts look very little to … the financial situation.'

In England and Wales, the result would not necessarily be different for a cohabiting couple (and could be worse if the property was not in joint names). However, if this couple were married, this result would be unlikely to meet the case law requirements for fairness[74] because it would leave the needs of the father and children unmet.[75] In contrast to the threefold objectives of need, compensation and

[72] MA Glendon, 'Is there a Future for Separate Property?' (1974) 8 *Family Law Quarterly* 315, 323.

[73] If the couple had been spouses, the only difference would be that the wife's savings would also form part of community, adding SEK 150,000 (circa £15,000) to the overall pot.

[74] *White v White* [2000] UKHL 54.

[75] *Miller v Miller; McFarlane v McFarlane* [2006] UKHL 24.

sharing in England and Wales, Swedish community of property only deals with the sharing of marital property. The responsibility for meeting needs falls on the individual or the state, subject to the provisions on spousal maintenance discussed in the next section. The extent of this sharing has the potential to be broader than in England and Wales in that pre-acquired assets are not so easily removed from its scope in cases where assets exceed needs. However, given that, at least in England and Wales, needs are more often a concern than sharing, the role of the state is likely to be of central importance in most cases. Viewing marriage as a relationship between two autonomous individuals who are expected to work explains this approach. It is, however, more problematic where caring responsibilities inhibit the ability of one spouse to compete in the labour market on equal terms.

C. Spousal Maintenance

Spousal maintenance in Sweden is rare. All participants to this research stressed its exceptional nature in practice. Bertil, for example, described it as 'very rare' and Gunilde, said that she '[v]ery seldom' saw it. Likewise, Ebbe suggested 'it's not very common at all' and Eric went so far as to say 'it doesn't really exist'. Anna and Clara gave examples of just how rare it was:

> **Anna**: … it's, like, very, very, very uncommon. Um, like … I've both been working here and at court, uh, and you, you never see it.
>
> **Clara**: You never get it …. Well, I think the last case I heard about, um, was a colleague of mine, and I think that was around 2010 somewhere.

This makes sense when considered in light of the goals of statist individualism and gender equality. In 1989, Bradley suggested:

> Of the three potential sources of income support for spouses on divorce – income from employment, social welfare from the state and maintenance from a former spouse – maintenance allowances are now of minor importance in principle and in practice in Sweden.[76]

This preference for individuals to support themselves through their own income (individual responsibility) and state benefits (vertical responsibility) is readily understandable in the Swedish context. As the preceding discussion explains, in Sweden it is expected that all adults will work. Further, dependence on the state is preferred to dependence on a partner.

Historically, spousal maintenance in Sweden, as in England and Wales, tended to be paid by husbands to wives. Sörgjerd explains that in 1978, 'financial independence after divorce was made the guiding principle, which signalled to society

[76] D Bradley, 'Sexual Equality and Maintenance Allowances in Sweden' (1989) 9 *Oxford Journal of Legal Studies* 403, 413–14.

that this was the desirable goal to strive for',[77] albeit that only 25 per cent of all married women were financially independent at the time.[78] Spousal maintenance remained available but 'primarily for a transitional period following the divorce'.[79] The Marriage Code of 1987 provides that '[f]ollowing divorce, each spouse shall be responsible for his or her own support'.[80] Spouses are, therefore, treated 'as two capable and independent individuals',[81] 'each responsible for his or her own material well-being'.[82]

Bradley explains, 'the attenuation in Sweden of a spouse's right to maintenance on divorce represents a conscious and deliberate effort to promote sexual equality',[83] and it is notable that this aspiration to move away from spousal maintenance post-dates other moves to make society more gender equal, for example, the introduction of individualised income tax in 1971 and the introduction of gender-neutral parental leave in 1974. Several participants recognised this interconnection between the rules on spousal maintenance and wider policy goals, in particular the goal of both men and women being in paid work. Eric, for example described 'the Swedish way of thinking' as 'self-support, get a job'. Clara commented that the tax regime in Sweden meant that most couples could not afford to have one parent stay at home:

> **Clara**: A-and since that is the basic structure, of the Swedish society, I do think that it's kind of fair. There is a possibility, but … it's very rare. And, uh, uh, since we have a pretty good, uh, social security network, um, I do think that it's ok.

Nevertheless, the difficulty in securing spousal maintenance could lead to outcomes that, at least from the perspective of reported case law in England and Wales, would appear unfair because they might not meet one party's financial needs. The potential unfairness of the rules on spousal maintenance was recognised by some participants. For example, Anna noted that whilst it was unusual in Sweden to have a stay-at-home parent, 'in some cases, or like most people Sweden, the, the wife, or like, the, the female are earning a lot less than the male'. Bertil described the rules as 'the brutal world that hits back, normally, on women'. Despite this, Gunilde was the only participant who expressed clear dissatisfaction with the system:

> **Interviewer:** Um, and what do you think about the law on alimony? Um, is it, is it good?
>
> **Gunilde:** No. It's … because, um, some women, there are still women they, that are home, at home very much and don't work, when the children are small as well. And um, they, they have an awful situation when they separate. I, I don't like it.

[77] Sörgjerd (n 67) 111.
[78] ibid.
[79] ibid.
[80] Commission on European Family Law, 'Marriage Code of Sweden' (official translation by the Swedish Government with amendments since 1994 unofficially translated by M Jänterä-Jareborg) http://ceflonline.net/wp-content/uploads/Sweden-Divorce-Legislation.pdf accessed 28 April 2023.
[81] Sörgjerd (n 67) 110.
[82] ibid 111.
[83] Bradley (n 76) 415.

> **Interviewer:** Ok.
>
> **Gunilde:** All the, Swedish law thinks that everyone are working full-time but it is not so.

Most participants supported the spousal maintenance regime. For example, Bertil, who jokingly referred to the rules as 'the black side of the feminist movement', was broadly supportive of the rules because 'there were very many reasons why people get married'. Ebbe also noted the role of the state in providing financial support, and stressed the importance of independence for the would-be recipient of spousal maintenance:

> **Ebbe:** And, um, I think it's good for, if you have been married for long time and just been, you know a house-, it's not just, but being in, being in a housewife, I think, just to keep up being a housewife wouldn't help the housewife in the long run, because she needs [to be] independent to be able to, uh, go on in the, in the real life. So even if it's hard in the beginning to be forced out to, to the working market again, I think that's, in the long run, is helping her. So that's why I think it's good to have this spouse, um … support in a limited way.
>
> **Interviewer:** And is that because it enables her to be independent and start a new life? Those sorts of –
>
> **Ebbe:** [Overspeaking] Yes. Otherwise she would be stuck in a, you know, in, in a prison really because she can't do anything and she's depending on somebody else. Or he.

Eric also felt that the absence of spousal maintenance was ultimately beneficial, even though it might be harsh in individual cases:

> **Eric**: … The equalities could be harsh for some people, but equality says that you are responsible for yourself, and you have to take care of yourself and the kids that you, sort of, bring up. Um, the other system, if you have a spouse alimony and support, could tend to do the opposite. It could be a, a trap for, for women really ….

The role of the state is crucial here. This is different from the position in England and Wales, where the emphasis on clean break settlements and reform proposals to limit spousal maintenance to exceptional circumstances occur in isolation. In Sweden, the state is active in both encouraging all adults to work during their relationship so that they can support themselves and in providing financial support where they cannot. There are, therefore, benefits to the Swedish approach if intra-partner (horizontal) support is limited. It is also worth noting the potential benefits of state support in relationships where there are significant power imbalances between the parties. The experiences of some participants to my research suggest that in such cases, not relying on a partner financially may be especially important, even where that person is not able to support themself financially.[84] Thus, the presence of state support may balance this desire for a form of autonomy against ensuring that financial needs are met.

[84] Heenan (2021) (n 10).

D. Pensions

The unique character of pensions rights demonstrates particularly clearly the disconnect between the underlying rationales for the division of marital assets, which is grounded in the community between partners, and the payment of spousal maintenance, which is limited because all adults are expected to work. Pensions have a capital value and therefore generally constitute deferred community property in Sweden.[85] However, under EU law pensions may constitute maintenance,[86] and the treatment of pensions under Swedish law provides at least some support for this view of pensions. Under section 10:3 of the Marriage Code, pension rights are exempted from deferred community if they are non-transferable and some special reason exists which can justify the exemption of those rights from the division of property.

There are three types of pensions in Sweden: occupational pensions, the state pension and private pensions. Of these, only private pensions form part of the community pot. As Brattström explains:

> The right to a state pension is always nontransferable, and the same is often true of the right to an occupational pension. The notion that pension rights should safeguard the entitled persons' ability to meet their economic needs in the future – when there is no mutual duty of maintenance between the spouses – has been deemed as a special reason for exempting them from a division of deferred community property.
>
> Transference of private pension saving is not prohibited during a division of deferred community. Consequently, in cases of divorce, private pension savings are included in the division of deferred community property. However, the entitled persons' possibilities of disposing private pension savings are limited by the rules concerning the tax advantages for such savings.[87]

The resistance to sharing pensions because of their role in securing spouses' economic needs in the future is consistent with a view of pensions as maintenance. Viewed in this way, there is no reason that a spouse should have any obligation to support his or her former partner in retirement if not obliged to do so immediately following divorce. The inability to share pensions was, however, considered problematic by several participants:

> **Bertil**: … You mention pension, and I would say that that is a very, very, very, very bad issue. Because when young people start, to form a family, and they start to work, they very little think about that. They very little think of that. And that ends up with the man with the good pension and the, the separate woman with the bad pension. I'm sorry to say. But that is, that is absolutely the main rule. Yes.

[85] Brattström (n 60) 334.

[86] A Heenan, 'Scuppering Schofield: The Impact of the EU Maintenance Regulation on Claims for Pension Sharing' [2012] *Family Law* 191.

[87] Brattström (n 60) 334.

> **Filippa**: [The law could be] a bit more generous and especially when it comes to the pension rights. So … I think that could also be good for the whole community because if one party doesn't have enough pension then it's the state that had to … cover that up.

Arguments about the desirability of pension sharing encapsulate both viewpoints on the nature of pensions (as property and as maintenance). For example, Brattström argues:

> … the size of a pension today is largely determined by a person's lifetime earnings. If those earnings are lowered as a consequence of part-time employment pension rights will to a certain extent be lost and will not be recoverable later. As long as their combined pension rights are not shared after a divorce, the spouse working part-time in favour of the family, will, on that situation, be obliged to alone bear the consequences of the spouses' division of employment during their marriage. This state of affairs does not harmonize well with the provisions, under property law for spouses, that their interests be paid due heed and cannot be a good way of balancing the spouses' interests. Moreover, a sharing of pension rights might be particularly desirable from a social welfare perspective, since their benefits would help provide for a spouses' subsistence at a time of life when gainful employment could no longer be expected. Sharing of accrued pension rights would indeed prove an important protection for the financially weaker spouse.[88]

On the one hand, the reference to the division of labour during the marriage draws on the marital property rationale. The division of marital property recognises the community in marriage and exists to protect the financially weaker spouse. Thus, a spouse whose ability to save for their own pension during the marriage has been compromised by part-time work has a legitimate claim to a share in the pension that has been built up during that period. On the other, the reference to the social welfare perspective under which pensions provide future support is suggestive of a perspective that views pensions as maintenance. The latter viewpoint is supported by the exemption of occupational and state pensions from the division of marital property, on the basis that pensions are seen to exist to meet the economic needs of the pension holder into the future. The rules on spousal maintenance assume that spouses are equally able to support themselves financially and are based on a premise of gender equality in society, despite the reality. It is, therefore, difficult to see why, on the basis of a maintenance or social welfare perspective, pensions should be treated differently from ongoing spousal maintenance or, indeed, why the role of the state should be considered differently. Pensions are, therefore, a good illustration of the tension between understandings of marriage, in which the idea of community is an exception to statist individualism, and the more individualistic approach which predominates elsewhere in the legal and policy framework.

[88] ibid 342.

E. Child Maintenance

The influences of statist individualism can also be seen when it comes to child maintenance. First, Singer explains that, '… parents are to provide maintenance for the child according to what is reasonable having regard to the needs of the child and their collected resources. This means that each parent should have a share in the costs for the child proportional to his or her economic ability.'[89] The exception to this is where there is shared residence (although child maintenance may still be payable if one parent has a much higher income than the other).[90] This is different to the position in England and Wales, where only the non-resident parent's income is used in the child maintenance calculation. The relevance of both parents' incomes reinforces the idea of both as workers. Second, the role of state support can be seen in the availability of maintenance support, a benefit which is available to the parent the children live with in the event that the other parent does not pay any child support, pays less than the amount they should have paid or does not pay on time.[91] Thus, the state provides a back up in the event that horizontal claims do not work effectively.

F. Child Arrangements

Earlier sections of this chapter discussed how state childcare is subsidised to allow all parents to work and how parents are encouraged to share parental leave. Alongside this, Duvander and Korsell explain that:

> Over time, the design of family policy has become increasingly individual; for example, giving fathers and mothers the same rights to parental leave and child allowance, with no distinction based on whether the parents live together. The focus on individual rights has not only strengthened the norm of gender equality but also fostered individual rights, and claims rather than rights directed to the family unit. This makes the concept of a single parent in some ways outdated, and reference is instead often made to parents living apart. In Sweden, this can be seen in, for example, official demographic statistics and information directed to parents on parental leave, preschool activities and other parental rights and responsibilities.[92]

[89] A Singer, 'Active Parenting or Solomon's Justice – Alternating Residence in Sweden for Children with Separated Parents' (2008) 4 *Utrecht Law Review* 35, 43. See also Försäkringskassan, 'Child Support When the Child Lives with You' www.forsakringskassan.se/english/parents/parents-who-do-not-live-together/if-your-children-live-with-you/child-support-when-the-child-lives-with-you accessed 28 April 2023.

[90] Försäkringskassan, 'The Child Lives with Both Parents' www.forsakringskassan.se/english/parents/parents-who-do-not-live-together/the-child-lives-with-both-parents accessed 28 April 2023.

[91] Försäkringskassan, 'Maintenance Support When the Child Lives with You' www.forsakringskassan.se/english/parents/parents-who-do-not-live-together/if-your-children-live-with-you/maintenance-support-when-the-child-lives-with-you accessed 28 April 2023.

[92] Duvander and Korsell (n 53) 263–64.

Chapter 5 will explore the extent to which this vision of parental sharing of care is achieved in reality. It is, nevertheless, important to understand this vision because it underpins the family law regime in Sweden, in which joint custody, which relates to joint legal decision-making, and shared residence are common upon separation. As regards joint custody, which does not necessarily entail shared residence, Bertil explained the Swedish approach as follows:

> **Bertil**: And, um, until one or two years ago there was a rule saying that, generally, there should be joint custody. Now the courts found that sometimes they forced people who couldn't even talk to each other to joint custody … today it's easier to get sole custody, if you can't co-operate [about] the children.

There is scope to depart from joint custody in cases where the parents cannot agree about key aspects of the children's upbringing; Anna suggested that the four key issues for this purpose were the child's healthcare, passport, the address where the child was registered and the child's schooling. Anna and Filippa suggested that such disagreements were present in some cases. Clara added that 'irreconcilable differences' would be another reason for sole custody. Despite this, most participants seemed to consider joint custody to be the default. Gunilde, for example, described it as 'very common' and in her experience the parents' failure to cooperate was not a reason to avoid joint custody: 'the courts say that, uh, if they can't, uh, cooperate now, perhaps they can cooperate later'. Other participants considered that joint custody functioned as a norm to guide negotiation:

> **Anna**: … And I think the courts almost always aim to, uh … it, it's possible to, that the parents have joint custody and, like, the courts in Sweden, always almost, want the parties to agree. So they try really hard to get the parties to agree before the case goes to a final hearing.
>
> **Clara**: You try to get them to agree. Uh, normally the base in Sweden is that joint custody what's best for the child always, uh, um, if one of the parents say no, you can still say that, yeah, the court can still say yes joint custody. But if both parties say no, then they have to choose one of the parents. And we try to tell them that, well, joint custody is almost always the best thing.

The role of joint custody as a default to help guide negotiations is consistent with the strong emphasis on private ordering discussed above: it provides a simple rule which helps to reduce the scope for argument. This may help to explain why some participants were critical of the changes to the rules on joint custody, perceiving them to have increased the scope for conflict:

> **Filippa**: … when it comes to, uh, think about children … uh … it sometimes feels like we don't really know what we're supposed, what's the best. I mean it's been like changing from, uh … for example … cooperation problems between parents and how much that is supposed to affect the process. Uh, first it was not supposed to affect the process, and then it was supposed to affect the process and now we see maybe its not so good that it affect the, uh, result. So now because it makes people fight instead …

The next chapter will consider in greater depth what these rules mean when thinking about how the Swedish system recognises and values caring responsibilities. It is, however, worth noting here Gunilde's concern that children were often lost in this emphasis on private ordering:

> **Gunilde**: … in Sweden we are making laws politically. Because now we have decided that every parent shall share the custody. So we make a law about it. Uh, and, uh, then everybody do so. And it's not quite sure that it's the best for the children. So I am, uh, I must say, I'm, I'm a bit disappointed about, uh, how, uh, now when they talk again about joint custody, that's the best for the children … I don't think they know what they are talking about.

Gunilde made similar observations about the approach to shared residence, suggesting that this was focused more on parental rights and perhaps resulted from misunderstandings of what the law said:

> **Gunilde**: And I think the, the most common is that, uh, the children live one week with their mother, one week their father. And, uh, some people think that that's the rule. But it isn't. You have to look at the children. But, um, ja. That's also about the rights, you know. The parent's rights. Rights of the parent.
>
> **Interviewer**: So, do you think that people, um, if, if they think that, that is the law, do you think it informs the, that misunderstanding, is that shaping the decisions that they reach.
>
> **Gunilde**: Ja.
>
> **Interviewer**: Ok.
>
> **Gunilde**: I think so.

Like joint custody, shared residence is prevalent following parental separation. In 2018, Statistics Sweden found that 'among children who do not live with both parents, nearly three out of ten have shared residence'.[93] Similar statistics from 2014 suggested that shared residence arrangements were even more common immediately following separation: '35 per cent of the children with parents who have separated share residence about equally with their mothers as with their fathers. Among children whose parents have separated recently, the share is roughly 50 per cent.'[94] Given that lawyers are most likely to be involved in cases at the point of separation, it is perhaps unsurprising that participants to my research perceived such arrangements as the most common:

> **Anna**: Yeah. It's pretty hard to say … because, uh, I have to know so much more about the, the parties of course. But, like, I think, if there are like no problems with the parents, they are like fully competent to be parents, uh, and there isn't any other like, um, difficulties, uh, I think it's pretty common that you have 50:50. Ja.

[93] Statistics Sweden, 'Nearly Three out of Ten Children Have Shared Residence' (11 July 2018) www.scb.se/en/finding-statistics/statistics-by-subject-area/living-conditions/living-conditions/living-conditions-surveys-ulfsilc/pong/statistical-news/childrens-residence-20162017/ accessed 28 April 2023.

[94] Statistics Sweden, 'Shared Residence for One in Three Children' (21 February 2014).

Clara: But it would also depend on the case. But 50:50 living is still seen as the magic answer to everything.

In the population as a whole (where nearly three in 10 children of separated parents live with both parents equally), 47 per cent of children of separated parents live only or mostly with the mother, with just over 10 per cent living only or mostly with the father.[95] The lower overall prevalence of shared residence in Swedish society than in those recently separated may suggest that, over time, shared residence arrangements break down and are replaced primarily by arrangements under which mothers again perform most of the caregiving. This will be discussed further in Chapter 5, where it will be suggested that despite efforts to achieve the statist individualism and gender equality that underpin the family law system, caring practices lag behind. As Chapter 5 will discuss, the danger of the appearance of equality without the reality can be unequal outcomes. Further, failing to understand and recognise care may serve to devalue it.

IV. Lessons from the Swedish Approach: A Role for the State in Supporting Autonomy

At this stage, and before considering the limitations of the Swedish approach in Chapter 5, it is worth reflecting on what lessons can be learned in England and Wales from the Swedish approach. First, if some form of autonomy is considered to be a worthwhile aspiration for the law, the Swedish vision of statist individualism more readily allows for the reconciliation of caring responsibilities and paid work than neoliberal understandings of autonomy. Parental leave allows parents a period of time at home with their children, and data suggests that 'Swedish fathers adjusted the length of their leave use in concert with the gender-equality-oriented parental leave reforms'.[96] This demonstrates the impact that state policy can have on gender equality in society. Further, well-funded state childcare frees up parents to undertake paid work and therefore achieve the sort of economic independence neoliberal norms of autonomy favour.

Second, accepting the Swedish vision of autonomy means accepting limitations on freedom of choice: after a period of parental leave, adults are expected to work. Nevertheless, it is only with this sort of support that economic independence is a remotely realistic goal. This model still has shortcomings. For example, as Chapter 5 will discuss, parental leave uptake is gendered and differs across income level. Adjustments would, therefore, need to be made to the Swedish model of parental leave. Another issue is that not all adults are able to undertake paid work.

[95] Statistics Sweden (n 93).

[96] L Ma et al, 'Fathers' Uptake of Parental Leave: Forerunners and Laggards in Sweden, 1993–2010' (2020) 49 *Journal of Social Policy* 361, 377.

This raises a question about the implications for those adults who cannot: how are they perceived by society, for example?

Third, even if we do not accept autonomy as our ultimate aspiration, Sweden illustrates the importance of a role for the state in supporting carers. For a whole host of reasons, horizontal (intra-partner) claims cannot help all carers. First, not all carers have partners. Erin, one of the participants to this research was not in a relationship with her child's father and had no financial claims against him. Parts I and II of this book outlined the shortcomings of the law in England and Wales in meeting the costs of care for both married and cohabiting couples: women continue to do worse financially on separation. Even if these shortcomings could be remedied, however, Erin would be unlikely to have sufficient financial claims to support herself financially. Without state support, carers in this position are, therefore, financially vulnerable. Second, horizontal claims are only effective if they are utilised. In 2000 it was suggested that a consent order is made in only around 40 per cent of cases,[97] a number which seems to have fallen since.[98] Further, a significant number of people have always divorced without legal advice (47 per cent of people divorcing between 1996 and 2011).[99] Thus, it is vital for the state to play a role if we want to provide meaningful support to all carers.

[97] G Davis et al, 'Ancillary Relief Outcomes' (2000) 12 *Child and Family Law Quarterly* 43.

[98] Gov.uk, 'Family Court Tables: April to June 2019 (Table 13)' (Ministry of Justice, 26 September 2019) www.gov.uk/government/statistics/family-court-statistics-quarterly-april-to-june-2019 accessed 28 April 2023.

[99] A Barlow et al, 'Mapping Paths to Family Justice: Briefing Paper and Report on Key Findings' (University of Exeter, 2014) http://socialsciences.exeter.ac.uk/media/universityofexeter/collegeofsocialsciencesandinternationalstudies/lawimages/familyregulationandsociety/pdfs/Mapping_briefing_paper_final_post_conference_version___ISBN.pdf accessed 28 April 2023.

5

Limitations of the Swedish Approach: The Invisibility of Care

> … I mean people can choose their lives, how to live their lives anyhow, regardless of these rules. I mean, if you want to live your life as a housewife or a houseman, you can choose that … So the system is not really the issue, uh, because it allows people to, to, uh, live their lives as they want to. But you have to know what you're doing …
>
> **(Eric, Lawyer, Sweden)**

Chapter 4 considered the goals of statist individualism, the idea that the state is responsible for dependency, and gender equality, and explored how they shape family law and policy in Sweden. It was suggested that the role played by the state in Sweden could provide a model for England and Wales, particularly if England and Wales continues to prioritise the goal of partners being financially independent of one another on separation. While supporting such a role for the state, this chapter makes the case that in Sweden the combination of an emphasis on paid work and a family law system that assumes equality, while overlooking the continued unequal sharing of unpaid work in society, serves to devalue care. Thus, while Sweden provides important lessons about the role of the state, it does not offer a complete model for dealing with caring responsibilities.

The chapter begins by exploring the idea that gender equality is an important aspect of Swedish identity, a result of which is to disguise the continued gendered inequalities that exist in Sweden. The chapter will go on to consider the potential causes of those inequalities, in particular ideas of motherhood and fatherhood. This raises questions about ideas of choice in the Swedish context. As Chapter 4 outlined, there seems to be a willingness to curtail choices about whether to engage in paid work in Sweden in order to facilitate economic independence for all adults. Nevertheless, as the extract from Eric's interview above reveals, ideas of choice persist when it comes to thinking about parenthood. These disguise gendered patterns of caring.

I. Gender Equality and Swedish Identity

It has been suggested that gender equality has become an aspect of Swedish identity,[1] and that not only does this serve to differentiate Sweden from other countries, but it 'also became central in the ongoing construction of "Swedes" and their various "immigrant" others among those living within Swedish state borders'.[2] de los Reyes explains:

> Swedish gender research has repeatedly pointed to enduring limitations in gender politics regarding salaries, working conditions, the organisation of care, distribution of paid and unpaid work etc. But, despite these shortcomings, the notion of Sweden as a gender equality paradise is one that is constantly enlisted in international comparisons and postulated as a national value threatened by the presence of immigrants or by the implementation of multiculturalism. In this way, gender equality is conceptualised on a discursive level not as an unfinished political project but rather as a distinctive national characteristic. Gender equality is thus constructed as a national (essential?) attribute closely connected to the notion of an exceptional Swedishness.[3]

Support for these ideas, that gender equality is an important part of Swedish identity, which serves to distinguish Sweden from other countries and which is threatened by immigration, can be found in interviews with participants in my research. Anna, for example, talked about the extent to which fathers wanted to be actively involved in their children's lives and suggested that the position in Sweden was different to that elsewhere:

> **Anna**: No, so it's, it's a little bit hard to, like, but I think it's, uh, maybe in, in like, difference to other countries, uh, like, par- or like fathers in, anyway my generation, really want to be home with the kids. And have like the opportunity to be home for a couple of months, anyway, in the beginning of the child's life. So, I think that's pretty good. Ja.

Anna draws a direct contrast between the position of fathers in Sweden and 'other countries'. The suggestion is that Swedish fathers want to be more actively involved with their children than fathers elsewhere. There has been a concerted effort through policy initiatives to try and encourage men to assume a greater share of domestic responsibilities. This is most obvious in the shared parental leave provisions in which three months of leave are reserved to each parent. It is, however, notable that Anna describes this desire as 'to be home for a couple of months,

[1] See, for example, S Eldén and T Anving, 'New Ways of Doing the "Good" and Gender Equal Family: Parents Employing Nannies and Au Pairs in Sweden' (2016) 21 *Sociological Research Online* www.socresonline.org.uk/21/4/2.html accessed 13 August 2021; A Towns, 'Paradoxes of (In)Equality: Something is Rotten in the Gender Equal State of Sweden' (2002) 37 *Journal of the Nordic International Studies Association* 157, 165 and L Martinsson et al, 'Introduction' in L Martinsson et al (eds), *Challenging the Myth of Gender Equality in Sweden* (Polity Press, 2016) 9.

[2] Towns (ibid) 165.

[3] P de los Reyes, 'Practising Intersectionality, Challenging Power' in K Dalborg and M Löfgren (eds), *Perspectives on Cultural Leadership. The Fika Project* https://europeanculturalleadershipdotorg.files.wordpress.com/2015/10/perspectives_web.pdf accessed 11 January 2023, 226–27.

anyway' rather than a complete sharing of caregiving responsibilities as such. This suggests that despite the focus on gender equality in Swedish society, there is at least some awareness that the roles of men and women remain different. These differences will be discussed further below.

The second dimension of gender equality as part of Swedish identity, the idea that it separates Swedes from immigrants, was evident in Eric's interview, where he commented on the particular difficulties faced by immigrant women on divorce:

> **Eric**: … The problem we have really is that a lot of … foreigners coming here. Or newly, new Swedes or whatever you wanna call them. Uh, come from countries with different cultures which means that the, the man is supposed to, uh, totally economically and otherwise, support the whole family and his spouse. When they come to Sweden, they find themselves marginalised, language-wise, um, economically-wise, because they tend to live their lives as they used to do in the country where they derived from, so to speak. So that's a, can be a very tough awakening for those women.
>
> So in that sense, this system is not, um, aligned, with the current situation …. But they haven't taken this [into] consideration. And, then suddenly they want to divorce here ….
>
> Then we have, uh, they are facing the Swedish way of thinking with, which is, uh, uh, self-support, get a job, and, and, um, and that could be tough. If you, sort of, you know, are married woman coming here – There are, this is ninety, over ninety-five per cent women I'm talking about now, the woman, the women's situation. And they comes here, and they don't find, if they don't, if they go into that culture, they don't find any purpose of education, finding a job, stuff like that. But things change over time.

This illustrates a particular concern for the position of women coming from other cultures where women are not expected to work. Eric's interview highlights the very real difficulty that traditional gender roles cause for women in Swedish society, particularly on divorce. Society is arranged around a different ideal that expects all adults to engage in paid work and the family laws that deal with the consequences of separation reflect this. Clara, for example, commented that 'since everybody works in Sweden and has been since the fifties, [the very limited availability of spousal maintenance is] not a big issue'. Ebbe explained, '[u]sually, it's kind of a luxury to be able to stay at home'.

There are differences in the employments rates of Swedish-born and non-Swedish-born women: for the former the relative activity rate (meaning the labour force as a percentage of the population) is 90 per cent, whereas for the latter it is 77 per cent.[4] Nevertheless, foreign-born women are not a homogenous group. Those with higher levels of education are more likely to be in employment.[5] There are also differences depending on country of origin; those born in Africa and Asia,

[4] Statistics Sweden, 'Women and Men in Sweden: Facts and Figures 2020' www.scb.se/contentassets/95ffcd4b3f394877abb3bd41e40df0a0/le0201_2019b20_br_x10br2002eng.pdf accessed 1 October 2021.

[5] MUCF, 'Unga utrikes födda kvinnors etablering i arbetslivet' [Establishment of Young Foreign-born Women in Working Life] (2021) www.mucf.se/publikationer/unga-utrikes-fodda-kvinnors-etablering-i-arbetslivet accessed 1 October 2021 (translated using Google translate).

for example, have the lowest employment rate.[6] Differences between Swedish-born and non-Swedish-born women also reduce with time spent by the latter in Sweden.[7] Caring responsibilities are a reason for these differences in employment rate, with foreign-born women more likely to be on parental leave.[8] This supports Eric's suggestion about the role of cultural understandings. This is not, however, the whole picture. First, foreign-born women in Sweden, and particularly those who wear veils, face discrimination and prejudice.[9] Foreign-born women are also more likely to work in occupations such as health and social care which have particular educational requirements, making it difficult to enter them in Sweden. They also lack contacts and networks.[10] Cultural understandings are not, therefore, the only explanation for different employment rates.

It is also important to recognise that foreign-born women are not the only ones for whom there is gender inequality in Sweden. There remain differences in the working patterns of mothers and fathers generally, as some participants to this research recognised:

> **Anna**: … it's not that common that someone in Sweden are like a stay at home mum. Uh, but is some cases, or like most people in Sweden … the female are earning a lot less than the male. And then, or it becomes like, uh, when … you have children, you always, almost, have the wife stay home.
>
> **Filippa**: … even though Sweden is much more … um … equal … when it comes to day-care, the child and so on, still we can see that there is, a, um … difference between women and men.

While these differences are perhaps more subtle because they do not entail women not working at all, they are significant, as the next section will discuss. The danger is that the focus on Sweden as a beacon of gender equality, and the concern with the position of immigrant women, may serve to disguise these wider gendered differences. As this Chapter will explore, gendered cultural ideas of motherhood and fatherhood continue to be influential in Sweden, with gendered financial consequences. Whereas, unlike the position in England and Wales, the state does help to mitigate those consequences in Sweden, the Swedish family law framework does not recognise these differences as it does in England and Wales: in England and Wales, the law of financial remedies on divorce (but not the law relating to cohabitants) may address the financial consequences of caring, in Sweden, as Bertil explained, 'what is done is done. And it won't be repaired by the law system.'

[6] ibid.

[7] ibid.

[8] ibid. See also 'Why Do Young Foreign-born Women Face Difficulties on the Swedish Job Market?' *The Local* (15 March 2021, updated 20 March 2021) https://www.thelocal.se/20210315/why-do-young-foreign-born-women-face-difficulties-on-the-swedish-job-market/ accessed 1 October 2021.

[9] MUCF (n 5). See also *The Local* (ibid).

[10] MUCF (n 5). See also *The Local* (n 8).

II. Gendered Difference in Sweden

In considering the role of the state in Sweden, Chapter 4 focused on two policies, state childcare and parental leave, and explored how they aimed to allow all adults to engage in paid work. This section explores those same issues and considers how the continued influence of gendered parenting norms impacts both parental leave uptake and working patterns. While gender is central to this discussion, it is important to recognise that it is not the end of the story. For example, wealthier parents have resources that better allow them to address the conflict between norms around paid work and care. Further, expectations of parents and how they should behave are not universal.

A. Working Patterns

Despite the emphasis on gender equality in Sweden, significant gender differences remain. As regards paid work, the gender pay gap in Sweden is 11.8 per cent,[11] but this figure disguises differences across age groups. Whereas for under 25s, the pay gap is 5.1 per cent, this increases to 12.4 per cent for the 35–44 age group and 15.8 per cent for the 45–54 age group, perhaps reflecting the impact of women's caring responsibilities.[12] There are also differences in the work that men and women do. For example, men are overrepresented at management level.[13] There is also significant occupational segregation in Sweden. For example, preschool teachers are overwhelmingly female, whereas the most male profession is 'woodworkers, carpenters etc'.[14]

Women are also more likely overall to work part-time than men: 16 per cent compared to 8 per cent.[15] Further, for mothers of young children these figures are even higher. For example, 27 per cent of mothers of a child aged 3–5 work part time compared to 7 per cent of fathers. For children aged 1–2 years the figures are 30 per cent and 6 per cent respectively, and for children aged 6–10 years they are 26 per cent and 9 per cent respectively.[16] Mothers' part-time work is also more likely to be because of childcare than men's part-time work.[17]

[11] Eurostat, 'Gender Pay Gap Statistics' (Data from February 2021) https://ec.europa.eu/eurostat/statistics-explained/index.php?title=Gender_pay_gap_statistics#Gender_pay_gap_levels_vary_significantly_across_EU accessed 4 October 2021.

[12] ibid.

[13] Statistics Sweden, 'Uneven Gender Distribution among Managers' www.scb.se/en/finding-statistics/statistics-by-subject-area/labour-market/employment-and-working-hours/the-swedish-occupational-register-with-statistics/pong/statistical-news/the-swedish-occupational-register-with-statistics-2015/ accessed 11 January 2023.

[14] Statistics Sweden, 'Women and Men in Sweden: Facts and Figures 2022 www.scb.se/contentassets/1fbf4f9815374356a786278faca6a7f0/le0201_2021b22_x10br2202.pdf accessed 11 January 2023, 74.

[15] ibid 61.

[16] ibid 67.

[17] ibid 68.

Underpinning these differences are very different expectations of mothers and fathers. The next section will explore how, despite the emphasis on gender equality, men are still expected to prioritise paid work when it comes to taking parental leave. This contrasts with the position of women, for whom norms of motherhood remain more traditional. Back in 2001, Elvin-Nowak and Thomsson suggested that '[m]others who live in Sweden have to construct their motherhood within the context of a gender-equality discourse, but in an everyday reality that is not gender equal'.[18] While this was some time ago and it is important to recognise changes since, such as the introduction of further reserved months of parental leave which are discussed in the next section, it is a widely quoted piece of research and appears to be supported by the later studies also discussed in this section. It is, therefore, important to explore the understandings of motherhood outlined by Elvin-Nowak and Thomsson.

First, it is suggested that 'accessibility' is an important aspect of motherhood: '[b]y spending as much time with their children as possible, especially when the children are young, the mothers see themselves as immunizing their children against future problems'.[19] This vision of motherhood is time-intensive, 'quality could never make up for quantity'.[20] It also means that a mother 'becomes an irreplaceable person of great significance'.[21] In addition to being time-intensive, Forsberg's research suggests that motherhood carries a mental burden. While both the mothers and fathers in his study were involved in children's everyday lives, '… involvement has somewhat different meanings for them … the women still assume greater responsibility for household work and childcare than the men do. The men are involved in all areas of family life, but they never assume the main responsibility – not for the planning nor for the accomplishment – for household work and childcare.'[22] Likewise, Collins' research suggests that middle class mothers feel guilt, about a range of issues:

> [they] felt that they didn't get enough time with their children and fretted over their wellbeing. They worried about daycare quality and whether their children were happy. They felt that working full-time meant they didn't spend enough time with their kids. All interviewees had internalized the idea that good mothers sublimated their own needs for their children.[23]

Despite the demands of motherhood, however, Elvin-Nowak and Thomsson suggest that '[e]mployment is constructed within a discursive position that, to a certain extent, excludes the woman as a mother'.[24] This is reminiscent of the

[18] Y Elvin-Nowak and H Thomsson, 'Motherhood as Idea and Practice: A Discursive Understanding of Employed Mothers in Sweden' (2001) 15 *Gender and Society* 407, 410.

[19] ibid 414.

[20] ibid 415.

[21] ibid 415.

[22] L Forsberg, 'Involved Parenthood: Everyday lives of Swedish Middle-Class Families' (DPhil Thesis, Linköping University, 2009) 167.

[23] C Collins, 'Is Maternal Guilt a Cross-National Experience?' (2021) 44 *Qualitative Sociology* 1, 22.

[24] Elvin-Nowak and Thomsson (n 18) 418.

conflict between neoliberal ideas of autonomy and care discussed in Chapter 2. In Sweden, despite the image of gender equality, it appears to be a conflict that is particularly experienced by mothers. Elvin-Nowak and Thomsson observe, for example, that whereas 'the father's activities and time seem to be understood as less negotiable', 'women's activities and time can be manipulated according to the needs and desires of other family members'.[25] Thus, despite the strong narrative of equality, women are seen as responsible for reconciling the conflict. This is reinforced by Kugelberg's research at a food production factory in Sweden, which found that '[p]arenthood was interpreted as motherhood and motherhood was seen as problematic, as the time-use norms were difficult for women with restricted timetables'.[26] Further, data from Statistics Sweden around absence from work suggests gendered patterns. Whereas a similar percentage of mothers and fathers of children under seven who have been absent for part of a week (8 per cent of mothers and 7 per cent of fathers) were absent because of childcare, the position is different where a parent is absent for an entire week. In this scenario, 18 per cent of mothers who were absent from work for a whole week were caring for children compared to only 6 per cent of fathers.[27] This challenges the idea of choice outlined in the extract from Eric's interview at the start of this chapter: if society expects mothers to behave in this way, prioritising their children, that shapes the choices open to them.

This potential for conflict between paid work and care is compounded by the idea that 'happy mothers make happy children'.[28] Elvin-Nowak and Thomsson suggest that this expectation is particularly challenging in Sweden:

> where almost every mother is in the labor market, this kind of discussion has a guilt-triggering effect. The individual task is not only to try and achieve an everyday life where work outside the home can be combined with caring for children but also to do this in a way that makes the mother happy and content and, most important results in the well-being of her child.[29]

As Swedish mothers are expected to be workers, it is not sufficient to be '*only* a mother'.[30] However, there is a need to balance the competing expectations of motherhood and paid work, which can be challenging.

The influence of these norms around motherhood are echoed by Roman, who suggests that '[r]egardless of socioeconomic background, the mothers … associated good mothering with meeting the children's needs, spending much time with them, and not letting them spend too long days in preschool'.[31] Nevertheless, while

[25] ibid 422.
[26] C Kugelberg, 'Constructing the Deviant Other: Mothering and Fathering at the Workplace' (2006) 13 *Gender, Work and Organization* 152, 159.
[27] Statistics Sweden (n 14) 70.
[28] Elvin-Nowak and Thomsson (n 18) 417.
[29] ibid 417.
[30] ibid 418.
[31] C Roman, 'Lone Mothers with Low Income Face Obstacles to Practice Their Mothering' (2017) 54 *Sociologisk Forskning* 303, 304.

norms are universal, the ability of mothers to meet them is not: 'culturally shaped ethical ideas of good mothering particularly constrained the low-income mothers' possibilities to reconcile paid work with caring commitments. While all mothers wanted to give appropriate care to their children, the opportunities to do so varied greatly.'[32] For wealthier mothers, it may be possible to achieve equality with a partner with outside help, for example by hiring a nanny or au pair. However, Eldén and Anving's research suggests that the decision to do this may be a response to gender inequality within their relationships:

> An important factor here seems to be that in most cases both fathers and mothers have demanding careers in well-paid jobs. However, in all the parent narratives, hiring a nanny/au pair was primarily related to the mother's career choices, and often involved both a critical reflection of men's unwillingness to follow gender equality ideals, and also criticism of perceived dominant motherhood and femininity ideals. Several mothers in our study were very frank about their husband's failure to share the care and housework equally.[33]

Once again, this challenges the idea of choice and illustrates how complex choices are. On the one hand, this scenario illustrates Lewis' observation that 'fathers' choices (for example, to work long hours) constrain those of mothers'.[34] Here, fathers' choices not to engage with gender equality ideals have the effect of constraining mothers' choices to engage in paid work. However, it is also important to recognise that there are constraints on fathers' choices too. For example, gendered norms around paid work and care have been found to constrain fathers' ability to choose to work part-time.[35] The next section will consider how parental leave is divided between parents in Sweden and how fathers' choices are also shaped by societal norms; the difference is that fathers are expected to prioritise paid work rather than care.

Another dimension of choice in this scenario is that these women have the resources to make a choice to work that other women do not have because of their socioeconomic position. Even if these women achieve a degree of equality with their partners, it does not further gender equality more widely, and may even serve to perpetuate inequality:

> Being a 'career mother' is defined by some of the participating women in opposition to other women: those women who choose less demanding and more traditional, caring jobs, and who then also do more care work at home. That is not the kind of femininity or motherhood ideal that these women value themselves, or want to pass on to their children. However, one could argue that their decision to hire domestic help does indeed signal to the children that this care work still needs to be done, but

[32] ibid 304.
[33] Eldén and Anving (n 1) 6.3.
[34] J Lewis, 'Childcare Policies and the Politics of Choice' (2008) 79 *The Political Quarterly* 499, 506.
[35] J Larsson and S Björk, 'Swedish Fathers Choosing Part-time Work' (2017) *Community, Work and Family* 142.

> that it can be performed by people other than themselves, in this case other (young and often migrant) women. By hiring other women to do parts of the care work the women distance themselves from 'traditional' ideals of motherhood and femininity, while simultaneously reaffirming those same ideals: care work is still to be performed by (other) women, not by men (Anderson 2000). The outsourcing of care becomes a new way of doing gender equality for the women in our study.[36]

Gender equality is, therefore, understood as a way of individual women achieving a level of equality with their partners. It is not about allowing all women to escape care work or about getting men to perform more care work. Further, and perhaps even more significantly, moves towards allowing tax deductions for domestic services in Sweden serve to render care even less visible:

> [tax deductions for domestic services] further cemented the gender equality discourse as being about the earner part of the dichotomy – about a woman's right to have a career on the same terms as a man – since the solution of 'dual earner/private outsourcing of care' makes the care part even *more* invisible. The talk about care as something 'others' do – especially the mundane everyday activities – signals a devaluation of the practice as such, something that is further emphasised by the exchangeability of the nanny/au pair (few stay in the family for longer than a year). In addition, this 'other' person is almost always a woman, and in many cases also a migrant woman … results in a very precarious position of the worker. Thus, the care carried out by the nanny becomes a kind of glue that ties the family together, but it is in its character almost invisible. This invisible glue is what enables the parents to pursue two careers, and thus also enables the ideal of gender equality to be superficially maintained: the parents manage to solve the jigsaw puzzle of life without compromising their work ambitions – and are thus 'equal'.[37]

Chapter 4 suggested that there were two strands to gender equality in Sweden: getting women into the workforce and getting men to do more at home. However, this suggests a focus only on the former, supporting Lewis and Åström's 1992 suggestion that '[d]espite a public commitment to achieving greater equality in the work of women and men, the Swedish system of promoting equal opportunities has only changed the position of women, leaving that of men relatively untouched'.[38]

The problem with this approach is that it leaves caring needs unaccounted for. While policies like parental leave aim to allow parents to share care, as the next section will explore, parental leave continues to be shared unequally. Further, caring needs go beyond what policies like parental leave and state childcare can meet. Someone needs to collect children from school or daycare or stay at home with them when they are sick. This discussion suggests that someone is disproportionately the child's mother or, in the case of some wealthier parents, another

[36] Eldén and Anving (n 1) 6.9.
[37] ibid 8.3.
[38] J Lewis and G Åstrom, 'Equality, Difference and State Welfare: Labor Market and Family Policies in Sweden' (1992) 18 *Feminist Studies* 59.

woman acting as a nanny. Caring also encompasses tasks like helping children with their schoolwork. Forsberg suggests that when it comes to schoolwork, teachers address letters to 'parents' and do not expect mothers to be more involved. Neither do the parents themselves. However, this work tends to fall to women.[39] He, therefore, suggests that 'mothers' involvement is taken for granted'.[40] This echoes my findings in this project that particular aspects of care may be invisible to the person not performing them.[41]

B. Parental Leave

Having explored working patterns and how these fit with ideals of gender equality, this section considers another key aspect of gender equality policy in Sweden: parental leave which aims to facilitate the sharing of care between parents. As explained in Chapter 4, Swedish parents are entitled to 480 days of paid parental leave, which can be taken until a child is eight years old. This leave is notionally divided between the parents, but only 90 days are reserved to each parent, meaning that the leave is lost if it is not taken. The presence of these reserved months means that significant numbers of fathers in Sweden take parental leave. Nevertheless, the overall division of this leave is gendered. In 2021, women took 70 per cent of parental leave days and 60 per cent of temporary parental leave days, which allow parents to stay at home with sick children.[42] Women also took greater amounts of unpaid time to care for children.[43] These overall figures, however, hide discrepancies within the population. For example, in an analysis of the impact of the introduction of the third of the reserved months of leave in 2016, the Swedish Social Insurance Agency (Försäkringskassan) noted that uptake differed between different groups of fathers.[44] Those with low education and/or low income, who used less parental leave than other fathers prior to the reforms, did not increase the number of days they took.[45] Conversely, those with higher education and/or income, who already used on average more than 90 days of parental leave, were also not affected by the reforms.[46]

Leave use also differs between Swedish-born and immigrant fathers.[47] Analyses suggest that it is more common for Swedish-born fathers than immigrant fathers

[39] Forsberg (n 22) 168.
[40] ibid 168.
[41] Discussed in Chapter 3. See also A Heenan, 'Neoliberalism, Family Law, and the Devaluation of Care' (2021) 48 *Journal of Law and Society* 386.
[42] Statistics Sweden (n 14) 54.
[43] ibid 56.
[44] Försäkringskassan, 'Jämställd föräldraförsäkring' (Summary) www.forsakringskassan.se/download/18.7fc616c01814e179a9f355/1656676749850/jamstalld-foraldraforsakring-socialforsakringsrapport-2019-2.pdf accessed 11 January 2023.
[45] ibid.
[46] ibid.
[47] E Mussino et al, 'Does Time Count? Immigrant Fathers' Use of Parental Leave for a First Child in Sweden' (2018) 73 *Population* 363.

to use amounts of leave that exceed the number of reserved months.[48] Conversely, immigrant fathers are more likely to use no leave at all than Swedish-born fathers.[49] Possible explanations for this difference include the idea that 'knowledge and dissemination of information about the leave system may be lacking in immigrant communities'.[50] Also, importantly, immigrants have lower employment rates than those who are Swedish-born; parental benefit is earnings-related and to be eligible it is necessary to have been employed for eight months before a child is born.[51] This link between labour market position and parental leave uptake is also reinforced when the differences between immigrant fathers based on their country of origin is considered. Those from Asian and African societies are less likely to use parental leave, whereas those from European, American and Oceanian societies are more likely to do so.[52] It is noted that the latter have 'education and skills to be used on the labour market [which] resemble those of Sweden at various degrees'.[53]

In addition to labour market position, the nature of a father's employer appears to make a difference to leave use: '[f]athers working in the private sector, at small workplaces, and in male-dominated workplaces, are less likely to use parental leave'.[54] Bygren and Duvander suggest that one reason that father's workplace norms are so important 'is the prevalent gender difference in the level of leave use'.[55] On average, fathers take considerably less leave than mothers:

> The marginal cost of another month of leave is arguably much greater at low levels of leave use than at high levels of leave use. Thus, the division of parental leave is not a gender-neutral question. Because of the initially skewed division of parental leave, the workplace and individual factors influence the division of parental leave use in gender-typical ways.[56]

Within the private sector, Haas and Hwang suggest that both workplace culture and the structure of workplaces can affect fathers' leave use, but that fathers often take these things for granted.[57] Culturally, these norms included things such as taking leave not being a strategic concern for the company or it being unusual for men to take such leave. Structural barriers included workers being seen as indispensable, insufficient personnel and a lack of infrastructure to support such leave. One effect of such norms might be to limit leave use altogether. However, it is

[48] ibid 368.
[49] ibid 368.
[50] ibid 365.
[51] ibid 365.
[52] ibid 368.
[53] ibid 368.
[54] M Bygren and AZ Duvander, 'Parents' Workplace Situation and Fathers' Parental Leave Use' (2006) 68 *Journal of Marriage and the Family* 363, 370.
[55] ibid 371.
[56] ibid 371.
[57] L Haas and CP Hwang, 'Policy is Not Enough – the Influence of the Gendered Workplace on Fathers' Use of Parental Leave in Sweden' (2019) 22 *Community, Work & Family* 58.

also important to note that workplace barriers might shape the way in which such leave is taken. The other cultural barriers identified by Haas and Hwang, were that 'leavetaking should minimally disrupt the workplace' and that 'the job came first'.[58] These influenced how leave was taken. For example, leaves were taken during quiet periods, such as around Christmas or in the summer, or they were taken part-time or spread out in small periods. Further, those taking leave were expected to 'solve their jobs while they were gone'[59] and those at managerial level 'were expected to keep close contact with work while on leave'.[60] These norms suggest very different expectations of fathers than mothers and have financial consequences. Nylin et al suggest that:

> … family policies have had an important, although small, impact on men whereas women's work has been more resistant to change since the late 1980s. This may be due to tenacious norms of mothers as caretakers, mothers' leave-taking for children's sick days and other care-taking accommodations, as well as a low return for investments in the labor market. Further, men's earnings seem to recuperate from childbirth over a relatively short period of time, indicating they may have greater opportunity to choose when to take parental leave, facilitating easier adaptation to employer preferences to leave-taking during slower periods.[61]

These different financial consequences may be particularly significant when parents separate, something that is considered further in the next section. These differences between expectations of mothers and fathers do appear, at least at some level, to be recognised in Swedish society. In Anna's interview, discussed above, she suggested that the expectation was that fathers would be at home 'for a couple of months', which reflects the how fathers typically take leave. Further, in research on parental leave, Evertsson et al found that:

> For some couples who stress the importance of gender-egalitarian ideals, other ideals and norms around motherhood and fatherhood counteract an equal sharing of the leave … The qualitative interviews show how women's wishes to be at home during the child's entire first year are connected with motherhood norms and ideals of intensive mothering that – in our interviews – often are embraced by fathers and mothers alike (in the couples that refer to them). Like all interviewed couples, these couples stress the importance of a close father–child relationship, but the first year of the child's life is seen as a special period, an exception. Even these couples often referred to their division of the leave as "rather equal", which highlights the strength of the equality discourse in Sweden.[62]

[58] ibid 67–69.
[59] ibid 67.
[60] ibid 68.
[61] AK Nylin et al, 'Trends over Time in His and Her Earnings Following Parenthood in Sweden' (Stockholm Research Reports in Demography no 2019:03) https://s3-eu-west-1.amazonaws.com/pstorage-su-4954321/14220869/SRRD_2019_03.pdf accessed 11 January 2023, 22.
[62] M Evertsson et al, 'Fathers on Call? A Study of the Sharing of Care Work between Parents in Sweden' (2018) 39 *Demographic Research* 33, 52–53.

Thus, while gender equality is a powerful narrative in Sweden, it is not fully recognised when it comes to the sharing of caring responsibilities. Despite the strong emphasis on all adults engaging in paid work, norms of motherhood continue to demand that mothers, but not fathers, also prioritise caring. This undermines the achievement of gender equality in society. However, key provisions of family law fail to recognise this; the impact of caring responsibilities remains hidden in Sweden.

III. The Invisibility of Care on Parental Separation

Having explored the contrast between pervasive ideas of gender equality in Sweden and the gendered differences in expectations of, and the care performed by, mothers and fathers, it is important to consider how this relates to the legal framework outlined in Chapter 3. The first part of this section considers the implications for the financial consequences of relationship breakdown and suggests that the result of the incompatibility between societal ideals of equality and gendered ideals of care is to disguise the work involved in care. Having done that, focus will turn to child arrangements on separation. In those arrangements, it might be expected that care would be more visible. However, this is not the case. Rather, much like the position with financial arrangements, the disconnect between ideals of equality and the reality of parenting norms serves to disguise the differences in the care performed by mothers and fathers.

While the overall effect of the Swedish position is, therefore, similar to the position in England and Wales in failing to account for the costs of care, there are important differences. As Chapter 3 explained, the legal framework in England and Wales is flexible and, at least in theory, can respond to financial needs generated by caring. Further, in cases where the assets exceed needs, it may be possible to make claims for compensation for the loss of a career. In this way, the legal framework can respond to gendered patterns of caring in society. This is important because, unlike the position in Sweden, gender equality and state responsibility for dependence are not policy priorities. In Sweden, much greater attempts have been made to change gendered caring patterns and to encourage all adults to be self-supporting. The challenge in Sweden is that the legal framework reflects these ideals but that they have not been fully implemented.

A. Financial Arrangements

As Chapter 4 explained, broadly the legal framework dealing with finances on divorce in Sweden is made up of three elements: community of property, spousal maintenance and pensions. For cohabitants, only the first of these elements is present: there is no possibility of making a claim for maintenance or to a partner's pension. Whereas community of property continues to be grounded in the idea of marriage as a community of individuals, both the rules on spousal maintenance and pensions are shaped much more by pervasive ideas of autonomy, which envisage self-support. These are, however, underpinned by both the idea of statist individualism – that the state will play a role in meeting dependency – and gender equality, which envisages the sharing of both paid and unpaid work.

Against this backdrop, Eric's suggestion that you could choose to do things differently from societal norms, you could 'live your life as a housewife or a houseman', makes sense. However, that statement disguises the complexity of social norms. While, as discussed above, it is unusual for women not to undertake paid work at all, it does not follow that men and women do the same paid work (or unpaid work). The very different working patterns and parental norms that apply to men and women are significant from a financial perspective. While state support is an important safety net, it does not necessarily act as a substitute for horizontal (intra-partner) claims. The practical impact of this approach is likely to differ across income levels. For those with very little, this lack of horizontal claims may make little practical difference and the benefits of state support are likely to be of paramount importance. Where it is likely to make a difference is for wealthier couples where the difference between the level at which the state would provide and the standard of living enjoyed during a relationship may differ significantly.

While there is good reason to be most concerned with the position of those who are least well off, a lack of horizontal responsibility is a concern if we want to recognise and value caring responsibilities. Such an approach signals that the partner performing a greater share of caring is solely responsible for the financial consequences even though, as discussed in Chapter 2, such choices are joint. In this way, privileged irresponsibility is perpetuated.

B. The Financial Consequences of Child Arrangements

As the next section will explore, in Sweden post-separation shared residence of children is very common. That section will also reflect on what the prevalence of shared residence reveals about the visibility and value of care in Sweden. Before that, however, this section considers the link between financial and child arrangements: how do post-separation child arrangements affect the financial position of the carer and, by extension, their children?

If equal shared residence is agreed in a case where the parents have previously adopted more traditional roles, then there can be financial consequences for the caregiver, which Singer suggests can create financial incentives for the parent with a higher income to seek shared residence and for the parent with a lower income to refuse it.[63] As in England and Wales, the default position in Sweden if there is a

[63] A Singer, 'Active Parenting or Solomon's Justice – Alternating Residence in Sweden for Children with Separated Parents' (2008) 4 *Utrecht Law Review* 35, 46.

shared residence arrangement in place is that no child maintenance is payable,[64] albeit that there is the possibility of child support if there is a big discrepancy in the parties' respective financial positions.[65] The potential unfairness of this situation was illustrated by one of the scenario questions that participants to this research were asked to consider. That scenario involved a married couple. The father worked full time earning a salary of SEK 1 million (circa £100,000) plus bonuses of up to SEK 1,500,000 (circa £150,000) and the mother had been at home with the children full-time for the last ten years. The children in this case were 12 and 10 years old which meant their views would carry significant weight, and in the case of the elder child these views would likely be determinative.

The limited availability of spousal maintenance in Sweden meant that some participants, such as Anna, thought it would be 'pretty unlikely' that the mother would receive any spousal maintenance. Further, even those who felt some spousal maintenance might be payable envisaged it for a very short period. Ebbe, for example, thought maintenance might be paid up to the point at which the divorce was granted, but that it was unlikely afterwards:

> **Ebbe**: … because she has no disabilities that, uh, help her getting into the working market as I can see it. As I know of. So it's um, if she gets a disease she might – Maybe [if her husband] wants out and, you know, pushing this divorce and she's ending up in a depression or something, she needs more time.

Bertil explained that the mother in this case would have 'to have a good argument and, um, be very concrete and, uh, so on'. Whilst payments might be made for a year to enable re-training, he felt it was unlikely that payments would be made for a three-year university course: 'he won't have to pay for that. Maybe the court might end up with one year and then she has to take loans or whatever. That's the brutal world that hits back, normally, on women.' Thus, if the parties were to agree to a shared residence arrangement, or the children were to live with their father following separation, the mother's only entitlement would be to a half share of the marital property (in this case circa £200,000). Whilst a financially superior position to that of many couples on separation, it is a result that leaves the mother solely responsible for the economic costs of caregiving.

A related issue to consider when looking at shared residence arrangements is their durability. As discussed in Chapter 4, shared residence is more common immediately after separation than in society more generally, where it is more common for children to live primarily with their mothers. This suggests that over time shared residence arrangements break down and are replaced primarily by arrangements under which mothers again perform most of the childcare. Bertil remarked on this experience in practice:

[64] Försäkringskassan, 'The Child Lives with Both Parents' www.forsakringskassan.se/english/parents/parents-who-do-not-live-together/the-child-lives-with-both-parents accessed 11 January 2023.
[65] ibid.

> **Interviewer:** … And so is [one week with each parent] the *most* common arrangement for children? Or does it vary?
>
> **Bertil:** I would say [pause] [laughs]. I would say, yes. Uh, no. Um, I would say, yes. When they divorce and the children are small this is quite a normal arrangement. Now after some years, the father, well you know, I have to work in Germany for two months here and I have to do, and now the chief has asked me to take a little more responsibility, can you take a little more of the children? So it changes of all the time, this is, life doesn't stand still.

Given the limited availability of spousal maintenance claims in Sweden this change perhaps makes less difference to the overall position of married carers than it might in England and Wales, where a court might be more inclined to make a clean break award in a case involving shared residence than in a case where one party was performing the bulk of the caregiving. However, this post-separation drift in caring arrangements may again serve to disguise gendered caregiving patterns in society. Lawyers, for example, advise on norms at the point of separation, rather than those afterwards. Thus, perceptions of the extent to which care is shared post-separation may differ from reality. This adds to an overall picture in which care is rendered invisible.

Finally, when considering the financial consequences of child arrangements, it is important to consider the extent to which shared residence denotes an equal sharing of time and/or care. As in England and Wales, shared residence is capable of a whole host of meanings in Sweden. Anna, for example, remarked that the 'limit' of shared care was not necessarily clear in Sweden. These sorts of labels may, therefore, serve to perpetuate the invisibility of caregiving after separation. Shared care or shared residence gives the impression of an equal division of time and care. However, the labels need not denote either. Further, even where time is shared equally, as the data from England and Wales suggest, this does not necessarily result in caregiving being shared equally.[66]

C. Post-separation Child Arrangements

Shared residence is particularly prevalent in Sweden following parental separation. Given that lawyers are most likely to be involved in cases at the point of separation, it is perhaps unsurprising that participants to this research perceived such arrangements as the most common. The discrepancy between this and the position in the general population (discussed above) raises several issues. First, given the gendered patterns of work and care described earlier in this chapter, the level of shared residence immediately following separation suggests that separation may be regarded as a catalyst for change. Gunilde's interview supported this view:

[66] Heenan (n 41).

> **Interviewer**: [Asking about scenario question] Um, and with the children here, what if Jonathan [the breadwinner] says, I want the children now to live with, half and half with both of us?
>
> **Gunilde**: I should say no … If I was the lawyer there.
>
> … And so typical. And he has had no interest before.

This suggests something about the value placed upon caring. In Sweden, mothers remain primarily responsible for childcare in intact relationships. Therefore, for both parents to be seen as equally capable of caregiving after separation suggests that past caring patterns are relatively unimportant; competence to care is assumed, rather than something that needs to be demonstrated. Clara, for example, suggested that:

> **Clara**: … we have a lot of custody fights, but normally one does agree because it is, by this time, so … well endowed in the society that both parents are equally good at, at giving care. We're, we're not … as it were, say fifty years ago, that dad was actually less competent as a parent. A-and now, the basic perception is that both parents are adept at being parents.

One possibility is that it is the gender gap in caregiving itself that is invisible, and the prevalence of professional care, particularly in the form of state nursery care, may serve to exacerbate this. If the expectation is that children are cared for by professionals then the caregiving that is carried out by parents, for example, in taking children to and from nursery and school or when they are unwell is even less visible than in England and Wales where there is not the same assumption that all adults will be fully engaged in the labour market. My data from England and Wales suggest that some fathers who perform less childcare perceive it as easier than the 'daily grind' of paid work. If caregiving is somehow seen as the easier or more enjoyable option, then it may be less important to have spent time doing it to qualify for the role post-separation. Anna's suggestion in the Swedish context that the requirement for 50:50 shared care is 'competence' may be indicative of this.

IV. The Shortcomings of the Swedish Approach: The Invisibility of Care

In considering the shortcomings of the Swedish approach, it is important not to lose sight of its strengths. As Chapter 4 revealed, a key strength of the Swedish approach is the important role played by the state. Nevertheless, while the Swedish approach serves to facilitate care and the reconciliation between paid work and care, it has not yet succeeded in sharing care in a gender equal way. Women still take more parental leave than men and are more likely to adapt their working hours around childcare responsibilities, and social norms expect this of them. Not all women face the same challenges. As the discussion above reveals, some women, particularly non-Swedish-born women, face barriers in finding appropriate paid work at all. Both Swedish-born and non-Swedish-born women also need to reconcile cultural expectations of motherhood with cultural expectations of paid work, albeit that the precise nature of those cultural expectations may vary significantly. For some groups of wealthier women the challenge of reconciling paid work and childcare can be resolved by paying someone else to do childcare for them. Yet, in all of these situations, an underlying problem is that the focus on gender equality still concentrates on engaging women in paid work rather than engaging men in care.

In the Swedish context, however, this gendered difference appears less stark than it does elsewhere. An important reason for this is the choice of comparators against which gender equality is judged. First, policies like parental leave and state-funded childcare are explicitly framed in terms of gender equality. These policies were and are markedly more progressive than those of key international comparators. To take the example of parental leave, this became gender neutral in Sweden in 1974 and the first reserved month of leave was introduced in 1995. In contrast, in the UK shared parental leave was not available until 2015 and uptake remains very low. Sweden is, therefore, incredibly progressive by international standards. It has not, however, achieved an equal sharing of parental leave or other aspects of unpaid caring.

A second way in which the choice of comparator serves to disguise gendered inequality in Sweden is the concern around immigrant women. It is important to recognise, as Eric pointed out in the start of this chapter, that not being employed creates a particular problem from the Swedish perspective of self-support. However, the focus on the lower employment levels and parental leave uptake of foreign-born women serves to disguise gendered difference in society more generally. More foreign-born than Swedish-born women are unemployed, but that does not mean that Swedish-born women are working the same hours, or earning the same wages, as Swedish-born men either. Crucially, neither does it mean that Swedish-born women have the same ability to support themselves financially on separation as men.

PART IV

Placing Care at the Heart of Family Law

6

Why and How to Make Care More Central

I. What Next?

Having outlined the problems of neoliberal-influenced ideas of autonomy and evaluated the Swedish approach involving a greater role for the state, this chapter suggests a new way forward: placing care at the heart of family law. The chapter begins by making the case for why a new approach is needed. It goes on to explain why that new approach focuses on family law, rather than family policy or the role of the state more broadly. Nevertheless, it is recognised that the state has an important role to play in supporting care. Finally, the chapter outlines two different mechanisms through which to place care at the heart of family law. These are: first, a framework that aims to embed a clear understanding of care in family law decisions; and, second, reforming elements of private family law in a way that recognises caring relationships. The first of these mechanisms is explored in this chapter. Chapter 7 considers the issue of reform.

II. Why is a New Approach Needed?

A. The Problems of Neoliberal-influenced Ideas of Autonomy

The discussion in previous chapters has considered the problems of neoliberal-influenced ideas of autonomy in some detail. Cumulatively, these critiques mean that neoliberal-influenced ideas of autonomy cannot be rehabilitated as a guiding principle of family law. First, the assumptions underpinning neoliberalism are flawed insofar as they relate to family life. When it comes to parental separation, the central tenets of financial independence and choice conflict with one another because the choices people make within families about how to share paid work and childcare between them frequently impact upon the ability of the carer to be financially independent after separation.

Second, and relatedly, even where attempts are made to resolve that central conflict, as in Sweden where there is strong state support and encouragement for both parents to prioritise paid work, disparities remain in how parents divide care between them. Caring relationships are messy and demanding. Neoliberal-influenced ideas of autonomy fail to understand and account for this. Even though the state can, and should, play a role in supporting care, there are limits to the care that the state can provide. The state can of course provide nursery care that enables parents to work. However, finding nursery care that works for everyone is tricky. For some of the participants in my research, like Gareth and David who worked shifts, nursery care would need to be flexible. For their children, this might entail staying at nursery overnight. Even if childcare for everyone could be achieved, what happens when children are unwell and cannot go to school or nursery?

Thus, not only are the assumptions of neoliberal-influenced ideas of autonomy incompatible with caring relationships, but the centrality of those relationships to family life means that it is vital to consider those relationships in their own right.

B. The Challenges of Relational Autonomy

Before entirely rejecting autonomy as the basis of the approach taken in family law, it is, however, important to think about whether autonomy might be reframed. One of the most important challenges to neoliberal-influenced ideas of autonomy are relational ideas of autonomy. Relational autonomy is:

> an umbrella term, designating a range of related perspectives … premised on a shared conviction … that persons are socially embedded and that agents' identities are formed within the context of social relationships and shaped by a complex of intersecting social determinants, such as race, class and gender.[1]

Whereas conceptions of relational autonomy vary, there are common themes between many of these approaches, as is the case with neoliberal-influenced visions of autonomy. It is, therefore, helpful to identify some of these common themes and reflect upon whether they are more consistent with the realities of caring relationships.

MacKenzie suggests that relational approaches 'reject social atomism and take as their starting point a socio-relational ontology of persons':[2]

> According to relational theories, persons are both causally and constitutively relational and social beings. Causally, because developmentally we only become persons through embodied social interaction with other persons with whom we exist in various relations of dependency. Constitutively, persons are relational because our identities and our sense of self are constituted through social relationships and through processes

[1] C MacKenzie and N Stoljar, 'Introduction: Autonomy Refigured' in C MacKenzie and N Stoljar (eds), *Relational Autonomy* (Oxford University Press, 2000) 4.

[2] C MacKenzie, 'Relational Autonomy: State of the Art Debate' in A Armstrong et al (eds), *Spinoza and Relational Autonomy: Being with Others* (Edinburgh University Press, 2019) 11.

> of enculturation into specific linguistic, political and historical communities. Given this commitment to a socio-relational conception of persons, relational theorists hold that an adequate conception of autonomy must be responsive to the facts of human vulnerability and dependency, and must be consistent with social relations of care.[3]

Connected to this, relational approaches to autonomy 'seek to provide a richer characterisation of individual identity and of the requirements for self-governing agency'.[4] As regards the former, this means recognising that 'our individual identities are shaped by the historical, social and relational contexts in which we are embedded, and by intersecting determinants of gender, culture, class, religion, ethnicity and race'.[5] Relational conceptions of autonomy are, therefore, superior to neoliberal conceptions in being able to understand individual and family decision-making. Rather than viewing choices as freely made by individuals who are, therefore, responsible for the costs of them,[6] it is possible to recognise that different choices may be available to different people and that choices may be made 'for the overall happiness of the family',[7] for example. When it comes to thinking about parental separation, this superior understanding of the nature of decision-making in intact families is beneficial. Whereas neoliberal-influenced ideas of autonomy assume partners are equally autonomous and fail to account for the sorts of caring responsibilities that interfere with such autonomy, relational ideas of autonomy not only recognise caring responsibilities but perceive them as valuable: relationships are seen as constitutive of autonomy. Thus, relational ideas of autonomy offer the potential to render care visible and recognise its value.

Relational ideas of autonomy may also offer the potential for a more nuanced understanding of the role of the state. When it comes to the 'requirements for self-governing agency'[8] MacKenzie suggests that 'relational theories understand self-governing agency as a complex competence, the development and exercise of which requires ongoing interpersonal, social and institutional scaffolding'.[9] This is connected to a third common feature of relational understandings of autonomy: a focus 'on the role of the interpersonal and social environment in shaping our agency'.[10] In addition to looking at individual relationships, such theories:

> … focus attention on broader social and political structures, and the ways these can undermine or defeat individuals' efforts at self-determination, for example, through curtailing important freedoms or restricting opportunities. Relational theories are thus

[3] ibid 11.
[4] ibid 12.
[5] ibid 12.
[6] T Lemke, '"The Birth of Bio-Politics": Michel Foucault's Lecture at the Collège de France on Neo-Liberal Governmentality' (2001) 30 *Economy and Society* 190, 201.
[7] *Radmacher (formerly Granatino) v Granatino* [2010] UKSC 42 [188].
[8] MacKenzie (n 2) 12.
[9] ibid 12.
[10] ibid 12.

> responsive to the concerns about social injustice, structural inequality and disadvantage that animate Fineman's critique of the 'autonomy myth'.[11]

Thus, unlike neoliberal-inspired conceptions of autonomy, relational ideas of autonomy may suggest that it is essential for the state to play an active role in facilitating autonomy.[12] In this respect they are once again preferable to dominant neoliberal understandings.

Given this potential of relational understandings of autonomy, it is important to consider how such understandings of autonomy might be used to reshape family law to address the issues that are caused by neoliberal understandings. This is where relational approaches to autonomy become problematic. While these ideas are crucial in understanding the type of autonomy exercised by those in intact families, it is very difficult to operationalise these understandings into a guiding principle for the law on separation.

Turning first to the financial consequences of separation, recognising that autonomy may be relational does not supply an obvious answer to the question of how to address the unequal financial consequences of decisions made through the exercise of such autonomy. Relational ideas of autonomy do, importantly, recognise that choices were not made in a vacuum and that, given the wider context in which they were made, it may be unjust for the decision-maker to be held solely responsible for all the financial consequences of their individual 'choice'. Practically speaking, relational ideas of autonomy might, therefore, provide an argument against a clean break settlement in every case. They do not, however, provide a principled basis for deciding how assets should be divided, whether maintenance should be paid and, if so, for how long. As Thompson explains:

> While in theory relational autonomy both challenges and undermines assumptions made by neo-liberal autonomy, in practice the term is almost impossible to apply without the court falling back on neo-liberal norms, because relational autonomy can be interpreted in a range of different ways. It appears then that the main difference between neo-liberal autonomy and relational autonomy is simply that the latter compels one to ask why the decision was made.[13]

A neoliberal-influenced concept of autonomy, whilst flawed for the reasons discussed above, is clear about what autonomy looks like on separation: partners are encouraged to be financially independent and expected to be able to move on with their lives, making decisions free from constraint. In contrast, it is not clear what degree of financial interdependence, if any, relational ideas of autonomy

[11] ibid 12–13.

[12] See, for example, E Gordon-Bouvier, *Relational Vulnerability* (Palgrave Macmillan, 2020) 9 and C Mackenzie, 'The Importance of Relational Autonomy and Capabilities for an Ethics of Vulnerability' in C Mackenzie et al (eds), *Vulnerability: New Essays in Ethics and Feminist Philosophy* (Oxford University Press, 2013).

[13] S Thompson, 'Feminist Relational Contract Theory: A New Model for Family Property Agreements' (2018) 45 *Journal of Law and Society* 617, 627.

require, or what it means for one's ability to make decisions about one's children, for example, going forward.

There are similar challenges in trying to operationalise relational ideas of autonomy when thinking about the arrangements for children. Where parents are in dispute about the arrangements for children, what do relational arrangements look like? Whose views matter? How do we weigh one person's interests against another? These difficulties are compounded because of the wider societal context in which we seek to apply these norms (although, of course, these features are relevant to how relational approaches understand autonomy). As was discussed in Chapter 3, for example, care is rarely thought about in court decisions relating to the arrangements for children unless the care a child is receiving is deficient.[14] Beyond this, when it comes to child arrangements orders there is generally considered to be a duty for resident parents (who are typically mothers) to facilitate contact[15] while there is no corresponding duty for non-resident parents (typically fathers) to have contact with their child.[16]

Relational ideas of autonomy would fall to be applied against this gendered backdrop. Thus, even though relational ideas of autonomy are capable of recognising these nuances, there is a danger that in practice relational ideas of autonomy would be interpreted according to prevailing societal norms. For example, an approach purporting to be influenced by relational norms of autonomy might provide support for arguments of a default position of shared time in child arrangements without any expectation that both parents are in a position to share care. It might also reinforce the expectations that those who were primary carers in intact relationships must undertake onerous work to facilitate the relationships between children and their other parent, without imposing any corresponding duty on that parent to maintain and develop the relationship.

Thus, whilst relational ideas of autonomy are crucial in understanding the decisions people make, and in challenging neoliberal understandings of individuals as rational beings who make individual decisions in their own best interests, they do not provide a framework for the law on separation. There is a need to find an approach that addresses the effects of decisions made through an exercise of relational autonomy.

C. Care as the Central Issue

An approach based upon care best addresses the shortcomings in the current legal approach. Throughout, this book has noted the invisibility of care in family

[14] A Newnham and M Harding, 'Sharing as Caring? Contact and Residence Disputes between Parents' (2016) 28 *Child and Family Law Quarterly* 175.

[15] F Kaganas and S Day Sclater, 'Contact Disputes: Narrative Constructions of "Good" Parents' (2004) 12 *Feminist Legal Studies* 1, 13.

[16] J Herring, *Family Law*, 10th edn (Pearson, 2021) 547.

law and wider society. While care is central to the functioning of the neoliberal order, it is not recognised: adults are expected to prioritise paid work. Care is thus both invisible and undervalued. Chapters 2 and 3 revealed the invisibility of care in the neoliberal paradigm and explored how this systemic invisibility translated itself into parental understandings of care on separation; for example, my data suggest that care is less visible to those who do not perform it. Chapter 3 then went on to explore the costs of this invisibility to carers, children and those who are unable to care.

Tackling this invisibility and devaluation of care requires going beyond simply trying to accommodate care. As was explained in the introduction, care is at the heart of what families do and is a valuable part of life.[17] Further, on parental separation, family law is inherently concerned with issues of care. It is, therefore, vital that the law on separation recognises care. The best way to do that is to focus on care.

III. Why Focus on the Law, Rather Than the State?

A. Why Think about Family Law at All?

The discussion in Chapters 4 and 5 revealed how state support can facilitate caregiving. The exploration of the state in those chapters was vital to understanding the legal framework in Sweden and how it operates; as explained in Chapter 4, the legal provisions may appear misleadingly harsh without this more holistic picture. Nevertheless, the central concern of this book remains the family law framework. This is not to deny the important role that the state can and should play in such matters. For example, as the discussion of Sweden shows, state measures to help parents care might reduce some of the consequences of unequal caring on parental separation. The state can also provide a vital safety net for all. Nevertheless, there are limits to what the state can do, and there remains an important role for family law for several reasons.

First, while the state may provide a framework for intimate relationships, it does not mandate the form those relationships take (whether legally or practically). For example, as the discussion in Parts I and II highlighted, the legal framework currently provides far greater protection for married couples than cohabiting couples. Nevertheless, cohabiting couples with children are the fastest growing family form in England and Wales.[18] Further, even where couples adopt the same

[17] J Herring, 'Making Family Law More Careful' in J Wallbank and J Herring (eds), *Vulnerability, Care and Family Law* (Routledge, 2013) 46; J Herring, *Caring and the Law* (Hart Publishing, 2013) 11.

[18] A Sharfman and P Cobb, 'Families and Households in the UK: 2021' (ONS, 9 March 2022) www.ons.gov.uk/peoplepopulationandcommunity/birthsdeathsandmarriages/families/bulletins/familiesandhouseholds/2021 accessed 28 April 2023.

form of relationship, as I have argued elsewhere,[19] not all marriages carry the same meaning to all married couples, and indeed parties to the same marriage may understand their relationship differently. How people understand their relationship is personal and, while it is important not to neglect the role of the state, it is also important to recognise that different couples organise their lives differently.

The second reason it is essential to think about individual relationships is that, as discussed earlier in this chapter, there are limits to what the state can do. Caring cannot be entirely outsourced, and arguably should not be. While the state could, and I argue should, play a greater role in facilitating the division of caring responsibilities between parents, for example by encouraging a particular division of parental leave as is done in Sweden by having periods of leave reserved to each parent, such policy initiatives do not necessarily apply in the same way to all families. As was discussed in Chapter 2, for example, the division of paid work and caring is particularly pronounced within certain ethnic groups, so imposing a one-size fits all approach affects different people differently. More generally, however, do we want the state to mandate how people must care?

Third, when it comes to thinking about caring relationships it is important to remember that while care is beneficial to the state, and indeed essential to the functioning of the neoliberal order, that is not why people care. People perform care in caring relationships for more nebulous reasons like love and commitment,[20] which the law does not readily recognise.[21]

The fourth way in which a focus only on the state is problematic is that it fails to provide a complete account of the consequences of an unequal division of caregiving in individual relationships. While the state may encourage the typical gendered division of care during intact relationships, the benefits of such a division are not only reaped by the state. Where one partner gives up work or works part-time and the other continues to work full-time, the latter often benefits financially in not having to make career sacrifices. In some situations, this might be recognised through the principle of compensation if the carer has sacrificed a lucrative career.[22] However, even where this is not the case – and even where the breadwinner cannot directly trace this into a promotion, for example, which Michael suggested might warrant financial compensation – the breadwinner has still avoided the detrimental financial consequences of caring through exercising 'privileged irresponsibility'.[23]

[19] A Heenan, 'The Meaning of Marriage and Approaches to the Division of Assets in Sweden, the Netherlands and England and Wales' in R Probert and S Thompson (eds), *Research Handbook on Marriage and Cohabitation* (Edward Elgar, forthcoming).

[20] J Herring, *Caring and the Law* (Hart Publishing, 2013) 2.

[21] R Grossi, 'Love as a Disadvantage in Law' (2018) 45 *Journal of Law and Society* 205; G Douglas, *Obligation and Commitment in Family Law* (Hart Publishing, 2018).

[22] *Miller v Miller; McFarlane v McFarlane* [2006] UKHL 24. Although note that the value of such awards may be limited in practice: see, for example, *RC v JC* [2020] EWHC 466 (Fam).

[23] J Tronto, *Moral Boundaries: A Political Argument for an Ethic of Care* (Routledge, 1993) 121.

B. The Danger of Privatisation

Nevertheless, there remain concerns around giving greater legal recognition to caring responsibilities. In the context of debates around the legal recognition of same-sex relationships, Boyd and Young observed that:

> The more the state recognizes private dependencies and responsibilities in the current neo-liberal economic climate, the more it is likely that it will tend to offload responsibility onto those private relationships, resulting in more expectations being made of those relationships in terms of taking care of 'their own'.[24]

Such privatisation has different impacts for different groups; for example, in the context of same-sex marriage, whereas middle-class spouses may benefit from tax exemptions, working-class spouses may simply lose benefit entitlements.[25] The context here is slightly different: neither of the mechanisms I am suggesting for placing care at the centre of family law involve recognising new forms of private relationship. In Chapter 7 I do suggest that family law should provide greater protection for cohabiting couples, but such couples are already often treated in the same way as married couples when it comes to state benefits.[26] Thus, a more protective family law regime would not of itself be the cause of greater privatisation. This is not to deny that financial claims on separation will most benefit middle-class cohabitants, for whom there are more assets to argue about. However, the point is that family law claims are envisaged here to sit alongside a greater role for the state and to fill the gaps left by state provision, even where that state provision is much more comprehensive, as in Sweden. More generally, while it is important to recognise political reality when thinking about the law and potential reforms, such as the potential for reforms to be used to support privatisation, this should not override the need for a principled legal framework that responds to the realities of people's lives.

C. The Interplay with the Role of the State

Having identified that the focus of this work is on family law but that a role for the state remains important, it is worth reflecting upon how the approach suggested in this chapter might fit with other theories that explore the role of the state. This

[24] SB Boyd and CFL Young, 'From Same-Sex to No Sex? Towards Recognition of (Same-Sex) Relationships in Canada' [2003] *Seattle Journal of Social Justice* 757, 784; see also N Barker, 'Why Care? "Deserving Family Members" and the Conservative Movement for Broader Family Recognition' in Wallbank and Herring (n 17).

[25] Boyd and Young (ibid) 784; N Barker, 'Sex and the Civil Partnership Act: The Future of (Non) Conjugality?' (2006) 14 *Feminist Legal Studies* 241.

[26] A Barlow et al, *Cohabitation, Marriage and the Law: Social Change and Legal Reform in the 21st Century* (Hart Publishing, 2005).

section does that by exploring vulnerability theory. There are two reasons for the choice to explore vulnerability theory. First, as Gordon-Bouvier observes, it is hard to overstate the impact of vulnerability theory on legal scholarship.[27] The theory, developed by Fineman, 'is based on a descriptive account of the human condition as one of universal and continuous vulnerability'.[28] Fineman, therefore, argues that 'state policy and the law should be responsive to human vulnerability' although 'the call for a responsive state does not dictate the form responses should take, only that they reflect the reality of human vulnerability'.[29]

Second, vulnerability theory is transformative in the way it thinks about the role of the state, and is therefore consistent with the arguments made about the need for a greater role for the state. For example, Fineman recognises the central role that the state plays in the family:

> Through the exercise of legitimate force in bringing societal institutions into legal existence and subsequently regulating them under its mandate of its public authority, the state also constitutes itself. For example, although we often experience entities such as the family and the corporation as 'natural' or inevitable in form and function, in reality such institutions are constructed and evolving; their identities are legitimated in law, hence by the state. Both intimate and economic entities are creatures of the state, in the sense that they are brought into legal existence by the mechanisms of the state. The state determines how both family and corporation, for example, are created as coherent entities entitled to act as such in society.[30]

Gordon-Bouvier develops this line of argument further in her exploration of the idea of relational vulnerability; a development of Fineman's vulnerability theory. She explains:

> The private family, as the institution with primary responsibility for dependency-work, exposes those who perform this work to various avoidable harms and hardships. I employ the umbrella term *relational vulnerability* to refer to these harms. I argue that the harms that constitute relational vulnerability are state-created and avoidable rather than inevitable.[31]

Thus, the state, which Gordon-Bouvier understands as including the legal framework, shapes the nature of the private family and is, at least to some degree, rightly to be held responsible for the consequences of that institution. This insight is a particularly important counter to neoliberal theories, which tend to understand the family as a private matter and not a matter of state concern.

Vulnerability theory is less focused upon relationships between individuals. For example, Gordon-Bouvier suggests that she is 'less concerned (although not

[27] Gordon-Bouvier (n 12) 1.
[28] M Fineman, 'Vulnerability and Inevitable Inequality' (2017) 4 *Oslo Law Review* 133, 134.
[29] ibid 134.
[30] M Fineman, 'The Vulnerable Subject: Anchoring Equality in the Human Condition' (2008) 20 *Yale Journal of Law and Feminism* 1, 6.
[31] Gordon-Bouvier (n 12) 43.

entirely unconcerned) with the individual behaviour of the parties than the ways in which relationships are structured by the state'.[32] This raises the question of whether it might be possible to have a distinct concept of horizontal responsibility that is separate from the sort of state responsibility envisaged through vulnerability theory: that is, could the approach of placing care at the heart of family law be used alongside vulnerability theory?

While there might be ways of doing this, the tentative suggestion of this chapter is that a better way forward for thinking about the role of the state in this regard is to think about how to make care central to family policy alongside taking a different approach to family law which places care at its centre. It is beyond the scope of this book to carry out such an undertaking, but the reason for favouring such an approach as a future development lies in the interconnected nature of horizontal and vertical responsibility. For example, in relation to the law of financial provision on divorce, Douglas has suggested that the law should move away from the principle of need and instead focus on the 'disadvantage generated by the *loss of the relationship*'.[33] Under this model not all losses would be remediable; only losses arising from the ending of the relationship and not those arising from structural disadvantage, such as from the way in which paid work and caregiving are divided in society, would be remedied. Significantly, women's lower earnings are seen to be the result of structural disadvantage.[34] The difficulty with this view is that it is not always possible to separate out the extent to which losses are related to the relationship as opposed to losses that result from the state's actions. In the leading case of *Miller v Miller; McFarlane v McFarlane*, Mrs McFarlane[35] was a City solicitor who gave up her career to look after the parties' children. While this decision might have been influenced by the expense of childcare and cultural norms around motherhood, it is not necessarily clear that she would have made the same decision outside of a secure relationship. As a single mother with her earning potential, it might have been possible, and considered prudent, to pay for help with childcare and maintain a career. This points to the need for a comprehensive approach to addressing the consequences of caring responsibilities on separation. That approach needs to consider both vertical and horizontal aspects of responsibility for care. These elements are interrelated, and practically speaking often inextricable, so a comprehensive approach should deal with both. Future work could address how best to do this. The Swedish experience can, however, provide insights into the potential role of particular policy measures.

[32] Gordon-Bouvier (n 12) 11.

[33] G Douglas, 'Sharing Financial Losses as Well as Gains on Divorce' (2018) 32 *Australian Journal of Family Law* 108, 123.

[34] ibid 125.

[35] *Miller v Miller; McFarlane v McFarlane* [2006] UKHL 24.

IV. The Potential Role of Policy Measures

While family law is the focus of this book and family law has an important role to play in dealing with the costs of care, it is nevertheless important to realise that truly recognising and valuing care requires a more holistic approach. The law that applies on separation is retrospective and is unlikely to help intact families in facilitating childcare. Further, not all children are ever part of an intact family. The lessons from Sweden provide a note of caution about the ability of the state to eliminate a role for family law; gender norms continue to shape the ways in which parents share care between them and so it is important for the law to remain able to address these unequal consequences. The fact remains, however, that the state benefits from care and the state has a role to play in regulating the family.[36] Therefore, it is worth reflecting on what the Swedish experience reveals about the potential role of policy measures in facilitating care and how these might intersect with the family law framework. The focus here is specifically on state-funded childcare and shared parental leave. While there may well be other policy interventions that could contribute to making care more visible and better valued in society, the focus is on these two measures because they are a key element of the Swedish approach.

A. State-funded Childcare

Childcare provision in England and Wales is a highly topical issue. Recent reviews suggest that childcare costs in England are high compared with other countries and have risen quickly over time[37] and that a 'universal childcare guarantee' would have significant economic benefits.[38] In terms of the relative costs of childcare in Sweden and England (an IFS report on the issue covers England only, rather than England and Wales), the maximum fee a parent would pay for one child in Sweden is circa £142 per month.[39] In England and Wales, there is no cap on fees. However, the IFS data suggests that while in Sweden gross childcare fees amount to around 5 per cent of net household income for a two-earner couple on an average wage, the figure in England is over 30 per cent.[40] For a single parent in England, the

[36] Fineman (n 30) 6.

[37] C Farquharson and H Olorenshaw, 'The Changing Cost of Childcare' (IFS, May 2022) https://ifs.org.uk/sites/default/files/output_url_files/R210-The-changing-cost-of-childcare.pdf accessed 28 April 2023.

[38] R Statham et al, 'Delivering a Childcare Guarantee' (IPPR and Save the Children, December 2022) www.ippr.org/files/2022-12/delivering-a-childcare-guarantee-dec-22.pdf accessed 28 April 2023.

[39] Stockholms Stad, 'Fees for Preschool' https://translate.google.com/translate?hl=en&sl=sv&u=https://forskola.stockholm/avgifter/&prev=search&pto=aue accessed 28 April 2023 (page translated using Google translate).

[40] Farquharson and Olorenshaw (n 37) 18.

figure is around 70 per cent.[41] No equivalent figure is given for Sweden, but this may because fees in Sweden are calculated based on parental income so fees will be reduced accordingly.[42] While the 2023 budget proposes to extend 30 hours of free childcare to children over nine months of age in England and Wales,[43] these proposals will not take effect until after the next general election and there are concerns that they are not fully funded.[44]

In the Swedish context, Chapter 4 explained that state-funded childcare is underpinned by the ideals of gender equality and creating opportunities for children from a range of different backgrounds. More affordable childcare in England and Wales would better allow parents to combine paid work and care and might, therefore, reduce the gendered financial consequences of separation. However, it is vital to remember that the neoliberal ideal of financial independence on separation is not the goal here. Rather, the goal is to help make care more central in family law and policy. Thus, it is important to reflect on how more accessible childcare could meet that goal.

First, prioritising childcare provision signals that care is a priority for society. While it is important to recognise the dangers, discussed in Chapter 5, that focusing only on the state can serve to disguise the role still played by parents, state provision alone does not cause this problem. Rather, state provision needs to be seen as part of an overall approach to making care more central in society.

Second, and relatedly, providing accessible and affordable childcare helps to ensure that all parents are supported to care and all children have access to the educational and other opportunities provided by such care. While accessible and affordable childcare should not be seen as a way to avoid a greater emphasis on parents sharing care, not all children are born within intact families, and policy must meet the needs of these children and parents too. The presence of only one parent does not reduce the amount of care to be performed; indeed, it increases the responsibility for that parent. While it is possible that even in these cases a greater emphasis on parental sharing may also be of use, this cannot be assumed to be the case.

State childcare can, therefore, play a role in helping to make care more visible and valued in society. This may, in turn, impact upon family law resolutions where parents separate. For example, the financial disadvantage suffered by primary carers may be reduced. However, these should not be the aims of the policy intervention.

[41] ibid 18.

[42] For further details about how fees work in Sweden, see Stockholms Stad (n 39).

[43] Department for Education, 'Budget 2023: Everything You Need to Know about Childcare Support' (16 March 2023) https://educationhub.blog.gov.uk/2023/03/16/budget-2023-everything-you-need-to-know-about-childcare-support/ accessed 28 April 2023.

[44] M Savage, 'This Will be the End of Nurseries': Preschools in England Warn of Closures amid Free Childcare Expansion Plan' (*The Observer*, 19 March 2023) www.theguardian.com/education/2023/mar/19/this-will-be-the-end-of-nurseries-preschools-in-england-warn-of-closures-amid-free-childcare-expansion-plan accessed 28 April 2023.

B. Shared Parental Leave

The link between shared parental leave and making care more central in society is perhaps more explicit than between this goal and provision of state childcare. Encouraging greater sharing of childcare between parents reinforces the idea that caregiving is central to what it means to be a parent. However, as with nursery care, shared parental leave does not guarantee that care is centred. Even in Sweden, which provides generous parental leave and the ability to take time off to care for sick children, research indicates that fathers find it difficult to adjust their work times according to children's schedules.[45] Further the fathers interviewed in England and Wales for this project who talked about the flexibility allowed by their jobs recognised that their positions were exceptional. Centering care means recognising that children's needs are ongoing. It is, of course, important for parents to be able to take occasional time off work to care for sick children. However, children also need to be picked up from nursery, school or after school care every day. Making care more central means engaging critically with the reasons that these aspects of care are complex. In many cases, this is likely to be a product of expectations around paid work and it may be that only radical changes to the nature of working patterns will truly tackle the invisibility of care in society.

This does not, however, preclude a role for less radical policies such as more effective shared parental leave provision. There is some evidence that enhanced pay for shared parental leave is less common than enhanced pay for maternity leave,[46] a policy which has been held not to be discriminatory.[47] Where maternity pay is enhanced and shared parental leave is not, there is a financial disincentive for the father to take the leave.[48] Changing this asymmetry would be an important step in facilitating fathers' shared parental leave use. However, it is important to recognise that not all employers enhance either type of leave. Where this is the case, there is a financial incentive for the lower earner to take leave (and the existence of the gender pay gap, together with the fact that women typically partner

[45] L Haas et al, 'The Impact of Organizational Culture on Men's Use of Parental Leave in Sweden' (2002) 5 *Community Work and Family* 319, 336.

[46] A poll of 375 employers by XPertHR found that while 65% of organisations offered some form of enhanced maternity pay, only 25% offered enhanced shared parental leave: F Churchill, 'Two-thirds of Businesses Now Provide Enhanced Maternity Pay, Poll Finds' (People Management, 24 May 2021) www.peoplemanagement.co.uk/article/1747219/two-thirds-of-businesses-now-provide-enhanced-maternity-pay accessed 28 April 2023. Employee benefits reports on Bright Horizon's (a nursery care provider) 'Parental leave benchmark' survey of 700 firms which found that 79% if employers enhance maternity pay compared with 48% who enhance shared parental pay: Z Wickens, '79% of Employers Offer Enhanced Maternity Leave Pay' (employee benefits, 1 October 2021) https://employeebenefits.co.uk/79-employers-enhanced-maternity-leave-pay/ accessed 28 April 2023.

[47] *Price v Powys County Council* [2021] UKEAT/0133/20.

[48] M Matthews, 'Working Fathers Experience Sex Discrimination' (2023) 45 *Journal of Social Welfare and Family Law* 84.

older men,[49] who are therefore often more advanced in their careers, means that this is likely to be the mother). Improving statutory rates of pay is, therefore, also likely to be important to try and facilitate greater uptake of shared parental leave.

Against a backdrop of better funded shared parental leave, it might be possible to go even further than Sweden and mandate an equal division of leave between parents to try and encourage a more equal sharing of caregiving. However, whilst superficially attractive, such an approach is potentially problematic for a variety of families. For example, in areas of England and Wales with a more ethnically diverse population, fewer women tend to work because they are caring for family.[50] Thus, such reforms are likely to have a disproportionate effect on families from minority ethnic communities. If choice is considered important, then mandating a particular division of leave is potentially problematic in a way that trying to address asymmetries in maternity and shared parental pay is not. Mandating a particular division of leave might serve to limit the options for parents to divide that leave in a way that works best for them. In contrast, addressing asymmetries in parental pay facilitates a more meaningful choice for both parents about how to divide leave between them by removing the economic barriers to choices that do not involve the lower earner taking the leave. If a family do choose to divide the leave unequally then it remains important that the family law framework is capable of dealing with the consequences of that choice.

On a different note, it is also important to recognise that an equal division of time does not necessarily translate into an equal division of caregiving. In Sweden, for example, there are seasonal peaks in fathers' leave use at Christmas and in the summer, suggesting that it may serve as additional vacation time.[51] This may become less of an issue if leave were divided equally, as it might help to create a culture in which both parents are seen as equally responsible. However, cultural change is not a quick or straightforward process and there is a possibility that gendered expectations of caregiving would persist, with mothers simply having less time to perform the tasks expected of them. Additionally, it is important to remember that not all families have two parents who can be, or want to be, involved in the day-to-day lives of their children. For Erin, for example, there was no possibility of sharing parental leave with her child's father who lived in a different city, and with whom she was not in a relationship.

[49] See F Mohammad et al, 'Marriages in England and Wales: 2019' (ONS, 19 May 2022) www.ons.gov.uk/peoplepopulationandcommunity/birthsdeathsandmarriages/marriagecohabitationandcivilpartnerships/bulletins/marriagesinenglandandwalesprovisional/2019#age-at-marriage accessed 28 April 2023 for relative ages of men and women who marry, and S Bradford, 'Birth Characteristics in England and Wales: 2020' (ONS, 13 January 2022) www.ons.gov.uk/peoplepopulationandcommunity/birthsdeathsandmarriages/livebirths/bulletins/birthcharacteristicsinenglandandwales/2020#age-of-parents accessed 28 April 2023 for average age of mothers and fathers.

[50] ONS, 'Women in the Labour Market: 2013' (25 September 2013) www.ons.gov.uk/employmentandlabourmarket/peopleinwork/employmentandemployeetypes/articles/womeninthelabourmarket/2013-09-25 accessed 28 April 2023.

[51] J Ekberg et al, 'Parental Leave – A Policy Evaluation of the Swedish "Daddy-Month" Reform' (2013) 97 *Journal of Public Economics* 131, 137.

As with better funded nursery care, shared parental leave policies might be used to encourage a greater sharing of care in society, which might have knock-on effects for family law. Once again, though, the goal of this policy should be to recognise and accommodate the essential role of care in society, rather than as a means of facilitating neoliberal-influenced ideas of autonomy on parental separation. As the Swedish experience illustrates, such policies are not a foolproof way of achieving this.

V. How Do We Make Care More Central to Family Law?

How then can family law achieve a shift from focusing on autonomy to focusing upon care? First, it is important that family law has a clear understanding of what it means to care. Tronto's understanding of the four phases of care – caring about, taking care of, caregiving and care receiving[52] – offers a way of interrogating the differences in the care provided by different carers. The next section suggests a framework for approaching questions of family law that employs Tronto's understanding of care to make caring relationships more visible in such decisions. This framework is the first mechanism for making care more central to family law. The second, and potentially more radical way, of placing care at the centre of family law is to draw on this understanding of the different aspects of care and use them to inform potential reforms to family law. Chapter 7 outlines some of the ways in which family law might be reformed to do this.

VI. A Framework for Approaching Family Law Questions

A. The Framework

The aim of the framework suggested here is to recognise the central role of care in family life and to try and ensure that legal decisions about family life consider caring relationships. When it comes to the arrangements on separation (whether financial or to do with arrangements for children) this requires a decision-maker to consider care both retrospectively and prospectively.

The first question this raises is what is meant by a decision-maker? Perhaps the epitome of a decision-maker is a judge in family law proceedings. The intention behind this framework is to help judges to approach legal questions on

[52] Tronto (n 23) 106–108.

separation in a more holistic way that recognises the central role of care. It is, however, important to recognise that in most cases these sorts of decisions are not made by a judge. Instead, parents might agree arrangements directly, or with the aid of solicitors, or through mediation or some other form of alternative dispute resolution. These different mechanisms may involve a range of different decision-makers. For example, in arbitration the arbitrator would be the decision-maker. In direct negotiations, the parents themselves would be. Where parents are using mediation or solicitor-led negotiation, the parents are likely to be the ultimate decision-makers, but the legal professionals help to shape the parameters within which those decisions are made. The aim of this framework is to provide guidance in all of these different processes. However, it needs to be recognised that the precise form of this framework may need to vary depending on who is using it. Judges and other legal professionals, for example, may want guidance that is clearly tied to the statutory framework. In contrast, parents may want a more practical set of questions tied to everyday experience.

A second issue to address at this stage is the importance of considering matters both retrospectively and prospectively. In short, while key aspects of the legal framework on separation are designed to look backwards and forwards, in practice, separation is dominated by a focus on the future. Turning first to the legal framework relating to financial remedies on divorce, the legal framework is explicitly backward-looking in considering the parties' standard of living prior to the breakdown of the marriage.[53] Nevertheless, case law makes clear that the standard of living is not the 'lodestar'[54] and that, rather than being seen as 'ceiling or a floor' it should be seen 'as a benchmark or starting point against which to assess needs'[55] but that '[u]sually, due to finite resources, it will not be possible for the marital standard of living to be maintained'.[56] Other provisions look at matters both retrospectively and prospectively. For example, the court is to have regard to the parties' financial resources,[57] financial needs,[58] and contributions[59] both at the time the court is considering these matters and 'in the foreseeable future'. Nevertheless, as Chapter 3 described, the practical emphasis on individual autonomy means that in practice clean breaks dominate despite the financial consequences of divorce being gendered. This suggests that perhaps in practice the forward-looking aspects of separation dominate.

When it comes to the arrangements for children, the legal framework again has retrospective and prospective elements. For example, the welfare checklist[60] directs a court to consider the likely effect on the child 'of any change in his

[53] Matrimonial Causes Act 1973, s 25(2)(c).
[54] *SS v NS (Spousal Maintenance)* [2014] EWHC 4183 (Fam).
[55] *BD v FD* [2016] EWHC 594 [114].
[56] ibid [116].
[57] Matrimonial Causes Act 1973, s 25(2)(a).
[58] ibid s 25(2)(b).
[59] ibid s 25(2)(f).
[60] Children Act 1989, s 1(3).

circumstances'[61] (often referred to as the status quo). This requires considering the arrangements that were in place during the relationship and is, therefore, retrospective albeit that there is a prospective element involved in considering the likely effect of any change in circumstances. Other elements of the welfare checklist also require a balance of retrospective and prospective analysis. For example, the court is directed to consider 'any harm which [the child] has suffered or is at risk of suffering'.[62] Further, assessments such as the capability of a parent of meeting a child's needs[63] are likely to require a holistic analysis. More recent developments in the legal framework are, however, more explicitly prospective. For example, the presumption of parental involvement directs the court to 'presume, unless the contrary is shown, that the involvement of that parent in the life of the child concerned will further the child's welfare'.[64] While this does not presume any particular division of a child's time,[65] this presumption is not grounded in the individual relationship between a parent and child but in assumptions about what is best for children in post-separation families.

Against this backdrop, I set out below a list of questions that provide a framework for considering the impact of care both retrospectively and prospectively. Beneath each question I have suggested some of the sorts of considerations that might be relevant to the answer to each in the context of parental separation. The idea behind this section is to give an overview of the framework based upon making care more central and to demonstrate how it addresses the shortcomings of the current legal approach: namely, the invisibility and devaluation of care.

Looking backwards

1. What caring relationships are there?

At this stage, the enquiry is very broad. The aim is simply to capture the existence of all possible caring relationships. When considering the example of parental separation, the sorts of relationships that might be identified include the relationship between the parents and the relationship(s) between the parents and children. There may also be other caring relationships, for example the relationship between the parents and their own elderly parents.

2. What role is each party playing?

This draws upon Tronto's four phases of care outlined above. The idea of this stage is to interrogate each of the caring relationships identified at the first stage, to gain a full understanding of how they impact the different parties.

In an intact family, it is likely that each party will be performing multiple phases of care and it is important to note this. However, it is also vital think about

[61] ibid s 1(3)(c).
[62] ibid s 1(3)(e).
[63] ibid s 1(3)(f).
[64] ibid s 1(2A).
[65] ibid s 1(2B).

the primary role that each parent plays. So, for example, in the context of a family consisting of two parents and a child it is likely that the child is primarily the care receiver. This does not preclude the possibility that the child at times plays a different role. They may, for example, recognise that a parent needs care, or take steps to put that care in place, or indeed provide care themselves.

When it comes to the parents, it is also likely that they have played a variety of caring roles. For example, parents are likely to recognise the need for care (care about), assume some responsibility for the need and determine how to respond to it (take care of) and meet those needs directly (caregive). However, as the discussion in previous chapters has revealed, in England and Wales (and to a lesser extent in Sweden) those roles are often shared unequally. Typically, families structure their lives so that one parent provides a greater share of caregiving with the other perhaps taking care of the situation by providing financial support. It is important to identify these different roles, which will require parents to think practically about day-to-day caring activities.

The experiences of participants to this research outlined in Chapter 3 suggests that it is important to think beyond a strict division of time when thinking about care. Based on those experiences, other considerations might include, but are not limited to:

— Who will be responsible for school pick ups and drop offs?
— Who will organise after-school clubs or other care?
— Who will be responsible for organising doctors, dentists and other appointments?
— Who will take children to those appointments?
— Who will organise buying clothing and school uniforms?
— Who will take the children to buy these items?

The role of the state is also relevant to this question. Where, as in Sweden for example, the state plays a greater role in supporting caring responsibilities then this will affect the roles parents play. Thus, if the state provides better-funded nursery care and as a result care is shared less unequally between parents then this will be evident in this section when thinking about the roles parents play. However, the need to identify the roles being played will mean that even where the state plays a greater role, the opportunity to understand caring practices fully is not lost.

3. What has been the impact on each of those parties of playing that role for the purposes of the question you are asking?

This stage is about recognising the real-world consequences of different caring roles. It allows, for example, for recognition of the relative financial costs of caregiving and other phases of care. If one parent has reduced their working hours to care and this has impacted their earning capacity, then this can be noted. Conversely, if there have been other costs, such as emotional costs, for the other parent in working more to take care of the situation by providing financial support then this can be recognised.

This stage is also where the impact of past caring relationships on the care receiver can be considered. Thus, if the care provided by a parent has had a detrimental effect on the care receiver, then this can be taken into account when considering the arrangements for children on separation.

Again, the role of the state is relevant here. If the state plays a greater role in facilitating care, then it might be that the financial consequences for parents, in terms of the impact on earning capacity, are reduced.

4. What should be done about this to ensure an outcome that meets the desired objectives?

This is the stage at which the interplay between relationships of care and the specific objectives of the law can be considered. So, for example, if the issue being considered is financial provision on divorce, then the question is how to address the consequences identified at stage 3 in order to reach a fair result[66] that upholds the principles of needs, compensation and sharing.[67] Thus, if one partner has sacrificed their earning capacity because of caregiving responsibilities, then fairness might require that they receive a financial settlement that meets the needs generated by those responsibilities or compensates them financially. It will, however, be important to consider the remaining stages of the framework (set out below) before reaching a final determination.

If the question being considered is the arrangements for children on separation, then the law's objective is to achieve an arrangement that is in the child's best interests.[68] It might be that the court would consider the extent to which the previous arrangements achieved this. Here too, though, it will be important to consider the remaining stages of the framework before reaching a final decision.

Looking forward

5. What will be the arrangements going forward?

This is where the proposals for the future are considered. Where a couple are in agreement, there may be one set of proposals to consider under this heading. Where they are not, this stage may involve considering competing sets of proposals to identify the potential outcomes.

6. What role will each party play?

This involves a similar undertaking to the one outlined at section 2 above. In exactly the same way, it is important to identify the multiple roles played by different parties. It will, however, also be important to think about who will hold primary responsibility for particular caring roles going forward. As at stage 2, this

[66] *White v White* [2000] UKHL 54.
[67] *Miller v Miller; McFarlane v McFarlane* [2006] UKHL 24.
[68] Children Act 1989, s 1(1).

requires practical thinking about the day-to-day activities of care, and it is not sufficient just to think about where children will live.

7. **What will be the impact on each of those parties of playing that role for the purposes of the question you are asking? How does this fit with the impacts identified at stage 3?**

As at stage 3, this stage involves thinking critically about caring roles and the impacts of them. Whereas stage 3 looked backwards at the roles played within an intact family, this stage initially involves asking that question while looking at the future. However, this stage also looks at the future consequences that follow on from the historic roles identified at stage 2.

Perhaps the best example of how this might work practically is to think about a situation where one parent had been the primary carer during the relationship, but a shared care arrangement has been agreed post-separation. If the question being considered is financial arrangements, then it will be important to first think about the impact of the future shared care arrangement on both parents' earning capacity. If, for example, the parents intend to share all aspects of the children's care and have identified those fully at stage 6 then both are likely to face financial consequences going forward. However, if one partner has been the primary carer historically whereas the other worked full-time then their relative abilities to balance paid work and care may be different. For example, the former primary carer may be limited by their past work experience whereas the former breadwinner may be able to make use of flexible working privileges because of the seniority gained in a career developed through the marriage. Thus, stage 3 cannot be neglected.

8. **What needs to be put in place to facilitate that role?**

At this final stage, the aim is to draw together all of the stages above to work out the best way forward that meets the objective of the relevant law.

VII. Contrasting Care and Other Approaches

Having suggested that placing care at the heart of family law is the best way to address the shortcomings of neoliberal-influenced ideas of autonomy and having outlined a framework for doing so, this section draws on real world examples from my data to contrast an approach based upon care and one based on a more neoliberal-inspired version of autonomy. I suggest that these examples illustrate that not only does an approach inspired by care better reflect the realities of caring relationships, which neoliberal-inspired approaches render invisible, but it may lead to substantively better outcomes.

The approaches of three participants – Elizabeth, Matthew and Jason – to questions arising on separation will be contrasted. Whereas the approach of Elizabeth and Matthew (who were married to each other) seems to be consistent with an approach informed by a nuanced understanding of care, Jason's approach is much more aligned with neoliberal-influenced visions of autonomy. Turning first to the question of child arrangements, Jason described the arrangements for his child, and the rationale for those arrangements, as follows:

> **Jason**: [I]t can get a bit floaty, flaky, and fluffy around the edges and I'd like that to be really trimmed, really clear. So, with –
>
> **Interviewer**: Can you explain what you mean by … 'floaty around the edges'? … [W]hat happens and what are some of the problems?
>
> **Jason**: So, handover as an example. … [G]ood example is last summer, so six weeks and … they were only on time for handover … once.
>
> **Interviewer**: OK.
>
> **Jason**: So it was like, that's flaky … – just leave a bit earlier … You know, I know that if you're half an hour late or an hour late, I'm just going to add it on Sunday or Saturday.
>
> **Interviewer**: OK.
>
> **Jason**: But why do that? … [I]t's that kind of stuff … – probably trivial but the more I try and keep it focused. If it had been the other way, if I hadn't really bothered about all this kind of stuff, it would be completely messy.
>
> **Interviewer**: OK.
>
> **Jason**: So.
>
> **Interviewer**: So in terms of … seeing your [child] at all or in terms of –
>
> **Jason**: In terms of me … receiving what's my right as a father.
>
> **Interviewer**: OK.
>
> **Jason**: And without becoming like one of the father doormats that are out there and like, 'Oh no, I don't have a right to see [them]. I can't see [them]. I'll only see [child] every other weekend.' That was never going to happen. That can't happen. And I've just tried to put the firm, clear boundaries in place because there can be confusion, there can be misunderstandings and actually if all this stuff is put in place now, then we know how it is, you know. You can't say five years down the line, 'Well, hold on – we never discussed this.' This has always been very clear. That's what I always wanted. And [child] is … very stable, I believe, because [child] understands boundaries. [Child] knows I'm very black and white.

Elsewhere in his interview, Jason outlined what this meant for his child:

> I think, [child] gets now, especially after last week, that actually, you've got your medicine at that house, and I've got mine and they're two different things, two different diets, two different ways of life.

This idea of two different ways of life even translated itself into school meals: Jason's child ate a vegan school meal for half of the school week because 'the official handover time … [in the shared care arrangement] is 11 on a Wednesday so that means [child's] lunch at school is actually within my time'.

This approach is heavily shaped by neoliberal-influenced ideas of autonomy. In particular, this approach venerates independence: here the two adults live entirely separate lives with distinct parenting styles. While that approach may work for children, and indeed Jason felt that it worked well for his child, the danger with this approach is that because it focuses on a clear separation between the parents, children's needs may be overlooked.

In contrast, Elizabeth and Matthew said this about their approach to child arrangements:

> **Elizabeth**: [T]he magnetic factor has to be the child and so stepping out of your own … you know, putting yourself in the child's position and, and basically every single decision what is better for them – doesn't matter what I think about it – what is better for them.
>
> **Matthew**: [T]he single most important thing are … the needs of the child, and everything else comes secondary to that. … [I]t may be that … you can barely bring yourself to speak to your ex-partner for whatever reason, but … if you can't get over that for your child, I think there's something seriously, seriously wrong.

Matthew explained what this meant practically for the adults:

> I'm not just managing my time and [child's] time but … I'm working … with Elizabeth and her partner, my partner, you know, and it's just almost like … you can't, you can never please anybody any of the time almost is, is how it sometimes feels to me.

This is the antithesis of Jason's approach. Here, the adults' lives are not entirely independent of one another. This could be described as a more relational form of autonomy in that autonomy is exercised within the context of relationships which provide meaning. However, it is not autonomy that is driving the arrangements here: it is a desire to provide care for their child.

Similarly contrasting approaches can be seen in relation to financial arrangements. For example, Elizabeth said this about how she and Matthew approached child maintenance:

> … when we first separated Matthew was paying an awful lot of child maintenance and it became, because at the time [child] was in nursery full-time … basically, he wasn't having [them] at all over night, and the nursery fees were extortionate so, it, it meant that he was having to pay over a lot of money, and at the point that he wanted to buy somewhere it became apparent that, that that level of maintenance was going to prevent him from getting a mortgage.
>
> So, we, um, it was at that point that we reduced the nursery hours … basically that, that reduced Matthew's liability down to – And we were most of all guided by … what could he pay and pay mortgage. Um, and then when [child] turned three so we got the free hours. I, I took the view that I didn't really need the maintenance even though we weren't on a 50:50 split [child's] dad needed to keep a roof over his head and, and meet all of those sorts of needs that I was meeting. So we just agreed at that stage that he would pay, we would both pay half of [their] nursery fees.

Again, this is very different from an approach informed by neoliberal-influenced ideas of autonomy. Unlike the clear-cut vision of financial independence envisaged by those norms, here Elizabeth and Matthew reached an arrangement that was flexible and informed by both their needs. Again, it would not be inaccurate to call this sort of autonomy relational, but this label is not necessarily helpful in trying to distil the decision-making process going on here. Relational autonomy does not specify a particular course of action. What Elizabeth is describing here is an attempt to think about what resources each partner requires to meet caring needs. While it is forward-focused in the sense that it draws on the considerations in questions 5–8 of the framework outlined above, the relationship position informs the options available. If, for example, Elizabeth had not worked during their relationship then she might not have been in a position to forgo child maintenance.

VIII. Conclusion

This chapter has argued that it is care, and not autonomy, that should be family law's focus on parental separation. It has also outlined two mechanisms that might help to place care at the centre of family law: a framework that aims to embed a clear understanding of care in family law decisions and reforming elements of private family law in a way that recognises caring relationships. Having outlined the first of these approaches, the framework, in this chapter, Chapter 7 goes on to suggest how care could be used in rethinking and refining the four key areas of family law with which this book is concerned: the financial consequences of separation for unmarried couples, the financial consequences of divorce and dissolution, the financial arrangements for children, and child arrangements on separation.

7

Reforming Private Family Law

I. Placing Care at the Centre of Family Law

Chapter 6 outlined a framework for decision-makers to use in approaching questions on parental separation. The aim of that framework is to render visible the caring relationships that are central to the functioning of family life. It is intended to work alongside current legal provisions and prompt a more direct engagement with caring responsibilities when applying them. This is important because, while care is at the heart of what families do, earlier chapters of this book have revealed that it is frequently invisible and devalued. This chapter undertakes a separate, but related, exercise. It aims to take a step back and consider the reforms we might make to family law if we truly want to recognise and value caring.

II. Statutory Reform or Other Interventions

When considering how best to place care at the centre of family law, it is essential to think carefully about what law reform can and cannot achieve. There are limits to the law's ability to create social and behavioural change. For example, as I have argued in the context of the law of financial remedies, financial remedy law reform alone is unlikely to create a more gender equal society; policy changes are also needed to facilitate a more equal sharing of work and care.[1] Further, it is important to be realistic about the sorts of decisions it is practical for judges to make. For example, in most financial remedies cases, courts tend to steer away from making decisions around chattels because it is time-consuming and the costs of doing so are disproportionate. Similarly, in child arrangement cases there are dangers in being too prescriptive about every detail because children's needs change as they get older, and arrangements need to be responsive to those changing needs.

When thinking about law reform, it is also important to recognise that judges are not the only ones making decisions on separation. As described in Chapter 2, private ordering has always been a feature of private family law, something which legal

[1] A Heenan, 'Neoliberal Autonomy and Financial Remedy Reform: Lessons from Sweden' (2020) 3 *Child and Family Law Quarterly* 263.

aid cuts are likely to have compounded. Thus, most decisions are made by parents themselves, with or without assistance from lawyers, mediators or other legal professionals. If bargaining in the shadow of the law[2] is to be a realistic possibility, then there is a challenge in ensuring that those without legal advice understand what the law is. This is not straightforward, and it is important to avoid simply conflating the content of the substantive law with the question of access to it.

Deech has argued that her suggested reforms in the Divorce (Financial Provision) Bill might assist litigants in person by making the law clearer to them.[3] In my view, there are two problems with this suggestion. First, simplicity should not be the primary goal of the law; the law should respond to the realities of people's lives. Family law is complex because the issues it deals with are complex and multifaceted. In the discussion of relational ideas of autonomy in Chapter 6, it was recognised that part of the instinctive appeal of neoliberal-influenced ideas of autonomy may be grounded in the relative simplicity of norms such as financial independence. However, the preceding chapters have demonstrated the problems with such an approach. The law should be capable of responding to the realities of people's lives; simplicity is not a justification for a legal framework that fails to do this.

The second problem with Deech's suggestion is that there is a need to be realistic about what the law, as opposed to procedural or other interventions, can achieve. First, my Swedish research suggested that even where the law is relatively simple, people do not necessarily know what the law is. Second, there are groups of litigants in person with specific vulnerabilities, such as learning disabilities,[4] for whom interpreting the law is likely to pose particular challenges. More generally, however, in a common law system, legal interpretation relies on the ability to identify and understand case law. This is a specialist skill, and it is not reasonable to expect those without legal training to possess it. Trinder et al's research with litigants in person found that '[t]here appeared to be no clear relationship between being highly educated, professional and articulate and being able to handle family law proceedings effectively'.[5] Thus, while it is vital to ensure access to justice, equating this goal with the content of the substantive law is misconceived.

For these reasons, in each of the four areas of law with which this chapter is concerned (the financial claims of cohabiting couples, financial remedies on divorce, financial arrangements for children, and child arrangements), the discussion will consider whether statutory reform is the most appropriate way forward. Where it is not, it will consider what other mechanisms might be useful in seeking to centre care in the relevant area of family law.

[2] R Mnookin and L Kornhauser, 'Bargaining in the Shadow of the Law: The Case of Divorce' (1979) 88 *The Yale Law Journal* 950.

[3] R Deech, 'Financial Provision Reform' [2018] *Family Law* 1251, 1252.

[4] L Trinder et al, 'Litigants in Person in Private Family Law Cases' (Ministry of Justice, 2014) https://assets.publishing.service.gov.uk/government/uploads/system/uploads/attachment_data/file/380479/litigants-in-person-in-private-family-law-cases.pdf accessed 28 April 2023.

[5] ibid 24.

III. Rethinking the Legal Framework for Unmarried Couples

Of the four areas of the law on separation being considered, the legal framework relating to cohabiting couples offers the clearest case for substantive law reform. As Chapter 3 explained, ideas of autonomy dominate the perception of cohabitants in the law and frame the very limited legal response. This creates dangers where care is systematically undervalued: without a formal legal entitlement, cohabitants who are carers are dependent on the goodwill of a former partner or on the support of the state. This leaves them and their children financially vulnerable. Barlow and Smithson's research reveals the challenges of seeking to address this issue in other ways, for example through raising awareness of the legal position.[6] First, different groups of cohabitants are likely to respond to this differently. Whereas the pragmatists and idealogues may be influenced to make legal arrangements by such information, those who are in uneven relationships are unlikely to respond in the same way. Even in these cases, though, the timing of information is likely to be important.[7] Further, 'romantic' couples, who are likely to be particularly optimistic about their relationship, may be unlikely to take steps to protect themselves, even if they are aware of the need to. Law reform is, therefore, key.

Before considering the options for substantive reform, it is important to note two things. First, and this is true of all the areas of law discussed in this chapter, the aim of making care more central in the law does not dictate a single outcome. Rather, the approach here is to use Tronto's[8] understanding of the different phases of care as a lens through which to critique the law. Second, the question of law reform is particularly complex when it comes to considering the position of cohabiting couples. Cohabitants are not a homogenous group. Unlike married couples, there is no ceremony of marriage (or equivalent) to give an easily identifiable measure of the nature of the relationship. The presence of a child could serve as a similar proxy and, given this work's concern with caring relationships, looking at this group of cohabitants is a useful focus. However, cohabitants with children are not the only group of cohabitants for whom legal protection might be necessary and appropriate; couples who have lived together for long periods of time without children also make decisions for the good of the unit, rather than purely in their own self-interest. Reforming the law for cohabitants, therefore, requires a coherent and overarching approach that considers a variety of circumstances. It is beyond the scope of this book to do that, but what follows is intended to inform such an exercise and to ensure that caring responsibilities are not neglected in any more comprehensive attempt to reform the law.

[6] A Barlow and J Smithson, 'Legal Assumptions, Cohabitants' Talk and the Rocky Road to Reform' (2010) 22 *Child and Family Law Quarterly* 328.

[7] ibid 338.

[8] J Tronto, *Moral Boundaries: A Political Argument for an Ethic of Care* (Routledge, 1993).

The first option would be to treat all parents of children in the same way, whether they are married or unmarried, and apply the same legal framework. The discussion later in this chapter suggests changes that could be made to the legal framework for married couples to place care at its centre. Option one would be to apply the same framework to all parents, regardless of relationship status. This could be justified on the basis that caregiving is valuable to society, and that it carries financial consequences. This approach places caregiving at the centre of family law, by placing the same value on it, regardless of who it is performed by. However, this justification would potentially mean that such a regime could apply in situations like Erin's.

Erin and her partner were never in a relationship. The idea that claims for financial provision should be available for the benefit of a parent in this situation, rather than for the benefit of the child, is radical, although not necessarily incompatible with placing care at the centre of family law. The question is whether, to return to the language of responsibility explored in Chapter 2, horizontal (intra-partner) responsibility is appropriate here. Is there a case for holding a partner responsible for the costs of care or is horizontal responsibility here a pragmatic approach, which attributes financial responsibility to a parent that should more properly be borne by the state?[9] The answer to this question is not straightforward. On the one hand, the carer is likely to suffer financial detriment and it could be argued that the other parent implicitly accepted responsibility for that child though the act of sexual intercourse. Indeed, Douglas suggests that:

> Willingly engaging in behaviour that runs the risk of creating a child, or failing to terminate a pregnancy that will result in the birth of a child, who will inevitably be vulnerable and dependent, seems a valid moral basis for imposing the prior obligation to 'take care of' that child in the sense used by Tronto on the child's progenitors. This means that the parent can either provide financial support, arrange for the child's care to be undertaken by someone else if she or he does not wish to provide it, or, of course, care for the child her or himself.[10]

However, while this might justify the imposition of an obligation in respect of the child, which seems to be what Douglas is suggesting, it is not necessarily clear that this should translate into a general financial obligation between the child's parents, albeit that there might be some justification for a more limited financial obligation based upon the costs incurred by that parent in performing childcare. Such obligations are perhaps best dealt with through the child maintenance regime.

A second option would be to apply the same regime to cohabiting parents as married couples where the relationship functions in the same way as marriage

[9] L Ferguson, 'Family, Social Inequalities and the Persuasive Force of Interpersonal Obligation' (2008) 22 *International Journal of Law, Policy and the Family* 61; A Heenan, 'Causal and Temporal Connections in Financial Remedy Cases: The Meaning of Marriage' (2018) 30 *Child and Family Law Quarterly* 75.

[10] G Douglas, *Obligation and Commitment in Family Law* (Hart Publishing, 2018) 29.

is assumed to. In *Miller; McFarlane*[11] Lord Nicholls suggested that '... to greater or lesser extent every relationship of marriage gives rise to a relationship of interdependence. The parties share the roles of money-earner, home-maker and child-carer. Mutual dependence begets mutual obligations of support.'[12] Thus, where cohabiting parents exhibit interdependence and make decisions in the interests of a family that may conflict with their own best interests, there would seem to be good reason to treat them in a similar way to married couples. This option would be consistent with the vision of state responsibility outlined here, which considers that there is a legitimate basis for the state to support caregivers because of the benefit of caring to society.[13] This state responsibility is separate from the responsibility of a partner. In Chapter 6, it was argued that a former partner should continue to have some financial responsibility for the costs of caring. This was partly because of the practical inability of the state completely to address all such costs. It was also grounded in the interdependent nature of relationships where there are children. Thus, the basis for the financial responsibility of a partner is the combination of caring responsibilities and an interdependent relationship in which those responsibilities are divided unequally.

This second option raises the question of how to identify cohabiting relationships that function in the same way as marriage is presumed to. One solution would be to develop a list of criteria which, if fulfilled, would lead to the regime applying unless a good reason was shown for it not to. In addition to the presence of children, criteria might include, for example, the length of the relationship and the degree of financial interdependence involved in it. The difficulty with this sort of approach is that such features are not necessarily a good indicator of when such a regime should apply. It is not difficult to imagine that in abusive relationships, or even in 'uneven couples'[14] where one partner is more committed than the other, it would be much harder to demonstrate the necessary measures of interdependence. In such cases it is hard to see why the carer alone should bear the financial consequences of having children. As Douglas explains, 'entering into an intimate relationship (including where it has been drifted into in a rather "contingent" way), and particularly having a child, generally entails the undertaking of forms of care'.[15] One way of addressing this might be for a regime to apply by default whenever a couple have a child, but with the possibility of arguing for a departure where it can be established that the parties did not have a relationship of interdependence.

[11] [2006] UKHL 24.

[12] *Miller v Miller; McFarlane v McFarlane* [2006] UKHL 24 [11] (Lord Nicholls).

[13] See also M Fineman, 'The Vulnerable Subject: Anchoring Equality in the Human Condition' (2008) 20 *Yale Journal of Law and Feminism* 1, 6 and E Gordon-Bouvier, *Relational Vulnerability* (Palgrave Macmillan, 2020) 43.

[14] Barlow and Smithson (n 6).

[15] Douglas (n 10) 29.

A third option would be to distinguish between married and cohabiting couples with children, but to provide some protection for them both. There is a difference between married couples and cohabitants, because the former have been through a ceremony of marriage and have actively chosen to enter into a legally recognised relationship. There are, however, difficulties with this distinction. For example, it is not necessarily the case that all married couples appreciate the financial consequences of their union. Conversely, as was reflected in the experiences of some of the participants in this study, a common law marriage myth[16] exists and many cohabitants fail to understand their lack of legal protection. Thus, the assumed differences between married couples and cohabitants are not necessarily a useful basis for treating them differently. That said, the diversity of cohabiting relationships may mean that there is value in a regime that is easy to apply automatically to a variety of such relationships. This could be combined with the possibility of offering a higher level of protection to those relationships that can demonstrate a relationship of care + interdependence.

As outlined above, placing care at the centre of family law does not dictate a single form that a regime applying to cohabitants should take. Nevertheless, it does offer a way of evaluating potential reforms. An approach that places care at its centre means that any regime must recognise the financial effects of caregiving. Regimes like the deferred community of property regime in Sweden, in which couples have a fixed entitlement to a share of certain property, are unlikely to achieve this. In contrast, the 2007 Law Commission proposals[17] explicitly consider the economic impacts of cohabitation. This scheme, which considers both retained benefit and disadvantage, reflects a compensatory principle that considers the position of both parties. This contrasts with the way in which the principle of compensation is understood to apply to married couples, where only the position of the claimant is relevant.[18]

Although the Law Commission proposals rejected financial needs as the basis of their scheme,[19] another alternative might be to develop a regime based on financial needs that both respected caring responsibilities and provided a principled basis for financial relief. For married couples, the law currently provides redress for needs that are both causally and temporally connected to a parties' relationship.[20] Whereas causal connections 'are concerned with whether a relationship is in some way responsible for creating a financial claim', temporal connections are concerned with 'the time at which the source of the unmet need for which provision is sought arose', and specifically, whether it arose during the relationship.[21]

[16] J Curtice et al (eds), *British Social Attitudes 36* (The National Centre for Social Research, 2019) www.bsa.natcen.ac.uk/media/39363/bsa_36.pdf accessed 28 April 2023.

[17] Law Commission, *Cohabitation: The Financial Consequences of Relationship Breakdown* (Law Com No 307, 2007).

[18] *Waggott v Waggott* [2018] EWCA Civ 727.

[19] Law Commission (n 17).

[20] Heenan (n 9).

[21] ibid 76.

As I have argued elsewhere, this is justified on the basis of the interdependence inherent in marriage.[22] If a distinction is to be drawn between married and cohabiting couples, then one option would be to limit the claims available to cohabitants to those causally connected to the parties' relationship. Financial needs arising from caregiving responsibilities are the paradigm examples of needs that are causally connected to the relationship. Such a regime would therefore place care at its centre.

Whichever of these options is chosen, an important consideration is whether such a regime should require couples to opt in or whether it should apply by default, perhaps with the possibility of an opt out. An opt-in regime would be largely meaningless for those who do not appreciate the legal significance of marriage – a significant number, given the prevalence of the common law marriage myth. Further, in couples where there is a heightened power disparity, for example in abusive relationships or uneven couples, an opt-in regime would favour the financially stronger party and offer limited protection to the other party. These factors would tend to favour a regime that applies by default.

In turn, this raises the question of whether opt outs from such a regime for cohabitants should be possible. In the case of married couples, pre-nuptial agreements offer the possibility of opting out of some of the financial obligations of marriage. However, it is not possible to opt out of a requirement to meet financial needs.[23] Pre-nuptial agreements are themselves not universally accepted. Herring, for example, argues that there are two primary reasons that such agreements should not be allowed.[24] First, intimate relationships are inherently unpredictable and 'any attempt to set down the parties' rights and responsibilities is likely to work against the interests of a partner who suffers an unexpected loss or sacrifice. These burdens are likely to fall on women as a result of care work …'[25] Second, '[t]here are important broader societal interests which will not be captured in an agreement between the parties'.[26] I am less convinced by arguments around the state interest in such agreements, for example that such agreements avoid costs to the public purse[27] or help to prevent gender inequality,[28] because I see the state as having an obligation in such matters too, which is separate from the obligation between the parties. However, it is possible to see the concern about opt outs as being grounded in the relationship between the parties.[29] If legal obligations are imposed because of the interdependence inherent in the relationship then, as

[22] Heenan (n 9).

[23] *Radmacher (formerly Granatino) v Granatino* [2010] UKSC 42.

[24] J Herring, *Family Law and the Relational Self* (Cambridge University Press, 2019) 154–55.

[25] ibid 154.

[26] ibid 155.

[27] J Herring, 'Why Financial Orders on Divorce Should Be Unfair' (2005) 19 *International Journal of Law, Policy and the Family* 218.

[28] Herring (n 24) 155; Herring (ibid).

[29] On the importance of such obligations being grounded in these relationships see, for example, Ferguson (n 9).

Herring's first objection recognises, the possibility of an opt out means that the burden of care falls on the carer and privileged irresponsibility is enabled. Given the concerns that I have outlined about autonomy, and my suggestion that care should be placed at the centre of family law, the need to recognise care outweighs demands for autonomy in this context. Nevertheless, this does not necessarily mean that pre-nups should be entirely prohibited.

More convincing justifications for pre-nuptial agreements are that they offer certainty in a discretionary system and that they enable parties to agree upon matters that lie beyond the scope of a court's powers, for example around the treatment of chattels. Allowing for pre-nups in some form may, therefore, be desirable. These should, however, be subject to the requirement that the provision made in such an agreement could not be less than the law would require. For example, provision would have to be the greater of a sum to meet needs or a half share of the marital assets. This is not without practical complexity: as Herring highlights, party needs may be very different at divorce from what was envisioned when the agreement was made. Nevertheless, provided safeguards are in place, in principle there seems to be no problem with allowing pre-nuptial agreements for these purposes.

What does this mean for cohabiting relationships? If there is a relationship of interdependence combined with caring responsibilities then, in principle, there appears to be no reason to offer the possibility for partners to opt out of these obligations. However, the diversity of cohabiting relationships means it may be difficult to identify the relationships to which these conditions apply. For that reason, there may be some merit in allowing couples to make an agreement to clarify that the scheme does not apply to them. It would, however, be important to think about the requirements for such an opt out. These would need to balance protection by ensuring that such opt outs were not misused against, for example, the costs of legal advice.

IV. Rethinking the Legal Framework for Married Couples

As Chapter 3 outlined, the legal framework dealing with the financial consequences of divorce is flexible and can, at least theoretically, respond to individual circumstances. Nevertheless, as that chapter explained, neoliberal-influenced ideas of autonomy have become increasingly important in the way that framework is employed. The result is that caregiving responsibilities are undervalued. In particular, research makes clear that women do worse financially on divorce than men, which is connected to their greater caring responsibilities.[30]

[30] H Fisher and H Low, 'Recovery from Divorce: Comparing High and Low Income Couples' (2016) 30 *International Journal of Law, Policy and the Family* 338; H Fisher and H Low, 'Who Wins, Who

This section suggests statutory reform of the law. It also goes further than the section dealing with the position of unmarried couples by setting out a concrete idea for reform, rather than a series of options. In contrast to the position of cohabitants, married couples are a more easily identifiable group because the presence of a marriage ceremony gives a straightforward measure of membership. Further, unlike the position of cohabitants, married couples have a bespoke legal framework. This means that reform has a clear starting point for comparison; for cohabiting couples there is no bespoke regime that provides a comparison. There may well be other options for reforming the law that would also place care at the centre. Nevertheless, it was felt important to offer a possibility here based on that objective for several reasons.

First, the Government has indicated its intention to review the law in this area,[31] as has the Law Commission.[32] The issue of reform is, therefore, highly topical. Second, and relatedly, the most prominent proposal for reform at present is the Divorce (Financial Provision) Bill, the provisions of which were outlined in Chapter 4. Given the emphasis in that Bill on individual ideas of autonomy, and the limitations of those ideas in the family law context which this book has identified, it seems important to offer an alternative option to inform debates around reform. Third, when the Law Commission previously reviewed the law in this area, the principles underpinning the law were not contested,[33] although specific problems with the law were identified. Thus, there is a framework upon which to base proposals for reform. For all of these reasons, and while the proposals outlined here are not intended to dictate the only possible outcome for a reform based upon placing care at the centre of family law, this section offers an option for reforming the law of financial remedies on divorce.

A. The Proposal in Outline

This section outlines one option for amending Matrimonial Causes Act 1973, s 25, to place care at the centre of family law. What follows is s 25 set out in this amended form. The subsequent sections explain the justifications for the changes made. In particular, the chapter will go on to explain how the reforms serve to make care more visible in the law.

Loses and Who Recovers from Divorce?' in J Miles and R Probert (eds), *Sharing Lives, Dividing Assets* (Hart Publishing, 2009).

[31] HL Deb 8 June 2020, vol 677, col 96.

[32] Law Commission, 'Financial Remedies on Divorce' (4 April 2023) www.lawcom.gov.uk/project/financial-remedies-on-divorce/ accessed 28 April 2023.

[33] Law Commission, *Matrimonial Property, Needs and Agreements* (Law Com No 343, 2014) para 1.24.

25 Matters to which court is to have regard in deciding how to exercise its powers under ss. 23, 24, 24A, 24B and 24E

(1) In deciding whether to exercise its powers under section 23, 24, 24A, 24B or 24E above, and if so in what manner—

(a) It shall be the objective of the court to meet the financial needs of the parties and of any children of the family who have not attained the age of 18. First consideration must be given to the welfare while a minor of any child of the family who has not attained the age of eighteen.

(b) If the resources available exceed the amount required to meet the financial needs of the parties and children of the family who have not yet attained the age of 18, then the court shall have regard to the principles of compensation and sharing in deciding how to divide the parties' assets.

(2) As regards the exercise of the powers of the court under section 23(1)(a), (b) or (c), 24, 24A, 24B or 24E above in relation to a party to the marriage, the court shall in particular have regard to the following matters when deciding how best to achieve the objectives set out in section 25(1) and 25(1A)—

(a) the income, earning capacity, property and other financial resources which each of the parties to the marriage has or is likely to have in the foreseeable future, including in the case of earning capacity any increase in that capacity which it would in the opinion of the court be reasonable to expect a party to the marriage to take steps to acquire;

(b) the financial needs, obligations and responsibilities which each of the parties to the marriage has or is likely to have in the foreseeable future;

(c) the standard of living enjoyed by the family before the breakdown of the marriage;

(d) the age of each party to the marriage and the duration of the marriage;

(e) any physical or mental disability of either of the parties to the marriage;

(f) the contributions which each of the parties has made or is likely in the foreseeable future to make to the welfare of the family, including any contribution by looking after the home or caring for the family;

(fx) the caregiving responsibilities which each of the parties has undertaken during the marriage and the likely impact of such caregiving responsibilities on their future financial needs.

(g) the conduct of each of the parties, if that conduct is such that it would in the opinion of the court be inequitable to disregard it;

(h) in the case of proceedings for divorce or nullity of marriage, the value to each of the parties to the marriage of any benefit which, by reason of the dissolution or annulment of the marriage, that party will lose the chance of acquiring.

(2A) For the purposes of this section—

'financial needs' means the sum required to meet the housing and income needs of the parties and any children of the family both at the time of the court's determination and in the future. That sum shall be determined in light of the parties' standard of living during the marriage and such other of the factors set out in section 25(2) as may be relevant.

'compensation' means that where either of the parties has suffered, or is likely to suffer, an economic disadvantage or receive an economic benefit arising from the way in which the parties have conducted their marriage, any financial award should reflect this.

'sharing' means that unless an unequal division of assets is required by the principles of financial needs or compensation, the parties' matrimonial property shall be divided equally between them. The proportions in which non-matrimonial property should be shared between the parties is to be determined by reference to the factors in section 25(2).

'caregiving' means the direct meeting of needs for care of family members.

B. How Does the Amended Section 25 Make Care Visible and Recognise its Value?

Chapter 6 argued that for the law adequately to deal with the unequal financial consequences of caring on separation, care must be placed at the centre of family law. The redrafted section 25 above attempts to reconcile this objective with the need for the law to respond to a wide range of circumstances including, for example, cases in which parties do not have children, or have caring responsibilities to family members other than children. This consideration informs the way in which caring features in the redrafted section 25. Rather than being the objective of the section, 'caregiving' is added to the factors to be considered in section 25(2).

As described below, the overarching objective of section 25 is, as within existing case law, to meet needs, or to share or compensate for relationship-generated disadvantage in cases where resources exceed needs. The inclusion of caregiving in section 25(2) is, however, designed to draw attention explicitly to the fact that caregiving creates financial needs that are not necessarily generated by other types of contribution. It is not suggested that the current incarnation of section 25 cannot take account of the costs of caregiving. For example, caregiving responsibilities are likely to impact on the assessment of a party's needs.[34] However, for section 25 to do so adequately requires a full appreciation of what caregiving responsibilities entail. As discussed, this sort of understanding appears absent at times in both case law and in the viewpoints of some parents. Thus, the inclusion of caregiving as a separate factor is designed to ensure that it is visible and properly considered in any analysis.

Adopting Tronto's definition,[35] 'caregiving' is defined as 'the direct meeting of needs for care of family members'. This is designed to make clear the difference between the sort of intensive day-to-day care which has economic ramifications and other forms of care. Additionally, the inclusion of caregiving as a separate factor from contributions is designed to draw attention to the difference between caregiving and contributions more broadly. Caregiving is different from other contributions because it often continues beyond the end of the relationship. Thus,

[34] Matrimonial Causes Act 1973, s 25(2)(b).
[35] Tronto (n 8) 106–108.

not only might past economic disadvantage have future effects, but there may continue to be an impact on the ability to engage in paid work into the future.

Caregiving is not limited to the care of children. It might also cover the care of elderly parents or the children of former relationships. This complicates matters: for example, it is perhaps easier to see the consequences of caring for the children of both parties as causally connected to a marriage than the care of one's own elderly parents.[36] However, the variety of different marriages, the interdependence that often characterises them, the extent to which the family is seen as being responsible for caregiving and the economic impact of caregiving for the party who performs it, makes it important for the law to be flexible enough to deal with these different situations.

This focus on caregiving is not designed to eliminate the objective of financial independence altogether. There are important reasons for parties to be able to move on with their lives after divorce. For that reason, it is not suggested that the encouragement in the statute to achieve a clean break should be amended.[37] Rather, the aim of making caregiving an explicit factor in section 25(2) is to make clearer the factors that may interfere with the ability to achieve a clean break. This is particularly important for those without legal advice. However, given the increasing moves towards a clean break in practice,[38] and the gendered financial outcomes of divorce,[39] there may also be reason to remind lawyers of this too.

In including the reference to caregiving, it is important to recognise that a court would be unlikely to engage in a forensic examination of the history of the parties' relationship. This does not, however, mean that the inclusion of this factor serves no purpose. At present, care is largely invisible and, as explained above, the inclusion of an explicit reference is designed to highlight that care has economic consequences. There may be cases where parents have spent equal time looking after their children during their relationship while performing different aspects of care. The revised framework would be capable of capturing this, although in practice a court is likely to shy away from this sort of enquiry. However, the greater concern is the much more common situation where there are clear differences in the roles that parents perform in terms of paid work and care, which have different economic consequences. The inclusion of 'caregiving' draws attention to this fact. This may mean that practically 'caregiving' is used in a broad-brush way. Nevertheless, the use of the language of 'caregiving' is important when we start to think about the law applying on separation more holistically. Consistently differentiating between different types of care within the legal framework is an important part of trying to embed more nuanced understandings of care into the law more generally.

[36] Heenan (n 9).

[37] Matrimonial Causes Act 1973, s 25A.

[38] E Hitchings and J Miles, 'Financial Remedies on Divorce: the Need for Evidence-based Reform' (2018) www.nuffieldfoundation.org/sites/default/files/files/briefing%20paper%20Jun%202018%20FINAL.pdf accessed 28 April 2023.

[39] Fisher and Low (2016) (n 30).

These suggested reforms to the law of financial provision are at odds with the reforms to periodical payments suggested in the Divorce (Financial Provision) Bill. The Bill limits periodical payments to a period:

> … of not more than five years from the date of the decree of divorce, such period not to be exceeded unless the court is satisfied that there is no other means of making provision for a party to the marriage and that that party would otherwise be likely to suffer serious financial hardship as a result.[40]

The amendments suggested here do not specify a time limit for periodical payments. Research demonstrates that joint lives orders are rare.[41] In many cases this is because they are simply unaffordable.[42] However, there remain cases where such orders are appropriate or necessary. The aim of the reform is not to revert to the pre-1984 version of the Matrimonial Causes Act and the minimal loss principle.[43] Neither is it to achieve a situation in which the marital standard of living becomes the benchmark for life after separation. Rather, it is to challenge the underlying assumptions of neoliberal-influenced ideas of autonomy, which fail to recognise that the ways in which families structure their lives can have ongoing economic ramifications. Instead of seeing financial independence as an abstract goal to be achieved at all costs, the aim of financial provision on divorce should be to achieve a transition to financial independence in a way that recognises context and, in particular, the fact that the decisions made as part of family life may affect individuals' ability to be financially self-sufficient when relationships break down.

V. The Financial Arrangements for Children

In Chapter 3, I explored the potential for caregiving to be shared unequally in situations where time was shared equally. A particularly stark example was Esther's situation in which she collected the children from school, fed them, took them to clubs and then dropped them at her ex-partner's house before bedtime. This meant that he would be entitled to the reduction for overnight stays under the child support formula while Esther bore many of the financial costs of caregiving on those evenings.

[40] Section 5(1)(c).

[41] Hitchings and Miles (n 38).

[42] G Douglas, 'Sharing Financial Losses as Well as Gains on Divorce' (2018) 32 *Australian Journal of Family Law* 108, 129.

[43] This principle provided that in exercising its discretion, a court should 'exercise those powers as to place the parties, so far as it is practicable and, having regard to their conduct, just to do so, in the financial position in which they would have been if the marriage had not broken down and each had properly discharged his or her financial obligations and responsibilities towards the other' (Matrimonial Causes Act 1973, s 25(1) as originally enacted).

An important way of making care more central to family law in this area would be to explore a new method of calculating child support based upon the costs of caregiving, rather than focusing exclusively on the division of time. This research looked at parents' experiences of separation in a holistic way. It did not ask specifically about the level of child support being paid or for financial information which would help to contextualise the level of those payments and the extent to which they met the costs of caregiving. For that reason, it is beyond the scope of this research to suggest the precise nature of such a reform. However, like the section on the financial arrangements of cohabiting couples above, this section attempts to provide insights that may inform future research.

A useful starting point for thinking further about alternative approaches to child support is the following extract from Neil's interview, in which he described his approach:

> So what I did was I started off by working out what the, what is the bare minimum that the Child Support Agency say I should, that I should pay and on looking at that it was, it was clear that it wasn't really very much and, you know, the jam would be spread very thinly. So, uh, what I did was try to work out the cost of keeping two [children] – so the additional cost. So a, a, a single woman can live for x, a single woman with two children needs a different house and consumes more bread in a week and can, you know, burns up more diesel in their car. I, I tried to work out what the difference was between single woman on her own and, um, single woman with two children for two thirds of the week. Um, I did lots and lots of sums. I found that, basically, how that worked was, say for example children go to football club, um, the football club costs thirty quid a) my earnings are 66 per cent of the, um, the total income between us so I will pay 66 per cent of the item. So it is in proportion to earnings you know.

This suggests two useful considerations when thinking about child support. First, Neil recognises that the costs of caregiving are wide-ranging. While some costs, such as food, are relatively obvious, others, such as fuel costs or housing are perhaps less apparent at face value. Going further, indirect costs such as working less to be able to pick children up from school (which might save the cost of after-school care for both parents) are also evident in situations like Esther's. Trying to account for these costs is complex and where married couples are concerned it will be important to ensure there is no double-counting; many of these costs could overlap with the calculation of adult needs or the calculation of compensation for relationship-generated disadvantage.

The second consideration in the extract from Neil's interview above is parents' relative incomes. In England and Wales, only the income of the paying parent is considered in the statutory formula. However, there is public support for an approach that takes the incomes of both parents into account.[44] Future research could usefully explore the feasibility of such an approach.

[44] C Bryson et al, 'Child Maintenance: How Would the British Public Calculate What the State Should Require Parents to Pay? (Nuffield Foundation, 2015) www.nuffieldfoundation.org/wp-content/uploads/2019/11/Attitudes_maintenance_v_FINAL28229.pdf accessed 28 April 2023.

In addition to the matters highlighted by Neil's interview, another consideration for future research is the impact of shared care arrangements. In England and Wales, where there is truly equal shared care, neither parent is required to pay child maintenance.[45] However, if one parent is receiving child benefit then there is a rebuttable presumption that that person is providing a greater degree of care (and is therefore entitled to child maintenance).[46] Whereas in cases where there is a non-resident parent, reductions in payments are based on the number of nights a child spends with them, here the assessment is more holistic. Overnight stays are not a 'trump card'[47] and it has been suggested that it is likely to be an 'unusual occurrence' for there to be no non-resident parent.[48] Given the emphasis on parents agreeing child maintenance between themselves, it is hard to assess the extent to which such cases exist in practice and whether there is truly shared care in such cases. However, this research has revealed that care is often invisible to those who are not performing it and that even in shared time arrangements care may not be shared equally. Therefore, something that it may be useful to explore further is how parents assess whether care is equally shared (if they even engage with that question at all) and whether parents are in agreement about this.

Finally, it may be worth considering whether, even in genuinely shared care cases, there is reason to depart from a position whereby no child maintenance is payable. In Sweden, child maintenance may be payable in such cases if there is a big income disparity between the parents ('In that case it may be good for the child if the parent with a higher income pays child support in order for the child's standard of living not to vary too much from one week to another'[49]). While top-up awards are possible in England and Wales where a parent's income exceeds £156,000 gross,[50] these sorts of claims would not be available in shared care cases. The effect of a case being classified as a case of shared care is that neither parent is a non-resident parent.[51] There is not, therefore, a non-resident parent who can be ordered to make a top-up award.

VI. Child Arrangements

When it comes to child arrangements, the question of how to make care more central to family law is more complex. Previous chapters have revealed that care is often invisible in this arena too. For example, Chapter 3 highlighted that care

[45] Child Support Maintenance Calculation Regulations 2012, reg 50.

[46] ibid.

[47] *JS v Secretary of State for Work and Pensions and another (CSM) (Child support – maintenance assessments – calculations)* [2017] UKUT 296 (AAC).

[48] *CF v SSWP & CG (CSM)* [2018] UKUT 276 (AAC).

[49] Forsakringskassan, 'The Child Lives with Both Parents' www.forsakringskassan.se/english/parents/parents-who-do-not-live-together/the-child-lives-with-both-parents accessed 28 April 2023.

[50] Child Support Act 1991, s 8(6).

[51] Child Support Maintenance Calculation Regulations 2012, reg 50.

is rarely discussed in child arrangements cases unless it is deficient. Likewise, in Sweden, the dominance of shared residence arrangements on separation without care being shared equally beforehand suggests that care is less important than other factors in these decisions. However, the question of how to address this is more difficult. There may be very good reasons for caring patterns to change on separation. Even where one parent has been the primary carer, in many cases the other parent will have played an active role in that child's life on a daily basis which will not be possible in the same way if parents are living separately (see the discussion of Louise's partner's experience in Chapter 3 for an example). There may, therefore, be very good reasons to reassess how care is provided after separation. What is important is that an understanding of caregiving is not lost in this process.

Douglas suggests that where arguments are made to recognise care in the law, 'what is actually entailed is not so much the imposition of an obligation to care for others in the relationship, as an obligation on those others to "recognise" (compensate) such care'.[52] This approach makes sense. Imposing an obligation to care is difficult to enforce[53] and does not guarantee the quality of that care. The reforms outlined in the preceding sections are, therefore, important to ensure that where caring is performed unequally the financial implications are addressed. However, this does not mean that care cannot be made more central in the law relating to child arrangements.

There are several aspects to consider. First, is the question of the legal framework itself. As with the law relating to cohabitation, the need to place care at the centre of family law does not necessarily dictate a particular form that the law should take. Nevertheless, reflecting on what care involves can offer insights into the shortcomings of the legal framework.

Chapter 2 highlighted that care within families has a relational element. Prominent critiques of the welfare principle centre on the suggestion that it places the interests of children above those of parents and any other relevant parties, regardless of the detriment that might be caused to them.[54] Alternatives typically consider ways in which the welfare principle could be recast or replaced so as to balance parental and child rights more explicitly.[55] Herring, for example, suggests a reconceptualised version of the principle in which the issue to be resolved is seen as 'deciding what is a proper parent-child relationship' rather than 'weighing two competing interests' with the goal of promoting welfare through ensuring that the child 'lives in a fair and just relationship with each parent'.[56] However, not

[52] Douglas (n 10) 7.

[53] K Lynch, *Care and Capitalism* (Polity, 2022) 22.

[54] See, for example, H Reece, 'The Paramountcy Principle: Consensus or Construct?' (1996) 49 *Current Legal Problems* 267; J Eekelaar, 'Beyond the Welfare Principle' (2002) 14 *Child and Family Law Quarterly* 237; J Herring, 'The Welfare Principle and the Rights of Parents' in A Bainham et al (eds), *What is a Parent? A Socio-Legal Analysis* (Hart Publishing, 1999).

[55] In relation to the former, see, for example Eekelaar (ibid). In relation to the latter see, for example, Herring (ibid).

[56] Herring (n 54) 102.

all academics share this concern with the welfare principle. George, for example, suggests that the welfare principle is already used in this way in practice: 'the harm to others – particularly a parent or other family member – will in itself impact adversely on the child, which will be a significant factor to take into account when deciding what is in the child's best interests in the first place'.[57] Given the central role of the welfare principle in the law relating to children, it is beyond the scope of this book to determine whether, and if so how, the principle ought to be recast or replaced. However, when thinking about the application of the principle to child arrangements, the need to recognise the relational nature of the care being performed is important.

This need to focus on care in the context of a particular relationship also raises questions about the role of presumptions in the application of the welfare principle. It is beyond the scope of this book to deal with this issue comprehensively, but the nuances of responsive caregiving discussed in previous chapters suggest a need for caution where presumptions, such as the presumption of continued parental involvement[58] and the case law 'assumption' of contact,[59] apply if the objective of the law is to achieve caring arrangements that best meet children's needs.

A second consideration when thinking about how to make care more central in child arrangements on separation concerns the type of information available to the court. Tronto's understanding of care suggests that to ensure good care it is vital to understand the perspectives of care receivers (children in this scenario). This final phase of Tronto's understanding of care allows an assessment of how well care is provided. My empirical research did not look specifically at this question, but there is a wide body of literature looking at how to ensure children's voices are heard in the court process and in mediation. Taking meaningful steps to engage with this issue would be an important way of centering care in the law relating to child arrangements.

It is also vital not to lose the focus on caregiving when thinking about child arrangements. As discussed in Chapter 3, this research has found that care is not always shared equally even where time is. This is a complex issue to address. As outlined at the outset of this chapter, it is important to think practically about the sorts of decisions that courts can make. Is it realistic for a judge to make an order than prescribes which parent buys school uniform, or takes children to the doctor? What happens when something arises that is not envisaged by the order? How would such an order respond to children's changing needs as they get older?

There may be a role for guidance in tackling this issue. For example, much like the Family Justice Council guidelines on Financial Needs,[60] there might be scope to develop guidance around what caring entails to inform the judiciary and also

[57] R George, *Ideas and Debates in Family Law* (Hart Publishing, 2012).

[58] Children Act 1989, s 1(2A).

[59] *Re L (Contact: Domestic Violence); Re V (Contact: Domestic Violence); Re M (Contact: Domestic Violence); Re H (Contact: Domestic Violence)* [2000] 2 FLR 334.

[60] Family Justice Council, 'Guidance on "Financial Needs" on Divorce' (FJC, 2016).

to support parents in making their own arrangements. Thought would need to be given as to how parents could access such guidance; research demonstrates the challenges that litigants in person face in trying to access information about the law.[61] Even for those who did find this guidance, there are also questions about how effective it would be in shaping behaviours. Research into the effectiveness of the Separated Parents Information Programme,[62] for example, found that whilst parents were positive about the course overall, it had limited impact on parental cooperation and conflict. Thus, even if this sort of guidance could be made a meaningful part of a parenting course, challenges are likely to remain. For example, such a course is most likely to affect those who take it, even if the materials are made available more widely. Further, trying to design a course that influences behaviour is likely to take time and require refinement.[63]

It is also vital to meaningfully address the financial consequences of an unequal sharing of care outlined in the preceding sections.

VII. Conclusion

Placing care at the heart of family law means thinking about family law differently and recognising the ways in which families live their lives. Rather than basing family law on ideas of autonomy (neoliberal or otherwise) the law must recognise the central role of care in family life. There is not a one-size fits all approach to this. Different families function differently. I have suggested two ways in which the law might better recognise caring responsibilities: through the use of a framework (outlined in Chapter 6) which works alongside the existing law, and through possible reforms of the law (outlined in this chapter).

As I have emphasised throughout, this should not be seen as an alternative to state support for caregiving. Rather, the purpose is to complement a state response and ensure a holistic approach to caring responsibilities. Finally, and relatedly, while my focus has been on the substantive content of family law this does not undermine the need to think seriously about issues of access to justice: my scepticism about the ability of the substantive law to improve access to justice does not mean we should ignore this pressing issue, albeit that this is a problem which it is beyond the scope of this book to solve. A perfect substantive law is useless if no-one has access to it.

[61] J Mant, 'Placing Litigants in Person at the Centre of the Post-LASPO Family Court Process' (2020) 32 *Child and Family Law Quarterly* 421.

[62] L Trinder et al, 'Building Bridges? An Evaluation of the Costs and Effectiveness of the Separated Parents Information Programme (PIP)' (Department for Education) https://assets.publishing.service.gov.uk/government/uploads/system/uploads/attachment_data/file/181695/DFE-RR140.pdf accessed 28 April 2023.

[63] ibid.

BIBLIOGRAPHY

Adams-Prassl, A, Boneva, T, Golin, M and Rauh, C, 'Inequality in the Impact of the Coronavirus Shock: Evidence from Real Time Surveys' (2020) 189 *Journal of Public Economics* 1.

Andrew, A, Bandiera, O, Costa Dias, M and Landais, C, 'The Careers and Time Use of Mothers and Fathers' (IFS, 12 March 2021) https://ifs.org.uk/publications/careers-and-time-use-mothers-and-fathers.

Attar Taylor, E and Scott, J 'Gender' in D Phillips, J Curtice, M Phillips and J Perry (eds), *British Social Attitudes: The 35th Report* (The National Centre for Social Research, 2018) www.bsa.natcen.ac.uk/latest-report/british-social-attitudes-35/gender.aspx.

Barker, N, 'Sex and the Civil Partnership Act: The Future of (Non) Conjugality?' (2006) 14 *Feminist Legal Studies* 241.

—— 'Why Care? "Deserving Family Members" and the Conservative Movement for Broader Family Recognition' in J Wallbank and J Herring (eds), *Vulnerability, Care and Family Law* (Routledge, 2013).

Barlow, A, 'Solidarity, Autonomy and Equality: Mixed Messages for the Family?' (2015) 27(3) *Child and Family Law Quarterly* 223.

Barlow, A, Duncan, S, James, G and Park A, *Cohabitation, Marriage and the Law: Social Change and Legal Reform in the 21st Century* (Hart Publishing, 2005).

Barlow, A, Hunter, R, Smithson, J and Ewing, J, 'Mapping Paths to Family Justice: Briefing Paper and Report on Key Findings' (University of Exeter, 2014) http://socialsciences.exeter.ac.uk/media/universityofexeter/collegeofsocialsciencesandinternationalstudies/lawimages/familyregulationandsociety/pdfs/Mapping_briefing_paper_final_post_conference_version___ISBN.pdf.

Barlow, A and Smithson, J, 'Legal Assumptions, Cohabitants' Talk and the Rocky Road to Reform' (2010) 22 *Child and Family Law Quarterly* 328.

Bhattacharya, T, 'Introduction: Mapping Social Reproduction Theory' in T Bhattacharya (ed), *Social Reproduction Theory* (Pluto Press, 2017).

Bix, B, 'Private Ordering and Family Law' (2010) 23 *Journal of the American Academy of Matrimonial Lawyers* 249.

Björk, S, 'Doing Morally Intelligible Fatherhood: Swedish Fathers' Accounts of Their Parental Part-time Work Choices' (2013) 11 *Fathering* 221.

Björnberg, U, 'Ideology and Choice between Work and Care: Swedish Family Policy for Working Parents' (2002) 22 *Critical Social Policy* 33.

Bloch, K and Taylor, T, 'Welfare Queens and Anchor Babies' in M Vandenbeld Giles (ed), *Mothering in the Age of Neoliberalism* (Demeter Press, 2014).

Booth, M, *The Almost Nearly Perfect People* (Random House, 2014).

Boyd, SB and Young, CFL, 'From Same-Sex to No Sex? Towards Recognition of (Same-Sex) Relationships in Canada' (2003) *Seattle Journal of Social Justice* 757.

Bradford, S, 'Birth Characteristics in England and Wales: 2020' (ONS, 13 January 2022) www.ons.gov.uk/peoplepopulationandcommunity/birthsdeathsandmarriages/livebirths/bulletins/birthcharacteristicsinenglandandwales/2020#age-of-parents.

Bradley, D, 'Sexual Equality and Maintenance Allowances in Sweden' (1989) 9 *Oxford Journal of Legal Studies* 403.

—— *Family Law and Political Culture* (Sweet & Maxwell, 1996).

Brattström, M, 'Bodelning mellan makar – verklighetens betydelse för framtidens regelutformning' (Särtryck från Tidskrift for Familierett, Arverett og Barnevernsrettslige Spørsmål (FAB), 2011) (translated using Google translate).

—— 'Spouses' Pension Rights & Financial Settlement after Divorce', *Scandinavian Studies in Law* (Social Private Law, Volume 50) 334.
Breach, A and Li, Y, 'Gender Pay Gap by Ethnicity in Britain – Briefing' (Fawcett Society and University of Manchester, March 2017) www.fawcettsociety.org.uk/gender-pay-by-ethnicity-britain.
Brewer, M and Nandi, A, 'Partnership Dissolution: How Does it Affect Income, Employment and Well-being? (Institute for Social & Economic Research, September 2014) www.econstor.eu/bitstream/10419/126462/1/79669074X.pdf.
Brewer, M and Patrick, R, 'Pandemic Pressures' (January 2021) www.resolutionfoundation.org/app/uploads/2021/01/Pandemic-pressures.pdf.
Brown, W, 'American Nightmare: Neoliberalism, Neoconservatism, and De-Democratization' (2006) 34 *Political Theory* 690.
Bryson, C, Ellman, IM, McKay, S and Miles, J, 'Child Maintenance: How Would the British Public Calculate What the State Should Require Parents to Pay? (Nuffield Foundation, 2015) www.nuffield-foundation.org/wp-content/uploads/2019/11/Attitudes_maintenance_v_FINAL28229.pdf.
Buckley, L, 'Relational Theory and Choice Rhetoric in the Supreme Court of Canada' (2015) 29 *Canadian Journal of Family Law* 251.
Bussemaker, J, 'Recent Changes in European Welfare State Services: A Comparison of Child Care Politics in the United Kingdom, Sweden, Germany and the Netherlands' 1997 Program for the Study of Germany and Europe 7.6 http://aei.pitt.edu/63647/.
Bygren, M and Duvander, AZ, 'Parents' Workplace Situation and Fathers' Parental Leave Use' (2006) 68 *Journal of Marriage and the Family* 363.
Carlson, L, *Fundamentals of Swedish Law*, 2nd edn (studentlitteratur Ab, 2012).
Chelliah, J, 'Austerity and Gender Neutrality' in M Vandenbeld Giles (ed), *Mothering in the Age of Neoliberalism* (Demeter Press, 2014).
Cheng, Z et al, 'Working Parents, Financial Insecurity, and Childcare: Mental Health in the Time of COVID-19 in the UK' (2021) 19 *Review of Economics of the Household* 136.
Chun, H '"Women's Work Penalty" in Access to Flexible Working Arrangements across Europe' (2019) 25 *European Journal of Industrial Relations* 23.
Chung, H, 'Return of the 1950s Housewife? How to Stop Coronavirus Lockdown Reinforcing Sexist Gender Roles' (*The Conversation*, 30 March 2022) https://theconversation.com/return-of-the-1950s-housewife-how-to-stop-coronavirus-lockdown-reinforcing-sexist-gender-roles-134851.
Chung, H and van der Lippe, T, 'Flexible Working, Work-Life Balance, and Gender Equality: Introduction' (2020) 151 *Social Indicator Research* 365.
F Churchill, 'Two-thirds of Businesses Now Provide Enhanced Maternity Pay, Poll Finds' (*People Management*, 24 May 2021) www.peoplemanagement.co.uk/article/1747219/two-thirds-of-businesses-now-provide-enhanced-maternity-pay.
Collins, C, 'Is Maternal Guilt a Cross-National Experience?' (2021) 44 *Qualitative Sociology* 1.
Commission on European Family Law, 'Marriage Code of Sweden' (official translation by the Swedish Government with amendments since 1994 unofficially translated by M Jänterä-Jareborg) http://ceflonline.net/wp-content/uploads/Sweden-Divorce-Legislation.pdf.
Cooke, E, Barlow, A and Callus, T, 'Community of Property A Regime for England and Wales?' (The Nuffield Foundation, 2006).
Costa Dias, M, Joyce, R and Parodi, F, 'The Gender Pay Gap in the UK: Children and Experience in Work' (IFS, February 2018) https://ifs.org.uk/publications/gender-pay-gap-uk-children-and-experience-work.
Cretney, S, 'Private Ordering and Divorce – How Far Can We Go?' [2003] *Family Law* 399.
Cretney, S, Masson, J and Bailey-Harris, R, *Principles of Family Law*, 7th edn (Sweet & Maxwell, 2002).
Croda, E and Grossbard, S, 'Women Pay the Price of COVID-19 More than Men' (2020) 19 *Review of Economics of the Household* 1.
Crowley, JE, 'Staying at Home or Working for Pay? Attachment to Modern Mothering Identities' (2014) 34 *Sociological Spectrum* 114.
Curtice, J, Clery, E, Perry, J, Phillips, M and Rahim, N (eds), *British Social Attitudes 36* (The National Centre for Social Research, 2019) www.bsa.natcen.ac.uk/media/39363/bsa_36.pdf.

Davies, R, 'Coronavirus and the Social Impacts on Great Britain: 17 July 2020' (ONS, 17 July 2020) www.ons.gov.uk/peoplepopulationandcommunity/healthandsocialcare/healthandwellbeing/bulletins/coronavirusandthesocialimpactsongreatbritain/17july2020#work.

Davis, G, Pearce, J, Bird, R, Woodward, H and Wallace, C, 'Ancillary Relief Outcomes' (2000) 12 *Child and Family Law Quarterly* 43.

de los Reyes, P, 'Practising Intersectionality, Challenging Power' in K Dalborg and M Löfgren (eds), *Perspectives on Cultural Leadership. The Fika Project* (2016) https://europeanculturalleadershipdotorg.files.wordpress.com/2015/10/perspectives_web.pdf accessed 11 January 2023.

—— 'Working Life Inequalities: Do We Need Intersectionality' (2017) 8 *Society, Health and Vulnerability* 14.

Deech, R, 'Financial Provision Reform' [2018] *Family Law* 1251.

Department for Culture Media & Sport, 'Attitudes towards Equality: Findings from the YouGov Survey' (June 2014) https://assets.publishing.service.gov.uk/government/uploads/system/uploads/attachment_data/file/316290/Attitudes_towards_Equality.pdf.

Department for Education, 'Budget 2023: Everything You Need to Know about Childcare Support' (16 March 2023) https://educationhub.blog.gov.uk/2023/03/16/budget-2023-everything-you-need-to-know-about-childcare-support/.

Dermott, E, *Intimate Fatherhood A Sociological Analysis* (Routledge, 2008).

Diduck, A, 'Autonomy and Vulnerability in Family Law: the Missing Link' in J Wallbank and J Herring (eds), *Vulnerability, Care and Family Law* (Routledge, 2013).

—— 'Autonomy and Family Justice' (2016) 28 *Child and Family Law Quarterly* 133.

Douglas, G, *Obligation and Commitment in Family Law* (Hart Publishing, 2018).

—— 'Sharing Financial Losses as Well as Gains on Divorce' (2018) 32 *Australian Journal of Family Law* 108.

Douglas, G, Pearce, J and Woodward, H, 'A Failure of Trust: Resolving Property Disputes on Cohabitation Breakdown' (Cardiff Law School, 2007) https://orca.cf.ac.uk/5186/1/1.pdf.

Duffy, M, *Making Care Count* (Rutgers University Press, 2011).

Duvander, AZ and Ellingsaeter, AL, 'Cash for Childcare Schemes in the Nordic Welfare States: Diverse Paths, Diverse Outcomes' (2016) 18 *European Societies* 70.

Duvander, AZ, Ferrarini, T and Thalberg, S, 'Swedish Parental Leave and Gender Equality – Achievements and Reform Challenges in a European Perspective (Institute for Futures Studies, 2005) www.iffs.se/media/1118/20051201134956filU8YIJLRAaC7u4FV7gUmy.pdf.

Duvander, AZ and Korsell, N, 'Whose Days are Left? Separated Parents' Use of Parental Leave in Sweden' in R Nieuwenhuis and LC Maldonado (eds), *The Triple Bind of Single-parent Families* (Policy Press, 2018).

Eekelaar, J, 'Beyond the Welfare Principle' (2002) 14 *Child and Family Law Quarterly* 237.

EIGE, 'Gender Equality Index 2019: Sweden' https://eige.europa.eu/publications/gender-equality-index-2019-sweden.

Ekberg, J, Eriksson, R and Freibel, G, 'Parental Leave – A Policy Evaluation of the Swedish "Daddy-Month" Reform' (2013) 97 *Journal of Public Economics* 131.

Eldén, S and Anving, T, 'New Ways of Doing the "Good" and Gender Equal Family: Parents Employing Nannies and Au Pairs in Sweden' (2016) 21(4) *Sociological Research Online* www.socresonline.org.uk/21/4/2.html.

Ellingsaeter, AL, 'Cash for Childcare: Experiences from Finland, Norway and Sweden' (Friedrich Ebert Stiftung, April 2012) https://library.fes.de/pdf-files/id/09079.pdf.

Elvin-Nowak, Y and Thomsson, H, 'Motherhood as Idea and Practice: A Discursive Understanding of Employed Mothers in Sweden' (2001) 15 *Gender and Society* 407.

Emma, 'The Gender Wars of Household Chores: a Feminist Comic' (*The Guardian*, 26 May 2017) www.theguardian.com/world/2017/may/26/gender-wars-household-chores-comic.

Eurostat, 'Gender Pay Gap Statistics' (data from February 2021) https://ec.europa.eu/eurostat/statistics-explained/index.php?title=Gender_pay_gap_statistics#Gender_pay_gap_levels_vary_significantly_across_EU.

—— 'Higher Employment Rate for Men with Children' https://ec.europa.eu/eurostat/web/products-eurostat-news/-/ddn-20210809-1 accessed 22 June 2023.

Evertsson, M, Boye, K and Erman, J, 'Fathers on Call? A Study of the Sharing of Care Work between Parents in Sweden' (2018) 39 *Demographic Research* 33.

Family Justice Council, 'Guidance on "Financial Needs" on Divorce' (FJC, 2016).

Farquharson, C and Olorenshaw, H, 'The Changing Cost of Childcare' (IFS, May 2022) https://ifs.org.uk/sites/default/files/output_url_files/R210-The-changing-cost-of-childcare.pdf.

Ferguson, L, 'Family, Social Inequalities and the Persuasive Force of Interpersonal Obligation' (2008) 22 *International Journal of Law, Policy and the Family* 61.

Fineman, M, *The Autonomy Myth* (The New Press, 2004).

—— 'The Vulnerable Subject: Anchoring Equality in the Human Condition' (2008) 20 *Yale Journal of Law and Feminism* 1.

—— 'Vulnerability and Inevitable Inequality' (2017) 4 *Oslo Law Review* 133.

Fisher, H and Low, H, 'Who Wins, Who Loses and Who Recovers from Divorce?' in J Miles and R Probert (eds), *Sharing Lives, Dividing Assets* (Hart Publishing, 2009).

—— 'Recovery from Divorce: Comparing High and Low Income Couples' (2016) 30 *International Journal of Law, Policy and the Family* 338.

Försäkringskassan, 'Child Support When the Child Lives with You' www.forsakringskassan.se/english/parents/parents-who-do-not-live-together/if-your-children-live-with-you/child-support-when-the-child-lives-with-you.

—— 'Jämställd föräldraförsäkring' (Summary) www.forsakringskassan.se/download/18.7fc616c01814e179a9f355/1656676749850/jamstalld-foraldraforsakring-socialforsakringsrapport-2019-2.pdf.

—— 'Maintenance Support When the Child Lives with You' www.forsakringskassan.se/english/parents/parents-who-do-not-live-together/if-your-children-live-with-you/maintenance-support-when-the-child-lives-with-you.

—— 'The Child Lives with Both Parents' www.forsakringskassan.se/english/parents/parents-who-do-not-live-together/the-child-lives-with-both-parents.

Forsberg, L, 'Involved Parenthood: Everyday lives of Swedish Middle-Class Families' (DPhil Thesis, Linköping University, 2009).

George, R, *Ideas and Debates in Family Law* (Hart Publishing, 2012).

Gilligan, C, *In a Different Voice* (Harvard University Press, 2003).

Giuliani, G and Duvander, AZ, 'Cash-for-care Policy in Sweden: An Appraisal of Its Consequences in Female Employment' (2017) 26 *International Journal of Social Welfare* 49.

Glendon, MA, 'Is there a Future for Separate Property?' (1974) 8 *Family Law Quarterly* 315.

Global Institute of Women's Leadership, King's College London, Working Families and University of East Anglia, 'Working Parents, Flexibility and Job Quality: What Are the Trade-offs?' (2021) https://workingfamilies.org.uk/wp-content/uploads/2021/11/Working-parents-flexibility-and-job-quality-what-are-the-trade-offs.pdf.

González, M, Miret, P and Treviño, R, '"Just Living Together": Implications of Cohabitation for Fathers' Participation of Child Care in Western Europe' (2010) 23 *Demographic Research* 445.

Gordon-Bouvier, E, *Relational Vulnerability* (Palgrave Macmillan, 2020).

Government Bill 1993/94: 147 Gender Equality Policy: Shared Power – Shared Responsibility. Translation from J Ekberg, R Eriksson and G Freibel, 'Parental Leave –A Policy Evaluation of the Swedish "Daddy-Month" Reform' (2013) 97 *Journal of Public Economics* 131.

Gov.uk, 'Child Maintenance Service' www.gov.uk/child-maintenance-service/payments#:~:text=You%20have%20to%20pay%20a,the%20payment)%20for%20receiving%20parents accessed 23 June 2023.

—— 'Family Court Tables: April to June 2019 (Table 13)' (Ministry of Justice, 26 September 2019) www.gov.uk/government/statistics/family-court-statistics-quarterly-april-to-june-2019.

—— 'How the Child Maintenance Service Works out Child Maintenance' www.gov.uk/how-child-maintenance-is-worked-out.

Grossi, R 'Love as a Disadvantage in Law' (2018) 45 *Journal of Law and Society* 205.

Gunnarsson, Å, 'Introducing Independent Income Taxation in Sweden in 1971' (2016) FairTax Working Paper Series No 2, Forum for Studies on Law and Society https://umu.diva-portal.org/smash/get/diva2:930244/FULLTEXT01.pdf.

Haas, L, Allard, K and Hwang, P, 'The Impact of Organizational Culture on Men's Use of Parental Leave in Sweden' (2002) 5 *Community Work and Family* 319.

Haas, L and Hwang, CP, 'Policy is Not Enough – the Influence of the Gendered Workplace on Fathers' Use of Parental Leave in Sweden' (2019) 22 *Community, Work & Family* 58.

Hale, B, 'Equality and Autonomy in Family Law' (2011) *Journal of Social Welfare and Family Law* 3.

Hamilton, P, 'The "Good" Attached Mother: An Analysis of Postmaternal and Postracial Thinking in Birth and Breastfeeding Policy in Neoliberal Britain' (2016) 31 *Australian Feminist Studies* 410.

Hankivsky, O, 'Rethinking Care Ethics: On the Promise and Potential of an Intersectional Analysis' (2014) 108 *American Political Science Review* 252.

Harari, D, Bolton, P, Francis-Devine, B and Keep, M, 'Rising Cost of Living in the UK' (House of Commons Library, 20 December 2022) https://researchbriefings.files.parliament.uk/documents/CBP-9428/CBP-9428.pdf accessed 10 January 2023.

Harman, T, 'Neoliberalism, Governmentality, and Ethics' (2009) 6 *Foucault Studies* 37.

Heenan, A, 'Scuppering Schofield: The Impact of the EU Maintenance Regulation on Claims for Pension Sharing' [2012] *Family Law* 191.

—— 'Causal and Temporal Connections in Financial Remedy Cases: the Meaning of Marriage' (2018) 30(1) *Child and Family Law Quarterly* 75.

—— 'Neoliberal Autonomy and Financial Remedy Reform: Lessons from Sweden' (2020) 3 *Child and Family Law Quarterly* 263.

—— 'Haley v Haley: Family Law Arbitration and the New Frontier of Private Ordering' (2021) 84 *Modern Law Review* 1385.

—— 'Neoliberalism, Family Law, and the Devaluation of Care' (2021) 48 *Journal of Law and Society* 386.

—— 'The Meaning of Marriage and Approaches to the Division of Assets in Sweden, the Netherlands and England and Wales' in R Probert and S Thompson (eds), *Research Handbook on Marriage and Cohabitation* (Edward Elgar, forthcoming).

Held, V, *The Ethics of Care* (Oxford University Press, 2006).

Herring, J, 'The Welfare Principle and the Rights of Parents' in A Bainham, S Day-Sclater and M Richards (eds), *What is a Parent? A Socio-Legal Analysis* (Hart Publishing, 1999).

—— 'Why Financial Orders on Divorce Should Be Unfair' (2005) 19 *International Journal of Law, Policy and the Family* 218.

—— *Caring and the Law* (Hart Publishing, 2013).

—— 'Making Family Law More Careful' in J Wallbank and J Herring (eds), *Vulnerability, Care and Family Law* (Routledge, 2013).

—— *Relational Autonomy* (Springer, 2014).

—— *Family Law and the Relational Self* (Cambridge University Press, 2019).

—— 'Ethics of Care and Disability Rights: Complementary or Contradictory?' in L Gelsthorpe, P Mody and B Sloan (eds), *Spaces of Care* (Hart Publishing, 2020).

——*Family Law*, 10th edn (Pearson, 2021).

Hill, K and Webber, R, 'From Pandemic to Cost of Living Crisis: Low-income Households in Challenging Times' https://michaelharrison.org.uk/wp-content/uploads/2022/05/From-pandemic-to-cost-of-living-crisis-low-income-families-in-challenging-times-Full-report.pdf.

Hill Collins, P, 'Shifting the Center: Race, Class, and Feminist Theorising about Motherhood' in E Nakano Glenn, G Chang, and L Rennie Forcey (eds), *Mothering: Ideology, Experience, and Agency* (Routledge, 2016).

Hitchings, E and Miles, J, 'Financial Remedies on Divorce: the Need for Evidence-based Reform' (2018) www.nuffieldfoundation.org/sites/default/files/files/briefing%20paper%20Jun%202018%20FINAL.pdf.

HL Deb 8 June 2020, vol 677, col 96.

Hourston, P, 'Cost of Living Crisis' (Institute for Government, 17 August 2022) www.instituteforgovernment.org.uk/explainers/cost-living-crisis.

IPSOS Mori, The Global Institute for Women's Leadership and Kings College London, 'International Women's Day 2019: Global Attitudes towards Gender Equality' (February 2019) www.kcl.ac.uk/giwl/assets/iwd-giwl-main.pdf.

Irvine, S, Clark, H, Ward, M and Francis-Devine, B, 'Women and the UK Economy' (House of Commons Library, 4 March 2022) https://commonslibrary.parliament.uk/research-briefings/sn06838/#:~:text=Most%20part%2Dtime%20employment%20was,compared%20to%20 13%25%20of%20men.

Jänterä-Jareborg, M, 'Marital Agreements and Private Autonomy in Sweden' in J Scherpe (ed), *Marital Agreements and Private Autonomy in Comparative Perspective* (Hart Publishing, 2012).

Jänterä-Jareborg, M, Brattström, M and Walleng, K, 'National Report: Sweden' (CEFL, October 2008) http://ceflonline.net/wp-content/uploads/Sweden-Property.pdf.

Kaganas, F, 'Justifying the LASPO Act: Authenticity, Necessity, Suitability, Responsibility and Autonomy' (2017) 39 *Journal of Social Welfare and Family Law* 168.

Kaganas, F and Day Sclater, S, 'Contact Disputes: Narrative Constructions of "Good" Parents' (2004) 12 *Feminist Legal Studies* 1.

Kahn-Freund, O, 'On Uses and Misuses of Comparative Law' (1974) 37 *Modern Law Review* 1.

Kalenkoski, C, Ribar, D and Stratton, L, 'The Effect of Family Structure on Parents' Child Care Time in the United States and the United Kingdom' (2007) 5 *Review of Economics of the Household* 353.

Kamba, W, 'Comparative Law: A Theoretical Framework' (1974) 23 *International and Comparative Law Quarterly* 485.

Kelly, J, 'Power Imbalance in Divorce and Interpersonal Mediation: Assessment and Intervention' (1995) 13 *Mediation* Quarterly 85.

Klinth, R, 'The Best of Both Worlds? Fatherhood and Gender Equality in Swedish Paternity Leave Campaigns, 1976–2006' (2008) 6 *Fathering* 20.

Kugelberg, C, 'Constructing the Deviant Other: Mothering and Fathering at the Workplace' (2006) 13 *Gender, Work and Organization* 152.

Lacroix, C, 'Freedom, Desire and Power: Gender Processes and Presumptions of Shared Care and Responsibility after Parental Separation' (2006) 29 *Women's Studies International Forum* 184.

Larner, W, 'Neo-liberalism: Policy, Ideology, Governmentality' (2000) 63 *Studies in Political Economy* 5.

Larsson, J and Björk, S, 'Swedish Fathers Choosing Part-time Work' (2017) 2 *Community, Work & Family* 142.

Law Commission, *Cohabitation: The Financial Consequences of Relationship Breakdown* (Law Com CP No 179, 2006).

—— *Cohabitation: The Financial Consequences of Relationship Breakdown* (Law Com No 307, Summary, 2007).

—— Law Commission, *Matrimonial Property, Needs and Agreements* (Law Com No 343, 2014).

—— Law Commission, 'Financial Remedies on Divorce' (4 April 2023) www.lawcom.gov.uk/project/financial-remedies-on-divorce/ accessed 4 April 2023.

Legrand, P, 'Beyond Method: Comparative Law as Perspective' (1988) 36 *The American Journal of Comparative Law* 788.

Lemke, T, '"The Birth of Bio-Politics": Michel Foucault's Lecture at the Collège de France on Neo-Liberal Governmentality' (2001) 30 *Economy and Society* 190.

Lewis, J, 'Childcare Policies and the Politics of Choice' (2008) 79 *The Political Quarterly* 499.

Lewis, J and Åström, G, 'Equality, Difference and State Welfare: Labor Market and Family Policies in Sweden' (1992) 18 *Feminist Studies* 59.

Lynch, K, *Care and Capitalism* (Polity, 2022).

Ma, L, Andersson, G, Duvander, AZ and Evertsson, M, 'Fathers' Uptake of Parental Leave: Forerunners and Laggards in Sweden, 1993–2010' (2020) 49 *Journal of Social Policy* 361.

Martinsson, L, Griffin, G and Giritli-Nygren, K, 'Introduction' in L Martinsson, G Griffin and K Giritli-Nygren (eds) *Challenging the Myth of Gender Equality in Sweden* (Polity Press, 2016).

MacKenzie, C, 'The Importance of Relational Autonomy and Capabilities for an Ethics of Vulnerability' in C Mackenzie, W Rogers, and S Dodds (eds), *Vulnerability: New Essays in Ethics and Feminist Philosophy* (Oxford University Press, 2013).

—— 'Relational Autonomy: State of the Art Debate' in A Armstrong, K Green and A Sangiacomo (eds), *Spinoza and Relational Autonomy: Being With Others* (Edinburgh University Press, 2019).

MacKenzie, C and Stoljar, N, 'Introduction: Autonomy Refigured' in C MacKenzie and N Stoljar (eds), *Relational Autonomy* (Oxford University Press, 2000).

Mant, J, 'Placing Litigants in Person at the Centre of the Post-LASPO Family Court Process' (2020) 32 *Child and Family Law Quarterly* 421.

Matthews, M, 'Working Fathers Experience Sex Discrimination' (2023) 45 *Journal of Social Welfare and Family Law* (forthcoming).

McRobbie, A, 'Neoliberalism, the Family and the New "mediated" Maternalism' (2013) 80 *New Formations* 119.

Miles, J, 'Responsibility in Family Finance and Property Law' in J Bridgeman, H Keating and C Lind (eds), *Regulating Family Responsibilities* (Ashgate, 2011).

Mnookin, R and Kornhauser, L, 'Bargaining in the Shadow of the Law: The Case of Divorce' (1979) 88 *The Yale Law Journal* 950.

Mohammad, F, Mill, N and Ghosh, K, 'Marriages in England and Wales: 2019' (ONS, 19 May 2022) www.ons.gov.uk/peoplepopulationandcommunity/birthsdeathsandmarriages/marriagecohabitationandcivilpartnerships/bulletins/marriagesinenglandandwalesprovisional/2019#age-at-marriage.

MUCF, 'Unga utrikes födda kvinnors etablering i arbetslivet' [Establishment of Young Foreign-born Women in Working Life] (2021) www.mucf.se/publikationer/unga-utrikes-fodda-kvinnors-etablering-i-arbetslivet (translated using Google translate).

Murphy, R, Dennes, M, Harris, B, 'Families and the Labour Market, UK: 2021' (ONS, 22 July 2022) www.ons.gov.uk/employmentandlabourmarket/peopleinwork/employmentandemployeetypes/articles/familiesandthelabourmarketengland/2021#employment-rates-for-parents-in-the-uk.

Mussino, E, Duvander, AZ and Ma, L, 'Does Time Count? Immigrant Fathers' Use of Parental Leave for a First Child in Sweden' (2018) 73 *Population* 363.

National Childcare Goals (Ds 2001:57; *Barnafödandet i fokus. Från befolkningspolitik till barnvänligt samhälle*, 57) quoted (and translated) in P Strandbrink and V Pestoff, *Small-scale Welfare on a Large Scale: Social Cohesion and the Politics of Swedish Childcare* (Södertörns högskola, 2006).

Newnham, A and Harding, M, 'Sharing as Caring? Contact and Residence Disputes between Parents' (2016) 28 *Child and Family Law Quarterly* 175.

NIKK, 'Increased Parental Choice Can Lead to Reduced Gender Equality' (Nordic Information on Gender, first published in (2007) 2 *NIKK*).

Nylin, AK, Musick, K, Billingsley, S, Duvander, AZ and Evertsson, M, 'Trends over Time in His and Her Earnings Following Parenthood in Sweden' (Stockholm Research Reports in Demography no 2019:03) https://s3-eu-west-1.amazonaws.com/pstorage-su-4954321/14220869/SRRD_2019_03.pdf.

Nyman, C, 'Gender Equality in "the Most Equal Country in the World"? Money and Marriage in Sweden' (1999) 47 *The Sociological Review* 766.

OECD, 'Net Childcare Costs' (2021) https://data.oecd.org/benwage/net-childcare-costs.htm.

The Official Site of Sweden, 'Children in Sweden' (last updated 18 July 2022) https://sweden.se/life/society/children-in-sweden.

—— 'Gender Equality' (last updated 18 November 2022) https://sweden.se/society/gender-equality-in-sweden/.

—— 'Work-life balance' (last updated 10 November 2022) https://sweden.se/life/society/work-life-balance.

ONS, 'Women in the Labour Market: 2013' (25 September 2013) www.ons.gov.uk/employmentandlabourmarket/peopleinwork/employmentandemployeetypes/articles/womeninthelabourmarket/2013-09-25.

—— '2011 Census Analysis: Ethnicity and the Labour Market, England and Wales' (13 November 2014) www.ons.gov.uk/peoplepopulationandcommunity/culturalidentity/ethnicity/articles/ethnicityandthelabourmarket2011censusenglandandwales/2014-11-13.

—— 'What is the Gender Pay Gap?' (ONS Digital, 12 February 2016) https://webarchive.nationalarchives.gov.uk/ukgwa/20171102124649/https://visual.ons.gov.uk/what-is-the-gender-pay-gap/.

—— 'Women Shoulder the Responsibility of Unpaid Work' (ONS Digital, 10 November 2016) www.ons.gov.uk/employmentandlabourmarket/peopleinwork/earningsandworkinghours/articles/womenshouldertheresponsibilityofunpaidwork/2016-11-10.

—— 'Is Hybrid Working Here to Stay?' (23 May 2022) www.ons.gov.uk/employmentandlabourmarket/peopleinwork/employmentandemployeetypes/articles/ishybridworkingheretostay/2022-05-23.

Pahl, J *Money & Marriage* (Palgrave, 1989).

—— 'The Gendering of Spending within Households' (2000) 75 *Radical Statistics* 38 www.radstats.org.uk/no075/pahl.htm.

—— 'Individualisation in Couple Finances: Who Pays for the Children' (2005) 4 *Social Policy and Society* 381.

Patrick, R et al, 'Covid Realities: Documenting Life on a Low Income during the Pandemic' (24 January 2022) https://cdn.sanity.io/files/brhp578m/production/dbb82337a5b6c6ad1fc2e524a75bb4123c5005b6.pdf.

Payne, C and Vassilev, G, 'Household Satellite Account, UK: 2015 and 2016' (ONS, 2 October 2018) www.ons.gov.uk/economy/nationalaccounts/satelliteaccounts/articles/householdsatelliteaccounts/2015and2016estimates#focus-on-childcare.

—— 'Coronavirus and How People Spent their Time under Lockdown: 28 March to 26 April 2020' (ONS, 27 May 2020) www.ons.gov.uk/economy/nationalaccounts/satelliteaccounts/bulletins/coronavirusandhowpeoplespenttheirtimeunderrestrictions/28marchto26april2020#main-points.

Platt, L, 'Ethnicity and Child Poverty' (Department for Work and Pensions, Research Report No 576, 2009) https://dera.ioe.ac.uk/11016/1/rrep576.pdf.

Power, K, 'The COVID-19 Pandemic Has Increased the Care Burden of Women and Families' (2020) 16 *Sustainability: Science, Practice and Policy* 67.

Pregnant Then Screwed, 'Press Release – 1 in 4 Parents Have Had to Cut Down on Heat, Food & Clothing to Pay for Childcare' (25 March 2022) https://pregnantthenscrewed.com/one-in-four-parents-say-that-they-have-had-to-cut-down-on-heat-food-clothing-to-pay-for-childcare/.

Raghuram, P, 'Care Ethics Beyond the Global North' (2016) 15 *ACME: An International Journal for Critical Geographies* 511.

—— 'Race and Feminist Care Ethics: Intersectionality as Method' (2019) 26 *Gender, Place and Culture* 613.

Reece, H, 'The Paramountcy Principle: Consensus or Construct?' (1996) 49 *Current Legal Problems* 267.

Rodriguez Castro, L, Brady, M and Cook, K, 'Negotiating "Ideal Worker" and Intensive Mothering Ideologies: Australian Mothers' Emotional Geographies during their Commutes' (2020) *Social and Cultural Geography* 1.

Roman, C, 'Lone Mothers with Low Income Face Obstacles to Practice their Mothering' (2017) 54 *Sociologisk Forskning* 303.

Savage, M, '"This Will be the End of Nurseries": Preschools in England Warn of Closures amid Free Childcare Expansion Plan' (*The Observer*, 19 March 2023) www.theguardian.com/education/2023/mar/19/this-will-be-the-end-of-nurseries-preschools-in-england-warn-of-closures-amid-free-childcare-expansion-plan.

Scott, J and Clery, E, 'Gender Roles' in A Park, C Bryson, E Clery, J Curtice and M Phillips (eds), *British Social Attitudes 30* (The National Centre for Social Research, 2013) www.bsa.natcen.ac.uk/media/38723/bsa30_full_report_final.pdf.

Sharfman, A and Cobb, P, 'Families and Households in the UK: 2021' (ONS, 9 March 2022) www.ons.gov.uk/peoplepopulationandcommunity/birthsdeathsandmarriages/families/bulletins/familiesandhouseholds/2021.

—— 'Civil Partnerships in England and Wales: 2021' (ONS, 9 December 2022) www.ons.gov.uk/peoplepopulationandcommunity/birthsdeathsandmarriages/marriagecohabitationandcivilpartnerships/bulletins/civilpartnershipsinenglandandwales/2021#:~:text=of%20civil%20partnerships-,There%20were%206%2C731%20civil%20partnerships%20formed%20in%20England%20and%20Wales,in%20opposite%2Dsex%20civil%20partnerships.

Singer, A, 'Active Parenting or Solomon's Justice – Alternating Residence in Sweden for Children with Separated Parents' (2008) 4 *Utrecht Law Review* 35.
Smart, C, 'The Legal and Moral Ordering of Child Custody' (1991) 18 *Journal of Law and Society* 485.
Smith, M, 'Global Report: Attitudes to Gender 2021' (YouGov, 8 March 2021) https://docs.cdn.yougov.com/cmzkyf80zr/YouGov%20-%20Global%20Gender%20Equality%202021.pdf.
Sörgjerd, C, *Reconstructing Marriage* (Intersentia, 2012).
Strandbrink, P and Pestoff, V, *Small-scale Welfare on a Large Scale: Social Cohesion and the Politics of Swedish Childcare* (Södertörns högskola, 2006).
Stanford Encyclopedia of Philosophy, 'Feminist Ethics' https://plato.stanford.edu/entries/feminism-ethics/.
Statens Offentliga Utredningar, 'Begränsningar i föräldrapenningen för föräldrar som kommer till Sverige med barn' (SOU 2016:73).
R Statham, S Freedman and H Parkes, 'Delivering a Childcare Guarantee' (IPPR and Save the Children, December 2022) www.ippr.org/files/2022-12/delivering-a-childcare-guarantee-dec-22.pdf.
Statistics Sweden, 'Shared Residence for One in Three Children' (21 February 2014).
—— 'Nearly Three out of Ten Children Have Shared Residence' (11 July 2018) www.scb.se/en/finding-statistics/statistics-by-subject-area/living-conditions/living-conditions/living-conditions-surveys-ulfsilc/pong/statistical-news/childrens-residence-20162017/.
—— 'Uneven Gender Distribution among Managers' www.scb.se/en/finding-statistics/statistics-by-subject-area/labour-market/employment-and-working-hours/the-swedish-occupational-register-with-statistics/pong/statistical-news/the-swedish-occupational-register-with-statistics-2015/.
—— 'Women and Men in Sweden: Facts and Figures 2020' www.scb.se/contentassets/95ffcd4b3f394877abb3bd41e40df0a0/le0201_2019b20_br_x10br2002eng.pdf.
—— 'Women and Men in Sweden: Facts and Figures 2022 www.scb.se/contentassets/1fbf4f9815374356a786278faca6a7f0/le0201_2021b22_x10br2202.pdf.
Stewart, K, Reeves, A and Patrick, R, 'A Time of Need: Exploring the Changing Poverty Risk Facing Larger Families in the UK' (Centre for Analysis of Social Exclusion, 2021) https://sticerd.lse.ac.uk/dps/case/cp/casepaper224.pdf.
Stockholms Stad, 'Fees for Preschool' https://translate.google.com/translate?hl=en&sl=sv&u=https://forskola.stockholm/avgifter/&prev=search&pto=aue (page translated using Google translate).
Sundström, E, 'Should Mothers Work? Age and attitudes in Germany, Italy and Sweden' (1999) 8 *International Journal of Social Welfare* 193.
Sutherland, JA, 'Mothering, Guilt and Shame' (2010) *Sociology Compass* 310.
Svensson, EM and Gunnarsson, A, 'Gender Equality in the Swedish Welfare State' (2012) 2 *Feminists@Law* http://journals.kent.ac.uk/index.php/feministsatlaw/article/view/51/160.
Swedish Government, Government declaration (18 September 2010) cited in M Nygård and AZ Duvander, 'Social Inclusion or Gender Equality? Political Discourses on Parental Leave in Finland and Sweden' (2021) 9 *Social Inclusion* 300.
Thompson, S, *Prenuptial Agreements and the Presumption of Free Choice* (Hart Publishing, 2015).
—— 'Feminist Relational Contract Theory: A New Model for Family Property Agreements' (2018) 45 *Journal of Law and Society* 617.
Towns, A, 'Paradoxes of (In)Equality: Something is Rotten in the Gender Equal State of Sweden' (2002) 37 *Journal of the Nordic International Studies Association* 157.
Trägårdh, L, 'Statist Individualism: The Swedish Theory of Love and its Lutheran Imprint' in J Halldorf and F Wenell (eds), *Between the State and the Eurcharist* (Pickwick, 2014).
Treloar, R, 'High-conflict Divorce Involving Children: Parents' Meaning-making and Agency' (2018) 40 *Journal of Social Welfare and Family* Law 340.
Trinder, L et al, 'Litigants in Person in Private Family Law Cases' (Ministry of Justice, 2014) https://assets.publishing.service.gov.uk/government/uploads/system/uploads/attachment_data/file/380479/litigants-in-person-in-private-family-law-cases.pdf.

Trinder, L, Bryson, C, Coleman, L, Houlston, C, Purdon, S, Reibstein, J and Smith, L, 'Building Bridges? An Evaluation of the Costs and Effectiveness of the Separated Parents Information Programme (PIP)' (Department for Education) https://assets.publishing.service.gov.uk/government/uploads/system/uploads/attachment_data/file/181695/DFE-RR140.pdf.
J Tronto, *Moral Boundaries: A Political Argument for an Ethic of Care* (Routledge, 1993).
—— *Caring Democracy* (New York University Press, 2013).
TUC, 'TUC poll: 1 in 3 Parents with Pre-school Children Spend More than a Third of Their Pay on Childcare' (17 March 2022) www.tuc.org.uk/news/tuc-poll-1-3-parents-pre-school-children-spend-more-third-their-pay-childcare.
Vandenbeld Giles, M, 'Introduction' in M Vandenbeld Giles (ed), *Mothering in the Age of Neoliberalism* (Demeter Press, 2014).
Vizard, T, 'Families and the Labour Market, UK: 2019' (ONS, 4 October 2019) https://www.ons.gov.uk/employmentandlabourmarket/peopleinwork/employmentandemployeetypes/articles/familiesandthelabourmarketengland/2019#balancing-work-and-family-life.
Waring, M, *Counting for Nothing*, 2nd edn (University of Toronto Press, 2004).
Webber, D and Payne, C, 'Chapter 10: Methodological Annex' (ONS, 7 April 2016) www.ons.gov.uk/economy/nationalaccounts/satelliteaccounts/compendium/householdsatelliteaccounts/2005to2014/chapter10methodologicalannex#annex-1-methodology-for-all-the-activities.
'Why do Young Foreign-born Women Face Difficulties on the Swedish Job Market?' (*The Local*, 15 March 2021, updated 20 March 2021) www.thelocal.se/20210315/why-do-young-foreign-born-women-face-difficulties-on-the-swedish-job-market/.
Wickens, Z, '79% of Employers Offer Enhanced Maternity Leave Pay' (1 October 2021) https://employeebenefits.co.uk/79-employers-enhanced-maternity-leave-pay/.
World Economic Forum, 'Global Gender Gap Report 2020' https://www3.weforum.org/docs/WEF_GGGR_2020.pdf.
YouGov, 'Global Report: Attitudes to Gender' (2015) https://d25d2506sfb94s.cloudfront.net/cumulus_uploads/document/43qhq95qwn/YouGov_Gender_Results_Share_Website2.pdf.
—— 'Global Gender Equality 2021' https://yougov.co.uk/topics/international/articles-reports/2021/03/08/global-report-attitudes-gender-2021.
Zweigert, K and Kötz, H, *An Introduction to Comparative Law*, 3rd edn (T Weir tr, Oxford University Press, 1998).

INDEX

www.ingramcontent.com/pod-product-compliance
Ingram Content Group UK Ltd.
Pitfield, Milton Keynes, MK11 3LW, UK
UKHW020819290926
15470UKWH00003B/1262

9 781509 959334